# Ethnic and Border Music

**Recent Titles in**
**Greenwood Guides to American Roots Music**

Jazz: A Regional Exploration
*Scott Yanow*

Folk Music: A Regional Exploration
*Norm Cohen*

Country: A Regional Exploration
*Ivan Tribe*

GREENWOOD GUIDES TO
AMERICAN ROOTS MUSIC

# ETHNIC AND BORDER MUSIC

## A Regional Exploration

*Edited by*
Norm Cohen

GREENWOOD PRESS
Westport, Connecticut • London

**Library of Congress Cataloging-in-Publication Data**

Ethnic and border music : a regional exploration / edited by Norm Cohen.
   p. cm. — (Greenwood guides to American roots music, ISSN 1551-0271)
Includes bibliographical references (p.   ) and index.
ISBN 978-0-313-33192-3 (alk. paper)
1. Folk music—United States—History and criticism. 2. Immigrants—United States—Music—History
and criticism. 3. Indians of North America—Music—History and criticism. I. Cohen, Norm, 1936–
ML3551.E73    2007
781.6200973—dc22       2007022746

British Library Cataloguing in Publication Data is available.

Library of Congress Catalog Card Number: 2007022746
ISBN: 978-0-313-33192-3
ISSN: 1551-0271

First published in 2007

Greenwood Press, 88 Post Road West, Westport, CT 06881
An imprint of Greenwood Publishing Group, Inc.
www.greenwood.com

Printed in the United States of America

The paper used in this book complies with the
Permanent Paper Standard issued by the National
Information Standards Organization (Z39.48-1984).

10  9  8  7  6  5  4  3  2  1

# Contents

# Series Foreword

If present trends are any indication, soon anyone with access to the Internet will be able to tune in to music from any part of the world. When that happens, listeners may well find Kentucky bluegrass bands playing Tex-Mex music along with banjo tunes and gospel favorites, while musicians in India may intersperse elements of American rap music with their own native raga traditions.

It's difficult to predict right now, but even to understand the significance of this revolution requires an appreciation for the fact that until recently all musical genres, like every aspect of human activity, were associated with relatively compact geographic regions, bounded not only by national boundaries but also by the more limiting barriers of language, religion, geography, and cultural heritage. In the United States, regional boundaries might enclose an area as large as the vast Southwest or as small as the immediate environs of Galax, Virginia.

This series of musical studies seeks to describe American musical traditions that are, or once were, associated with geographic regions smaller than the nation as a whole. These musical varieties include jazz, blues, country music, Hispanic American music, Irish American music, polka music, Franco-American music (including Cajun and Zydeco), Native American music, and traditional folk music. Jazz music originated in New Orleans and other cities along the lower Mississippi River in the early 1900s, but by midcentury it was equally at home in New York and San Francisco as in New Orleans or Memphis. Jazz was in turn heavily influenced by blues music, an African American creation born in the broader regions of the Deep South.

Country music of recent decades is a merger of two regional Anglo-American musical traditions, one from the Appalachians and other southeastern states, and the other from the southwestern plains. Its earlier name of country-western music reflects more clearly that parentage. Irish American music, brought to these shores mainly in the 1840s and later by emigrants from Ireland, flourished best in the big cities where the Irish made their new homes: Boston, New York, Philadelphia, and Chicago.

Hispanic (Latino, Tex-Mex) music migrated north from Mexico and other Latin American countries. In the early 1900s it could be heard only in Texas, New Mexico, and California; a century later, Spanish language radio stations reach almost everywhere in the lower forty-eight. Polka music was brought to the New World by musicians from Central Europe—Germany, Switzerland, and what used to be Czechoslovakia. It was fruitfully transplanted to the Midwestern states from Texas north to Nebraska and the Dakotas.

The music of First Nations (Native Americans) was spread across the continent in varieties associated with particular groups of peoples, but as a result of ethnocentric federal policies that forced their relocation to "Indian Reservations," was subsequently located in regions that were often at great distances from the original homelands. Traditional folk music, the product of evolved music of European American and African American immigrants, had developed distinct regional characteristics in the New World by the eighteenth and nineteenth centuries, but as a result of internal, primarily western migrations, had changed considerably by the early twentieth century.

Four of these musical styles—jazz, blues, country, and traditional folk—are treated in separate volumes; the other "ethnic" traditions (Hispanic, Cajun/Zydeco, Polka, Irish, and Native American) are presented together in a fifth volume.

American music continues to evolve. Readers of these volumes can doubtless think of changes in music that have taken place in their own lifetimes. The many musical heritages of the nineteenth and twentieth centuries laid the foundations for today's music. The advent and growth of national media —radio, television, digital recordings, Internet—exert powerful forces on the nature of musical genres that were once regional. Ironically, national media permit two contradictory phenomena. At first, they introduce listeners to the regional musical forms that a wider audience otherwise might never have known about. Eventually, though, they provide the mechanism for the scrambling and cross-pollination of what were once distinct styles.

This does not mean that American musical regionalism is gone forever, doomed to a homogeneous culture that is the same in Key West, Florida, as in the San Juan Islands of Washington. If the past is any guide, new regional styles will continually emerge, gradually to become part of the national mix.

As long as immigration to these shores continues, the influx of new musical styles will contribute to and invigorate the old. It is an exciting prospect.

Norm Cohen
Portland Community College, Oregon
Series Editor

# Introduction

This is the fourth of a series of five volumes treating regional music in America. The first, *Folk Music*, dealt mainly with Anglo-American traditional folk music. The other three volumes were concerned with musical genres that all grew out of the music of specific regional communities but were transformed over time into commercial music idioms: blues, jazz, and country music. All emerged from the American Southeast: blues and jazz from the African-American culture and country music from the Anglo-American. These transformations have taken place over most of the past century, and today the roots of all three genres are hidden by the overgrowth of decades of development, but they are not completely obliterated.

The present volume concerns five representative ethnic musical traditions. "Ethnic" here refers to communities that have managed to maintain some distinctiveness with respect to the mainstream culture surrounding them. Four of the five originated with distinct immigrant groups in the nineteenth or twentieth centuries; all still retain distinctions in language, community mores, religious practices, and social customs; the fifth has been here much longer. The five are: (1) Native American, (2) Irish-American, (3) Polka music from central European nationalities, (4) Franco-American, and (5) Hispanic-American music.

These are by no means the only ethnic musical traditions within our nation's boundaries, but each presents some unique characteristics that make it worthy of examination.

*Native American Music.* Native American peoples have not been on the North American continent "forever," but they have been here so long relative to any other humans that we can comfortably regard them as having always been here. The other four groups all came ultimately from Europe or the British Isles; they share an Indo-European culture whose roots reach back one to two millennia. By virtue of constant contact, all the cultures of Europe and Britain shared enough features that their musics were not totally alien from one another. The same cannot be said of Native American culture. Both cultural isolation and a profoundly different relationship between people and their environment helped to make Native American music substantially different in social function from the musics of the European Americans.

To dismiss the cultural differences as the result of what is pejoratively labeled a more "primitive" society is both reprehensible and, ultimately, inaccurate. Consider, for example, the attitudes of certain communities when first confronted by the machinery for making reasonably accurate sound recordings. Apart from the completely magical nature of recordings to someone whose experience holds nothing comparable, there is the separate question of who is entitled to "own" a person's clothing, photographic image, hair, or voice. (To put a modern spin on it: who is entitled to own someone's genetic code? We are still wrestling with this conundrum.) When orthodox Jewish cantors were first offered the opportunity to record particular holy prayers early in the twentieth century, there were many who demurred because of the concern that they would have no control over how their recordings might be used once they were available for commercial distribution. The conflict is not a result of technological naivete but of different attitudes toward extension of self, ownership, property, and propriety.

Because Native American music has been, for the most part, intimately a part of religious and ceremonial activities, not to mention its musical characteristics that are distinctive from European music, it has been more resistant to cross fertilization with other musics on American soil than, say, Hispanic music (think of Marty Robbins' song, "El Paso") or Cajun music (Hank Williams' "Jambalaya"). The resistance has not been impenetrable, however; in the last few decades we have seen more of an amalgamation of Native American with country music and rock in forms such as "chicken scratch" music.

*Franco-America Music.* French exploration and settlement in the New World paralleled that of Britain in the sixteenth and seventeenth centuries. If Napoleon had not been so cash-poor in 1803 he might not have felt obliged to sell French lands to America (as the Louisiana Purchase). What we now consider an ethnic cultural subgroup would then be the dominant element of probably another country. Because of the strong French presence in Louisiana and elsewhere, the region provided a haven to French Huguenots who were driven out of Nova Scotia (Acadia) in the middle of the eighteenth century. It was this group that provided most of the foundations for the musics that we now label "Cajun" and "Zydeco" in Louisiana.

*Hispanic American Music.* Like the Franco-Americans, Spanish Americans trace their New World roots back for centuries. In much of the southwest, Spanish settlements preceded those of English-speaking pioneers. By the time the southwest states were ceded by Mexico to the United States at the conclusion of the Mexican War (1848), the populations had already intermarried heavily with the native populations, and their musical traditions had had ample opportunity to evolve from the purely Castilian elements that at one time must have predominated. In the twentieth century in cities in New Mexico and elsewhere, collectors found, along with the familiar Tex-Mex border musics, ballads and songs that were directly traceable back to seventeenth century Spain.

*Irish-American Music.* As Paul Wells points out in his chapter, while Irish immigration to America experienced an enormous jump in the 1840s, there has been a significant Irish presence in colonial America ever since the first settlers debarked on New World shores. By the end of the Revolutionary War, perhaps 200,000 Irish had emigrated to America. Mainly as a result of the potato famine of the 1840s, two million Irish emigrated to the United States between 1820 and 1860, and another 1.6 million by 1890. Though percentage-wise they established the greatest presence in New England and the Mid-Atlantic states, there were significant numbers elsewhere—in the Midwest and even in California. While, as Wells notes, there are other elements of Irish music in this country, such as music of the stage, most of what we consider "Irish" music is fiddle and dance music.

*Central European (polka) Music.* The music discussed in this chapter comes not from a single country but from a wide swath of Central Europe, including countries whose names no longer appear on European maps, such as Bohemia, Slovenia, and Ruthenia. Immigration from these countries was boosted in the 1840s by political and economic upheavals in Europe. Of the five groups examined in this volume, this represents the latest arrivals to the New World, and also the most diverse in terms of cultural heritage.

In addition to the obvious difference in national background, each of these groups discussed came to America for different reasons, which meant different socio-economic groups participated in emigration. Spanish immigration was voluntary, and attracted the upper classes as well as the working classes who hoped to better their fortunes by careers in the army or New World bureaucracies. Central Europeans in the 1840s and 1850s fled for political reasons that affected all social classes equally, but by the end of the century economic opportunities had more appeal for the underemployed working classes. Other groups not discussed here—for example Scandinavians in the last decades of the nineteenth century—were farming families who came to the American midwest in search of the abundant land that was no longer available in Europe. Some—for example, East European Jews—came mainly because of religious persecution. Others—for example, Chinese in the middle of the nineteenth century—came in spite of racial prejudices and persecutions for economic opportunities in the frontier states, often with little intention to remain permanently in America.

As a result of class differences, the musics that the immigrants brought to the New World varied greatly from one cultural group to another—and not just because of language distinctions. What we now lump in one category of "ethnic" music is therefore not purely folk music, nor pop music, nor classical music, but whatever musics these various groups brought with them and strove to perpetuate after they arrived in their new homeland.

Two themes surface repeatedly in the several chapter studies of this volume: (1) the conflict between tradition and innovation, and (2) the problem of participatory exclusivity. The first of these confronts any cultural genre that is presented with the possibility of commerce across the community's boundaries. How to respond to the pressures of the outside culture? In the case of musical traditions, this takes the form of whether or not to adapt the instruments, styles, language, and/or music of the neighboring or surrounding culture group. Should polka bands discard the button accordion in favor of the piano accordion? Should cajun bands sing in Cajun-French or English? Should Irish singing groups adopt the instrumentation and harmonies (and language) of American folk revivalists or adhere to hibernian customs? These are recurring conflicts, and they become foci of intense disagreement in music circles. It does little good to remind the adversaries that in every case, what the traditionalists want to promote as the genuine and original product was itself once the result of innovation and assimilation. This is truly an instance of those not learning from history being condemned to repeat it.

The second theme concerns the ownership of the music and who has the right to represent or perform it. Can an Anglo-American fiddler lead a Norwegian-American band? Should a white boy from the big city play the blues? Should a Jewish boy from Brooklyn play old time Appalachian banjo? Can an African-American play klezmer clarinet? The stumbling block is not so much the question whether there is intent do misrepresent oneself–this once-common issue has generally been resolved in recent decades. The question is more whether a cultural artifact such as music can (or should) be separated from the rest of the cultural matrix in which it is normally embedded. One generation sees the cultural artifacts—whether music, foodways, costumery, or language—as the icons of the community itself; the glue that bonds the community together; the shibboleths that distinguish insider from outsider. Another generation sees the artifacts is discreet commodities—produce in a cultural marketplace from which we freely pick and choose what we fancy and discard the remainder.

The authors of the following chapters do not offer advice on these matters, but they are all aware of the issues and have dealt with them in one form or another in their respective roles of scholars, performers, and/or cultural representatives.

What are our sources of information on the musics of these groups? For the most part, we have little to go on before the end of the nineteenth century.

In the case of the four groups from Europe, we have, of course, some knowledge of the musical cultures they came from, and can make some extrapolations based on such clues. For the native Americans, though, we have nothing of the kind, and are further handicapped by the fact that their culture was entirely oral, and nothing was preserved in writing until the encounter with European peoples. So, by and large, our knowledge base commences in the 1890s with the invention of the phonograph and its utilization in recording community musics. In some cases this was done by anthropologists and ethnomusicologists interested in preserving (or at least documenting) ethnic culture. The earliest Native American recordings were made in 1890 by Harvard University anthropologist Jesse Walter Fewkes among the Passamaquoddy Indians in Maine. Soon after, commercial companies were producing and selling cylinder recordings: Berliner in 1894, Victor in 1904, Edison in 1921. Spanish-language ethnographic music documentation in the southwest began in 1903 with cylinder recordings by Charles F. Lummis of the Southwest Museum in Los Angeles, but even before the turn of the century Berliner and Edison had made some recordings of singers in New York. The first ethnographic recordings of Franco-American music were made in 1934: in Missouri by Joseph M. Carriére and in Louisiana by John A. Lomax. But again, commercial record companies had beat the academics to the punch: Brunswick, Columbia, and Victor field representatives had already visited Louisiana and recorded cajun musicians and singers on location by 1929. As Wells notes in his essay on Irish-American music, Patrick Touhey was selling homemade cylinder recordings in 1901, and Zonophone had made commercial discs of accordionist John Kimmel in 1904. Even earlier, Edison had recorded Irish bagpipe music in 1899. In the Central European communities that originated polka music, Bohemian, Serbo-Croatian, Slovak, and Slovene commercial recordings had been produced by Columbia and Victor in the first two decades of the twentieth century.

Within a few years, however, a more extensive means of music documentation opened up. Commercial recording companies realized that there were potential profits to be made in recording the music of ethnic and regional communities and marketing the published recordings in those very communities themselves, advertising in newspapers and other media that catered exclusively (or nearly so) to those communities. For about two decades, until the economic hardships of the Great Depression and then wartime materials shortages during World War II forced a halt to recording activity, these commercial record companies recorded and issued tens of thousands of 78 rpm discs featuring local ethnic musicians. More than 1,300 Spanish-language artists recorded nearly 9,000 selections in those years. French-language recordings feature over 200 musicians and a total of nearly 2,200 selections. More than 200 Irish-American musicians and singers recorded close to 3,000 songs and tunes. In each case, these selections included not only folksongs and tunes but also popular hits, religious numbers, and light-classical compositions, as well as some spoken word recordings. What distinguished them was not the type of material but the fact that it was created by and for a very specific regional or ethnic community.

After World War II concluded and the economy, including the music industry, began to recover, the proliferation of recording and pressing equipment made it feasible for small independent record producers to start up their own companies. This trend continued with the invention of the long playing (LP) record, and accelerated even more with the advent of tape recording. By the 1960s it was no longer possible to track and catalog all the recorded output of thousands of small producers, some of whom may have issued only a few recordings in quantities that major record companies could never find profitable. The proliferation of inexpensive high quality digital recording equipment meant that any musical aggregation could (and still can) make its own recordings and sell them directly to fans at local concerts and in other venues—in quantities anywhere from a dozen to a thousand. All of this wealth of product provides an enormous potential for cultural documentation, but a headache to anyone who tries to inventory just what is available.

The advent and spread of recording technology wrought a remarkable transformation on America's musical landscape. It must rank as one of history's preeminent ironies that while this new invention facilitated the documentation of aural culture in a way previously impossible—yet that very process contributed to, if not the destruction, at least the transformation of what it sought to preserve. While in nineteenth-century America, a Kentucky fiddler was unlikely to have ever heard the musicians of two hollers away, by the middle of the twentieth century an Italian street musician in lower Manhattan could listen to a Chicano band from Los Angeles as easily as to his neighbors down the block. Older musics didn't vanish, nor did they undergo entirely unprecedented changes, but the transformations that ensued happened on a time scale orders of magnitude shorter than anyone had previously experienced.

This collection of essays merely hints at the wealth of cultural material that remains to be investigated. Each of the five essays includes references to significant recordings and written publications. In addition, a selected bibliography at the end of the volume lists some of the more general studies, as well as books concerning some of the musical traditions other than the five presented here.

Norm Cohen

# 1

# You Can't Go Wrong, If You Play It Right: Cajun Music and Zydeco

*Kevin S. Fontenot*

Southern Louisiana, west of the Atchafalaya basin, is home to two of the most distinctive American musics—Cajun music and zydeco. Often confused, the two genres are actually complementary musics that grew up in close proximity and heavily influence each other. The accordion forms the basic distinctive sound of both Cajun music and zydeco, but the styles based around the instrument are only one facet of a diverse musical culture that embraces influences from country music, rhythm and blues, jazz, and, more recently, rap and urban styles. Cajun music and zydeco reflect the cultures of the Cajuns and Creoles as these once rural populations moved into the twentieth century.

Louisiana's Cajuns descend from French settlers who originally colonized Nova Scotia (then called "Acadie") during the seventeenth century. The colony was founded in 1604, but major settlement did not occur until the 1630s when people of western France fled their homeland due to war, disease, and religious turmoil. The ancestors of the Acadians came primarily from Poitou and, unlike other French colonists, usually migrated in family or community groups. Thus, the early Acadian community demonstrated a strong sense of community solidarity that mixed with frontier individualism. From the mid-seventeenth century, Acadie shifted between French and English control on a regular basis, and the Acadians developed an identity that centered on the group rather than national allegiance. In 1713 the colony fell under English control, this time permanently. After a 50-year struggle to force the Acadians to declare unconditional loyalty to the British crown, the English and their allies from Massachusetts expelled Acadians from Nova Scotia in 1755. This event became known as the Grand Derangement ("Great Upheaval"), and some 8,000 Acadians were displaced throughout the British colonies along the Atlantic, France, and the Caribbean. Some 3,000 would eventually make their way to Louisiana, originally a French colony that had been transferred to Spain.

The Acadian exiles settled the prairies and swamps of southwestern Louisiana and prospered until the coming of the Civil War. The war devastated the region and pushed the Acadians down the economic ladder as many lost their farms and ranches and became tenant farmers. These people eventually came to be called "Cajuns," a corruption of the pronunciation of Acadian. The Cajuns intermarried with Irish, German, and Anglo Americans, but the Cajun culture proved remarkably resilient. As a result, outsiders were quickly absorbed into the group and added elements of their own culture into the Cajun culture. At the heart of the Cajun culture lay the extended family.

Few words generate as much controversy as Creole. The definition varies in Louisiana widely from group to group, almost from speaker to speaker, and has been applied to everything from vegetables to people to styles of cooking. At the most basic level, "Creole" means native to the Americas, with any person born in a French colonial region being a creole. In New Orleans, Creole is used to describe the descendants of elite French and Spanish colonials of both white and mixed racial heritage. These two groups often refuse to recognize each other as Creoles and also tend to hold rural Creoles in disdain. In rural Louisiana, Creole has come to mean almost exclusively the racially mixed descendants of French, Spanish, and African colonials who are Francophone and whose ancestors were free during the antebellum era. Rural Creoles, sometimes called Creoles of Color, lived in communities based around extended families and often kept to themselves.

Cajuns and Creoles shared many cultural traits. Both held the family as the central economic and social unit. Though never truly isolated, Cajuns and Creoles clung to their Francophone culture, and this set them apart from other groups in Louisiana. They remained wary of outsiders but readily accepted those who expressed an interest in becoming part of the fabric of the community. Cajuns and Creoles have traditionally practiced the Catholic faith, though often tempered with strong anti-clericism. Language was a marker of Cajun identity well into the twentieth century, with French being the primary language. Following World War II, the French language fell into disuse and has struggled to remain relevant. Today most Cajuns and Creoles speak English as their primary language, with French spoken at home with older relatives. French remains mandatory for singing, and in many ways music has kept the language alive.

## FOLK BACKGROUND

Cajuns and Creoles share a reputation of loving good times, especially music and dance. Dances served as important sites of social interaction where the community came together after a hard week toiling in the fields. Early dances, called "bals de maison," were held in the home, with music usually provided by fiddle players. Furniture would be pushed against the walls or moved into the yard to create a dance floor inside the house. Bals de maison often lasted deep into the night, the dancers fortified with meals of gumbo or jambalaya. A lively instrumental tradition developed around the dances, and a distinctive Cajun style of fiddle playing formed as well. Cajun fiddlers performed a double string bowing technique with a drone played beneath the melody. This sound could be heard over the feet of the dancers. Fiddlers often performed in pairs. An excellent example of the old time style of Cajun fiddle duets is heard in the work of Dennis McGee and Sady Courville. The duo began performing together early in the twentieth century, and McGee's style had formed before the advent of the accordion. Other examples of this early fiddle style can be found in the recordings of the Soileau cousins, Wade Fruge, and Rodney Fontenot. Creole fiddle styles were poorly recorded until the 1960s, but performers such as Canray Fontenot and Bebe Carriere harken back to the early days before the accordion. The only Creole fiddler to record before World War II was Douglas Bellard, who made the very first Creole recordings with accordionist Kirby Riley.

Cajun balladry, once vibrant, has faded in recent years. For most Cajuns, their first exposure to music was the singing of their mother as she worked around the home or calmed babies to sleep. This repertoire drew on French and English ballads, songs of lost love and romantic lands across the ocean. A wide range of Cajun balladry was recorded by John and Alan Lomax during their 1930s field recording trips through Louisiana. Most significant was the 1934 trip that preserved the vast repertoire of New Iberia's Julian Hoffpauir and his daughters. Drinking songs (la chanson de bamboche) were enjoyed, as were bawdy songs, particularly by men. Cajun men also sang songs associated with their Mardi Gras celebrations. Cajun Mardi Gras differs greatly from the staged pageantry of New Orleans. On Mardi Gras, Cajun men would dress in costume and roam the countryside begging for gumbo ingredients (this was called courir de Mardi Gras or running the Mardi Gras). They stopped at each house and danced and sang for the people, who then rewarded the troupe with rice, sausage, or a live chicken, which the "Mardi Gras" then had to chase and catch. At the end of the day, everyone who contributed was invited to a communal gumbo and dance. The Cajun Mardi Gras is deeply rooted in traditional European carnival and spring celebrations in which excessive consumption of food and alcohol preceded a period of fasting. Today Cajun Mardi Gras is often viewed as a wild drunk by outsiders who fail to connect the excess with the restraint that follows. Traditionally, Mardi Gras is a male centered activity, but many women now participate. Creoles practice similar Mardi Gras celebrations, though theirs often lack the rough and tumble frontier edge of the Cajun tradition. Songs associated with Mardi Gras often reflect the hunt for food or alcohol and emphasize camaraderie as basic elements, all of which are integral to the celebration.

Creoles preserved African derived song traditions as well. This survival is particularly illustrated by jurer, the Creole form of the ring shout common in other parts of the South. Jurer was performed by clapping the hands and stomping the feet, resulting in a polyrhythmic dance beat. In 1934 the Lomax team recorded some stunning jurer performances by Jimmy Peters and accompanying dancers. One of these songs, "J'ai Fait Tout le Tour du Pays," included the line "les haricots sont pas sales," which eventually provided the name for zydeco. "Les haricots" is roughly pronounced "zarico" and has been standardized as zydeco. The phrase literally means, "the beans are not salty," and is a reference to impoverished times when no salt meat is available to flavor beans. Creoles also possessed a vibrant ballad tradition that included drinking and Mardi Gras songs. Unfortunately, little work was done to record these traditions until late in twentieth century.

The Lomaxes made significant efforts in recording Cajun and Creole folk music with their field trips in the mid-1930s. Their guide to Acadian folk song was Irene Therese Whitfield, who conducted the first widely known academic study of the genre as her master's thesis from Louisiana State University in 1935. In 1939 she published *Louisiana French Folk Songs*. Her work made her the unofficial academic guide to southern Louisiana's Francophone music. Whitfield's relative Lauren Post further expanded the academic study of Cajun culture with his important *Cajun Sketches* (1962), and he published "Joseph C. Falcon: Accordion Player and Singer," the first academic profile of a Cajun musician (in *Louisiana History* in 1970). Louisiana State University professor Harry Oster broke new ground in 1958 with "Acculturation in Cajun Folk Music," which considered the contemporary Cajun music scene amid a changing region. Oster continued to carry out field recordings throughout his career, leaving an invaluable collection documenting the vibrant club scene of the mid-twentieth century.

In the late nineteenth century, the ubiquitous fiddle was joined by many newly available and affordable instruments that expanded the sound of Cajun music. Guitars, mandolins, and bass fiddles added rhythmic and melodic elements to the music. One major instrumental addition transformed the genre. The diatonic accordion (invented in Vienna in 1828) entered the music after the Civil War and seems to have established itself by the turn of the century and proliferated after the first world war. Limited to a range of 20 notes (10 each pushing and pulling), the diatonic accordion was portable and easily heard in the loud dance halls of Louisiana. The accordion's limited range tended to modify and simplify song arrangements, and often frustrated adventurous fiddlers who felt constrained by the "tit noir," or "little black," as the diatonic accordion came to be called. The most popular models were the German-made Monarchs and Sterlings. Until World War II, most accordions were imported, but the war years forced Cajuns to learn to repair or build their own accordions. The first Cajun accordion craftsman was Sidney Brown of Lake Charles. Marc Savoy, a master accordionist, is one of the finest accordion craftsmen and has experimented with hardwoods and inlays to produce instruments that are works of art as well as functional. Savoy and his wife Ann are respected musicians. Their family includes their sons Joel and Wilson, widely acclaimed musicians and producers.

## EARLY RECORDINGS (1928–1934)

The first phase of commercial recording demonstrated the diversity of Cajun musical styles. Accordion-fiddle or accordion-guitar duets dominated, but fiddle duos, fiddle-guitar bands, and polished parlor singers were all recorded. This period also revealed strong regional styles within the tradition, from the smoother vocal stylings of the eastern edge of Acadiana to the rough dancehall sounds of the western prairies. This first phase also provided the early stars of the genre such as Joe and Cleoma Falcon, Leo Soileau, Lawrence Walker, and the great Amede Ardoin.

Evidence indicates that the first "Cajan" record was recorded by Dr. James F. Roach from New Orleans in 1925. A report from *Talking Machine World* of July 15, 1925, stated that Roach had cut the "Song of the Crocodile" for Okeh. The song was later released on Roach's personal label, backed with a piano performance by his wife. The identity of Dr. Roach and any ties he might have had to the Cajun community remain clouded in mystery. The song he recorded is not part of the Cajun repertoire, thus indicating that Roach may have recorded a polished middle class version of a Creole folk song. Since the recording has not surfaced, little is known of this "Cajan" title.

Accordionist Joe Falcon and his fiance Cleoma Breaux, a strong rhythm guitarist, cut the first commercial Cajun record on April 27, 1928, in New Orleans. The record featured "Lafayette" (later known as "Allons a Lafayette") backed with "The Waltz That Carried Me to My Grave." Shortly after the Falcon-Breaux recording, fiddler Leo Soileau and accordionist Mayeus LaFleur cut several sides in Atlanta. The success of these recordings proved that a viable market existed for Cajun recordings and companies responded enthusiastically.

Joe and Cleoma Falcon were among the most extensively recorded Cajun musicians before World War II. Though often regarded as traditional Cajun artists, the Falcons drew on a wide range of popular culture for musical inspiration. In addition to standard Cajun songs, they recorded French versions of Fats Waller's "Lulu's Back in Town" and various country and western songs that indicated the influence of Jimmie Rodgers. Cleoma's brothers, who recorded under the name Breaux Freres, also made numerous recordings. The most famous had been written by Amede Breaux and was titled "Ma Blond Est Parti." Eventually this song would become known as "Jole Blon" and gain status as the Cajun national anthem. Cleoma died in 1941, and Joe Falcon continued to perform until his death in the 1960s. He was also a drummer, as was his second wife Theresa.

Though both Joe Falcon and Amede Breaux were important accordionists, neither exerted the same influence as Amede Ardoin, a Creole from west of Eunice. Ardoin was a highly accomplished accordionist, his style being a mixture of Cajun and blues. His fine playing often garnered him well-paying white dances. Amede also possessed a deeply emotional vocal style that ranked him among the finest singers in the region. Ardoin made a series of records with the Cajun fiddler Dennis McGee that formed the basis of the standard Cajun repertoire. His recordings inspired generations of Cajun musicians, such as Nathan Abshire, Iry Lejeune, and Marc Savoy. Ardoin's extended family included the renowned accordionist Bois Sec Ardoin and his children. Ardoin met an untimely end. He was severely beaten during a racially motivated attack and as a result, began to lose his sanity. He died in a mental hospital in 1941. While he was the most influential Creole to record before World War II, Ardoin was not the first. That honor went to fiddler Douglas Bellard and accordionist Kirby Riley, who on October 2, 1929, recorded the earliest version of the standard "Flames d'Infer" ("The Flames of Hell").

The Soileau-LaFleur recordings anticipated the direction of Cajun music in the post-war era. Soileau was a driven, highly focused fiddler who often struggled with the limitations of the accordion. This was not the experience with Mayeus LaFleur, who added distinctive elements of swing to his style. The resulting titles, such as "Basile," demonstrated the ability of the accordion to adapt to the emerging jazz dance scene. Unfortunately, LaFleur was killed in a barroom brawl, ironically in Basile, shortly before his record's release. Soileau continued to record during the early phase. His recordings with accordionist Moise Robin are tension-filled blues numbers, and his fiddle duets with cousin Alius Soileau came out of the pre-accordion repertoire. By the early 1930s, Soileau abandoned playing with the diatonic accordion and moved to a string-band format that increasingly revealed the influence of commercial country music.

Other prominent figures to record during the initial phase of commercial recording included Dudley and James Fawvor, Blind Uncle Gaspard, and John Bertrand. Little-remembered today, these artists revealed the vocal lyricism in Cajun music. The Fawvors sang beautiful duets, a rarity in Cajun music, and Gaspard and Bertrand were far smoother and melodic than the dancehall singers of western Acadiana. Angleas Lejeune, an accordionist from Acadia Parish, cut the standards "La Valse de la Pointe Noire" and "Bayou Pom Pom" and accompanied the early Cajun humorist Walter Coquille, "The Mayor of Bayou Pom Pom," on several sides. Lejeune would later influence his cousin Iry Lejeune. Accordionist Lawrence Walker also made his earliest recordings in 1929, but these were in a stringband format. The Segura brothers also enjoyed regional success during this period.

## THE STRINGBAND ERA (1935–1950)

The 1935 RCA Bluebird sessions exposed a shift in Cajun music. Though the accordion-based groups such as the Falcons continued to wax sides, the next decade would be dominated by hot stringbands. These bands abandoned the limited abilities of the accordion and explored the full range of their instruments. The stringbands added drums, steel guitars, lead guitars, mandolins, and occasionally trumpets and saxophones to the lineup. The result was an intense dance music that drew heavily from jazz and western swing, a big band form of country music best illustrated by Bob Wills and his Texas Playboys and the bands of Cliff Bruner and Milton Brown. Jimmie Rodgers, the "Father of Country Music," also exerted great influence on young Cajun musicians such as Crawford Vincent, Roy Gonzales, and Leroy "Happy Fats" LeBlanc.

At the center of the stringband movement was Leo Soileau. During the early 1930s he created his Three Aces stringband, later called the Rhythm Boys, and incorporated popular country music into his playbook. He especially enjoyed the songs of Jimmie Davis, a north Louisiana country singer and politician who wrote "You Are My Sunshine" and later was elected governor of Louisiana. Soileau's "Personne m'aime pas" was a French version of Davis' "Nobody's Darling But Mine." Soileau's band lasted until his retirement in the 1950s and was breeding ground for talent such as Crawford Vincent, Julius "Papa Cairo" Lamperez, and Harry Choates.

The most successful and long lasting stringband was the Hackberry Ramblers, led by the ethereal fiddler Luderin Darbonne. Formed in 1933, the first members of the band included Darbonne, guitarist Lennis Sonnier, and multi-insturmentalist Edwin Duhon. The Ramblers specialized in hot dance music and regularly recorded in English as well as French. Their English language records were released under the name "Riverside Ramblers" after the Riverside Tire Company that sponsored their radio show. The Ramblers were the first Cajun group to use amplification, running the equipment off of an idling Model T. Among the Hackberry Rambler's most successful recordings were "Une Piastre ici, une piastre la-bas" and "Jolie Blonde," the first time Amede Breaux's classic was given that name. The Ramblers experienced a long career that ended only in 2005 with the death of Edwin Duhon. Darbonne was the constant center of the band, and he proved to be remarkably flexible in his approach to music. Under his leadership the band adapted to changing tastes, playing rock and roll in the 1950s and adding an accordion in the 1960s. The band won numerous awards, was nominated for a Grammy, and appeared on MTV.

Other prominent stringbands included the Alley Boys of Abbeville, J. B. Fuselier and Miller's Merrymakers, and the Dixie Ramblers. Joe Falcon adapted to the new situation by switching to the drums and doing shows that alternated stringband and accordion sets. Meanwhile, Lawrence Walker revolutionized the accordion by adding strong swing elements to his playing style. This revolution was caught in several exciting and innovative sides cut in 1935, including "What's the Matter Now" and "Alberta," a swinging rendition of the blues classic "Corinne Corinna." Walker's accordion playing anticipated the fusionist style that emerged in the post-war years and established him as one of the most important artists in the music's history.

The stringband era produced the first Cajun artist to break out of the region and to heavily influence country music. Harry Choates was a brilliant fiddler, but personal demons haunted him until his early death. Born near Rayne, Choates performed on the fiddle and guitar with equal skill. He grew up in the east Texas oilfields where he absorbed the emerging hot western swing sound. By the late 1930s he was playing guitar in Shelly Lee Alley's hot stringband. Alley, who enjoyed great success in eastern Texas as a bandleader and had once backed the famous Jimmie Rodgers, provided Choates with an entrée into the country music circuit. Choates returned to southern Louisiana and the bands of Happy Fats LeBlanc and Leo Soileau. Choates' French was rough, but he made a great splash on the stage, dancing as he played and hollering in the style of Bob Wills when the band hit the groove. His popularity spread west toward Austin, and he spent most of his last years playing in Texas honky tonks. Choates' recordings sat firmly in the western swing genre, with heavy emphasis on his dramatic fiddle playing. Among his better recordings were "Grand Texas," "Port Arthur Blues," and "Austin Special." But it was his fiddle-driven version of "Jolie Blonde" that took the Gulf coast circuit by storm and turned Choates into a regional hero during the mid-1940s. The song gained such popularity that Roy Acuff and Moon Mullican cut English versions and spawned numerous spoofs and answer songs using "Jolie Blonde" as a motif. Choates suffered from alcoholism and mounting personal problems inhibited his moving into the higher ranks of country music. He died under mysterious circumstances in an Austin jail cell in 1950.

Jimmy C. Newman succeeded where Choates failed. Hailing from a small town outside Mamou, Newman joined Chuck Guillory's stringband in the mid-1940s. Guillory's band included the innovative steel guitar player Julius "Papa Cairo" Lamperez, whose version of "Grand Texas" helped to inspire Hank Williams' "Jambalaya." By the early 1950s Newman had moved to Nashville and established himself as a mainstream country star with hits such as "Cry Cry Darling." In the early 1960s he started recording Cajun music again, with heavy country influences. Newman joined the Grand Ole Opry, the only Cajun member of that institution, and was for many years the national face of Cajun music.

Another Cajun artist who emerged from the stringband era enjoyed brief success in Nashville. Vin Bruce (Ervin Broussard) had a rich baritone that made him one of the finest Cajun singers of all time. He possessed equal vocal facility in both French and English. His early years were spent in country groups such as Gene Rodrigue's Hillbilly Swing Kings. In 1951 he signed with Columbia Records and cut several beautiful records for the label, including "Dans La Louisianne." The emergence of rockabilly crippled his career, but Bruce remained popular in Louisiana. In 1961 he recorded for the Swallow label and enjoyed a renewed success that lasted into the twenty-first century.

Creole music was not recorded during the stringband era. However, the stylistic shift made its presence known among the Creoles. Canray Fontenot, a fiddler who belonged to the extended Ardoin family complex of musicians, formed a stringband called the Duralde Ramblers and played hot string music during the period. Like their Cajun neighbors, Creoles absorbed the sounds coming over the radio waves and via recordings. The emerging sound of rhythm and blues and jump blues, as played by artists such as Louis Jordan, proved deeply influential. That influence slowly fused with traditional la-la music and would explode in the 1950s.

## THE DANCEHALL ERA (1950–1980s)

World War II brought an economic boom to southern Louisiana. For the first time, Cajuns earned steady salaries in the oil fields and shipyards. Disposable income was used to buy appliances, electrify homes, and purchase records. The result was an increasing demand for Cajun records. Major record labels ignored the Cajun market, except for the stringbands, which could be

Buckwheat Zydeco performs during the 2006 New Orleans Jazz and Heritage Festival in New Orleans on Saturday, May 6, 2006. Courtesy AP Images.

sold to the country audience as well as Cajuns. In the decades following the war, entrepreneurial Louisianians filled the demand by establishing labels that catered to local tastes. Disposable income, new products, and a growing sense of pride in being Cajun and Creole combined to reinvigorate Cajun and Creole music. The new situation demanded a new music, one that fused elements of various styles to produce the dancehall sound. That sound placed the accordion in a stringband complex and was hammered out in the dance halls during war and early post-war periods.

Local record companies facilitated the spread of the dancehall sound. These companies were led by enterprising men who combined business with culture and in the process nurtured south Louisiana musics of all types. Record company owners J.D. Miller, Eddie Shuler, George Khoury, and Floyd Soileau all exhibited catholic tastes in music and a willingness to allow musicians to explore sounds that could turn a profit. Eddie Shuler founded Goldband in Lake Charles, which would release the first records in both the dancehall and zydeco styles. J.D. Miller of Crowley (Mastertrack Studios) was a prolific recorder of Cajun, zydeco, blues, and country. He also penned Kitty Wells' hit "It Wasn't God Who Made Honky Tonk Angels" and acted as a talent scout for national record companies. Floyd Soileau entered the record business in 1956 and was soon producing music for a variety of labels such as Swallow, Jin, and Maison de Soul. Shrewd businessmen, these producers and company owners often rubbed musicians the wrong way, and complaints about royalties and song ownership haunted some of them. But without them, the recorded legacy of Cajun and Creole music would be much poorer, and the music might have died without the recording opportunities provided by men such as Miller and Soileau.

The first artist to benefit from the post-war boom was Iry Lejeune, a nearly blind accordionist from Acadia Parish. Lejeune was heavily influenced by his cousin Angelas Lejeune and the great Amede Ardoin, but he also absorbed the stringband sounds of Leo Soileau and the country music coming in over the airwaves. He learned to play the fiddle while attending a school for the blind in Baton Rouge. While visiting his brother in New Orleans, Lejeune met Virgil Bozeman's Oklahoma Tornadoes, a country band that played in the Magazine Street honky tonks that catered to rural immigrants who moved to New Orleans during the war. In 1948 Lejeune traveled with the Tornadoes to a Texas recording session. There he cut "La Valse du Pont d'Amour," the first accordion record in the dancehall style. The record proved immensely popular, and soon Lejeune was recording for Eddie Shuler's Goldband label. Lejuene composed new songs such as "Grand Bosco" and "J'ai Fait Une Grosse Erreur." These titles featured his accordion playing in a stringband context with wailing, emotional vocals. Lejeune's career was cut tragically short when he was killed in an automobile accident in 1955.

Though Lejeune was the first to record in the dancehall style, the form had been percolating in the western prairie dance halls for years. Basically, the dancehall sound consists of a driving, swinging accordion accompanied by the fiddle, drums, guitars, and a "crying" steel guitar. The music was amplified to cut through the noise of the dancehall. Waltzes, two-steps, and jitterbug tunes dominate the repertoire. More than anything else, it was music for dancing and socializing. Among the formulators of the dancehall tradition were men who were older than Lejeune and had probably worked out the basic framework by the time he recorded. These innovators included Nathan Abshire, Lawrence Walker, and Austin Pitre, all accordionists with experience in the stringbands, ironically as fiddlers.

Nathan Abshire was born in Gueydan but spent most of his professional life in the prairie town of Basile, known as a hard living, hard dancing place. Basile sported some of the most famous dance halls and honky tonks of the post-war era. Abshire and his band, The Pine Grove Boys, held the house band position at the most famous Basile club, the Avalon. Abshire's music was rooted deeply in the blues as indicated by some of his most important recordings, "French Blues," "Offshore Blues," and "Pine Grove Blues," now a standard in the Cajun repertoire. He made his earliest recordings in 1935 with Happy Fats' band, but he struggled to integrate his rough accordion style to the stringband format. By the late 1940s, Abshire had refined his style and placed the accordion firmly in the midst of strings. Abshire's music maintained a steady dance groove that kept him popular until his death in 1981. An humble man somewhat overwhelmed by the fame he garnered, Abshire was always more comfortable in the dance halls than on festival circuit.

Born in Scott in 1907, Lawrence Walker transformed the Cajun accordion style by adding strong elements of swing to his playing. This transformation is revealed in Walker's historic 1935 Bluebird recording of "Alberta," a reworking of the blues standard "Corinne, Corinna" that he performed in English. By the post-war years, Walker put together a stellar band (the Wandering Aces) that exemplified the dancehall sound. Walker was a perfectionist, both as a band leader and a musician, and demanded high standards from his musicians. The Ace's performances were tight and smooth. A gifted singer and composer, Walker's classic recordings include "Chere Alice," "Reno Waltz," and "Petits Yeaux Noir." Walker regularly incorporated new styles into his repertoire. He recorded an early Cajun rock song, "Allons a Rock and Roll," but his sound always came out Cajun. His reputation gained him the title "King of the Cajun Dancehalls," and he remained popular among dancers until his death in 1968. Despite his popularity, Walker has not received the attention he deserves from historians of Cajun music.

If Abshire represents the blues tinge in the dancehall era and Walker the elegance of sound, Austin Pitre was the raucous, loud, hard-edged voice. A powerful accordionist, Pitre hailed from Eunice. His band, the Evangeline Playboys, played hot dance music punctuated by Pitre's pulsating accordion and a cutting steel guitar sound that pierced the dancehall atmosphere. Pitre cut a series of stunning records in early 1960s for the Swallow label that included "Opelousas Waltz," "Rene's Special," and the blues-drenched "Don't Shake My Tree." Pitre also waxed the seminal version of "Les Flumes d'Enfer." Pitre's vocals were highly emotional, crying over the music.

Pitre's sound was hard Cajun and among some urban and upwardly mobile Cajuns, too much a reminder of the hard rural existence from which they sprang. The urban group gravitated to the dance sounds of Aldus Roger and Belton Richard. Roger and his Lafayette Playboys had a driving sound that was tight and used little improvisation. Roger's vocals were often criticized for lacking emotion. Nevertheless, Roger quickly gained popularity and was a staple on Lafayette television. Belton Richard polished the dancehall sound, smoothing out the rough edges and singing in a detached manner. He reintroduced twin fiddles to Cajun music and incorporated influences from 1960s country music. The dancehall era produced numerous fine bands and innovative performers such as Alphe Bergeron, Shirley Bergeron, Joe Bonsall, Blackie Forrestier, Walter Mouton, the Michot brothers, Eddie Lejeune, and many others.

The finest singer of the dancehall era was D.L. Menard from Erath. Heavily influenced by Hank Williams, Sr. (as were many Cajun singers), Menard sang in a nasal style that sliced into noisy dance halls, and wrote songs dealing with the problems of love and a fading rural lifestyle. His biggest hit, "La Porte d'en Arriere" ("The Back Door"), dealt with drinking, while the lovely "Rebecca Ann" is a fine ballad opining on a difficult love. He also regularly sang country music, demonstrating the close ties between the genres, and especially favored the work of his idol Williams.

## ZYDECO

Creole music was poorly recorded before World War II. Only three Creoles recorded commercially in the 1920s and 1930s: Douglas Bellard, Kirby Riley, and Amede Ardoin, and of these, only Ardoin left an extensive legacy. In years following Ardoin's recordings, Creole music underwent a process similar to Cajun music, molding outside influences into a regional style. This process resulted in a music that came to be called "zydeco" based on the pronunciation of the phrase "les haricots sont pas sale," literally meaning "the beans are not salty" but actually signifying a state of poverty. Zydeco formed in the 1940s with a fusion of rhythm and blues into the Creole accordion tradition.

Zydeco had reached its basic form several years before the first recording was made by Boozoo Chavis in 1953. The blues singer Lightnin' Hopkins recorded "Zolo Go" about 1948, a song that tried to approximate the sound he heard among the Creole expatriates in Houston. "Zolo Go" is a straight blues song performed over a strange organ sound in which Hopkins tries to suggest an accordion. In 1949 Clarence Garlow released the rhythm and blues song "Bon Ton Roula," which included a reference to "zydeco" as a dance. Thus, the form was well established by the late 1940s to be referenced in the rhythm and blues scene. The man most responsible for zydeco's rise was the accordionist Clifton Chenier.

Clifton Chenier fused rhythm and blues into Ardoin's style and produced the driving sound of zydeco. Chenier included saxophones and drums in his band and began playing the piano accordion. He also sang many of his lyrics in English, reflecting not only the bilingual nature of Creole society, but also the growing fan base among non-French speakers. Additionally, Chenier developed a new instrument for the genre. Creoles had long played the washboard in a raspy rhythmic fashion. Chenier designed a harnessed vest version of the washboard ("frottoir") to be played by his brother Cleveland. The vest rubboard was played with bottle openers or thimbles, and the player could adjust the sound by the amount of space between the vest and the player's chest. Chenier was a remarkable blues performer, and the revival of his career in the early 1960s did much to expand the popularity of zydeco.

In 1954 Chenier recorded his first session in Lake Charles, the titles later released on the Elko and Post labels. Chenier's records eventually were picked up by the Specialty label, and he enjoyed his first substantial hit, "Ay Tete Fee," in 1955. Chenier's newfound popularity took him to the rhythm and blues circuit, where he performed with such artists as B.B. King, Ray Charles, and Big Joe Turner. After two sessions with Specialty, Chenier moved to the Chess label. During this period, his music took a decided rhythm and blues feel, perhaps the result of his touring experience. This fusion of the Creole accordion style with rhythm and blues helped define burgeoning zydeco sound. Chenier also adopted the piano accordion as his primary instrument as opposed to the smaller diatonic (or "tit noir") accordion favored among traditional artists. The music was both bluesy and propulsive, with an intensity accentuated by the power of the piano accordion. Chenier developed a national popularity and toured extensively. In 1955 he toured with a very young Etta James .

The emergence of rock and roll dimmed Chenier's national career, and by 1960 he was firmly back in Louisiana. He recorded for J.D. Miller's Crowley-based Zynn label in the late 1950s, but produced no significant hits. His career stalled until Lightnin' Hopkins introduced him to Chris Strachwitz. Chenier began recording with Strachwitz's Arhoolie label, inititating one of the most productive and rewarding careers in zydeco music. In 1964, Chenier cut his first record for Arhoolie. The resulting single, "Ay Ai Ai," restarted his career. Chenier deeply appreciated Strachwitz's unfailing promotion of his career.

Chenier started touring Europe in the late 1960s and in 1969 performed at the American Folk Blues Festival in Germany. During the 1970s, he kept up a hectic touring and recording schedule. Chenier became a popular regular at such festivals as the Montreaux Jazz and Pop Festival, the New Orleans Jazz and Heritage Festival, and the Berkeley Folk Festival. He released albums on Arhoolie, Bayou, Jin, Maison de Soul, and other labels. He recorded several live performances that come close to capturing the intensity of a live Chenier show. Chenier was equally at home playing traditional Creole tunes and blues, but he developed a strong affinity for rhythm and blues tinged dance music. He took to wearing a crown on stage and proclaimed himself the "King of Zydeco." In 1983 Chenier won a Grammy for his *I'm Here* album (Alligator 4729), and the following year he played for President Reagan at the White House. He also received a National Heritage Fellowship, awarded by the National Endowment for the Arts.

Zydeco enjoyed great popularity outside Louisiana. The region of southeast Texas from Orange to Houston experienced a heavy Cajun and Creole migration during the war years. South Louisianians often jokingly refer to the area as "Cajun Lapland" because Cajuns "lapped" over into Texas. Houston nightclubs provided a venue for the development of zydeco, particularly the more rhythm and blues style. In Acadiana, an older, more rustic sound dominated, perhaps best illustrated by the highly percussive and syncopated work of Boozoo Chavis. His best work is simple yet mesmerizing, and focuses a hard dance rhythm. Chavis regularly participated in zydeco trail rides in which groups of mounted ranchers and farmers rode through the countryside and then held a party at the end of the ride. Band battles are also common between zydeco musicians. Following the death of Clifton Chenier, Chavis and his archrival Andrus "Beau Jocque" Espre often competed for the title of "King of Zydeco."

Innovation is a basic element of zydeco. Just as Chenier added rhythm and blues elements, Beau Jocque mixed funk into the zydeco gumbo. During the 1970s, the Sam Brothers fused the decade's soul music into zydeco and came

Rosie Ledet of Rosie Ledet and the Zydeco Playboys performs during the 2006 New Orleans Jazz and Heritage Festival in New Orleans on Sunday, April 30, 2006. Courtesy AP Images.

to be known as the Creole Jackson Five. Rockin' Sidney enjoyed a national hit with "My Toot Toot" in 1985 after years of struggling on the south Louisiana circuit. "My Toot Toot" was a novelty song which was released at a time when Cajun and zydeco entered the national conscience, led by the efforts of such artists as Buckwheat Zydeco. In recent years, musicians such as Keith Frank have experimented with rap and soul elements. Zydeco has also been friendly to female performers. Queen Ida, centered in the expatriate community in California, was an early female star. With Rosie Ledet, zydeco found its first sex symbol. Easily fusing blues, zydeco, and soul, Ledet presented a smoldering image on stage and readily turned old male images on their heads. Geno Delafosse performs in a style closer to Cajun music, and this has allowed him to break down many racial barriers, including performing at previously exclusive white clubs such as Angele's Whiskey Landing.

## SWAMP POP

During the 1950s and 1960s young Cajuns and Creoles fell under the spell of rock and roll. Especially strong was the influence of Fats Domino and Jerry Lee Lewis. These young musicians forged a South Louisiana style of rock and roll that eventually came to be called "Swamp Pop." The new style featured a front line of saxophones and trumpets with lead guitars played in the rock style, a strong rhythm laid down by the drums, and a tinkling piano sound drawn from country music. This style was exemplified by the Boogie Kings, a band that often provided backing for major Swamp Pop singers. The Boogie Kings referred to their music as "blue-eyed soul." The hallmark of the Swamp Pop sound was an aching vocal style delivered in English.

Singers occupied the heart of Swamp Pop and among the best were Tommy McLain, Johnnie Allen, Joe Barry, and Rod Bernard. All had smooth vocal styles that drew upon the mainstream pop tradition and preferred to sing love ballads. Several Swamp Pop singers gained brief national recognition. Rod

Bernard performed his major hit "This Should Go On Forever" on American Bandstand, and Dale and Grace reached the number one position on the national charts with "I'm Leaving It Up to You" in 1963.

With such an emphasis on singing, Swamp Pop songwriters were particularly strong. The best was Bobby Charles (Guidry) who penned numerous hits for Fats Domino, including "See You Later Alligator," "Walking to New Orleans," and the Louisiana chestnut "Before I Grow Too Old." Jimmy Donley came from Mississippi but melded easily into the Swamp Pop scene, which spread out along the Gulf coast. Donley wrote several of the genre's standards, including "Think It Over," "Hello, Remember Me," and "Born to Be a Loser."

Swamp Pop was an interracial musical movement with African American performers enjoying great success and garnering white fans. Huey "Cookie" Thierry and the Cupcakes reached #47 on the national charts with their standard "Mathilda," still a favorite on Louisiana jukeboxes. Shelton Dunaway, Lil' Alfred, and King Karl all experienced regional fame. Phil Phillips' "Sea of Love" became a national hit for the disc jockey from Jennings.

Subgenres of Swamp Pop include rockabilly and "hippie" music from the region. Many Cajuns embraced the rockabilly style of Elvis Presley and Jerry Lee Lewis. These acts usually performed in English and differed little from their mainstream contemporaries. Among the best rockabillies from southwestern Louisiana were Al Ferrier, Jay Chevalier, and Johnny Janot. "Hippie" music reflected the counter culture of the 1960s and added a psychedelic edge to Cajun music. Rufus Jagneaux ranks as the best of these bands. Their funky harmonica-driven version of "The Back Door" reveals the possibilities of the style, and "Opelousas Sostan" was a regional hit for the group.

Swamp Pop was widely derided by critics, most of whom were purists from outside of Louisiana or academics who saw the music as too "American." But Swamp Pop musicians simply continued a tradition of adapting popular trends to the region. Singing in English did promote a national career, but it also reflected the reality of the decline of French as a primary language among Cajuns and Creoles in the post-war era. Adapting to rock and roll differed little from Leo Soileau's acceptance of country music influence in the 1930s or zydeco's embrace of rhythm and blues. What mattered was that the popular style was refashioned to meet local standards. Swamp Pop remains deeply popular in southern Louisiana and continues to produce new artists of high quality, such as Don Rich. The form deserves to be ranked with Cajun music and zydeco as one of the great forms to emerge from Louisiana. The local public has already given it that honor.

## THE RENAISSANCE YEARS (1970s & 1980s)

While the dancehall and zydeco sounds dominated the post-war years and constituted a grassroots cultural movement, the civil rights movement of the 1960s radicalized some Cajuns and caused them to attempt to preserve traditional culture. The first step in this process was taken by a veteran of the Louisiana dance halls.

Dewey Balfa had played with his brothers for years in the honky tonks of the prairie region. In 1964 Balfa, Gladius Thibodeaux, and Louis Lejeune traveled to the Newport Folk Festival to demonstrate Cajun music. Many of Balfa's friends warned him not to go, fearing that the crowd would make fun of his music. Other elite Cajuns felt that Cajun music, derided as "chank-a-chank," provided a horrid example of the culture. An editorial from the Opelousas paper opined,

> Cajuns brought some mighty fine things down from Nova Scotia with them, including their jolly selves, but their so-called music is one thing I wished they hadn't...All we can do is sit back and wait for the verdict from Newport. I am not sure Cajun music is on trial in Newport. It may be us. Their verdict could subject us to tortures like the world has never known.

Balfa met with stunning success in Newport. He came back radicalized and deeply aware of the value of his native culture. Balfa began an almost one man campaign to raise the image of both Cajun music and culture. He was supported by such national figures as Alan Lomax and Ralph Rinzler. With the national spotlight on the Balfas, the brothers recorded a series of stunning albums for Swallow titled *The Balfa Brothers Play Traditional Cajun Music*. Balfa presented musicians as cultural heroes and began to urge the academic study of Cajun culture.

The state of Louisiana officially recognized the grassroots movement in 1968 when it founded the Council for the Development of French in Louisiana, called CODOFIL. The Council focused on reviving the French language, by which it meant standard French, not Cajun or Creole. The Council's leader, politician James Domengeaux, came from an elite group called the genteel Acadians. While proud of their French heritage, the group was embarrassed by the rural Cajun culture. It was only with great effort that Barry Ancelet convinced Domengeaux to support the 1974 Tribute to Cajun Music festival, held in Lafayette. The astounding success of the festival opened Domengeaux's eyes to the importance of the regional culture. The festival became an annual event under the title Festivals Acadiens, and is now the major celebration of the region's culture.

Coinciding with the official and academic movement was a rebirth of pride in Cajun ethnicity. Cajun music and zydeco became fashionable, and dance halls flourished alongside restaurants such as Mulates and Prejeans, which featured music as well. Many younger musicians embraced Cajun and Creole music, often with a radical edge.

At the heart of the radical fringe were the cousins Zachary Richard and Michael Doucet. Both highly intelligent and skillful musicians, Richard and Doucet spent several years abroad and returned hoping to raise cultural and ethnic awareness through music. Richard made brash statements about ethnicity in his early years, calling for a radical rebuke of modern urban American culture. His calls for action confused many Cajuns who were happy with their lives in prosperous 1970s Louisiana. Though he has tempered his rhetoric, Richard remains an active advocate for Cajun culture. A provocative and interesting performer, Richard's greatest success has come outside of his native Louisiana. In many ways, his greatest contribution can be found in his deeply introspective songwriting and his talent for integrating rock into Cajun music while respecting its boundaries. Richard is also an accomplished poet and has written several children's books.

Doucet became the national face of Cajun music with his band BeauSoleil, named after the leader of the Acadian resistance to the Grand Derangement. Doucet immersed himself in Cajun music history, studying with fiddle legends Dennis McGee, Varise Connor, Dewey Balfa, and others. As a result he formed BeauSoleil in 1976 to play traditional Cajun music while adding elements from such genres as jazz and Caribbean (best seen in "Zydeco Gris Gris"). The band has recorded widely and included an all star set of members, including Jimmy Breaux, David Doucet, Al Tharp, Bill Ware, Tommy Alesi, and Mitch Reed. BeauSoleil enjoys considerable popularity outside of Louisiana and have appeared on recordings with such artists as Mary Chapin Carpenter.

Stanley Dural, known as Buckwheat Zydeco, mirrored the national and international fame of Richard and BeauSoleil. Buckwheat Zydeco continued the urban zydeco style pioneered by Clifton Chenier by performing with the piano accordion and utilizing front lines of horns and electric keyboards. Dural launched his own zydeco career in 1979. He and his group, the Ils Sont Parti band, enjoyed great success with a sound that fused zydeco with 1980s funk and soul. In 1986 he signed with Island Records, the first zydeco group signed to a major label. His high profile led to recordings with several mainstream acts including Paul Simon and Dwight Yoakam. Buckwheat Zydeco's work has been criticized over the years for being too commercial, yet Dural remains highly popular, especially outside of Louisiana.

While acts such as Zachary Richard, BeauSoleil, and Buckwheat Zydeco took the sounds of Cajun and Creole music to the national and international stages, the music continued to evolve in Louisiana. Wayne Toups introduced his fusion of Cajun and zydeco, called Zydecajun, in 1984. Toups mixed Cajun, rhythm and blues, Caribbean, and Southern Rock to produce a potent, hard edged music that offended purists and delighted younger listeners who enjoyed a wide range of music. Toups combined his music with a flamboyant performance style. Other acts, such as Mamou, fused rock elements into Cajun music, following the path forged by Michael Doucet's earlier band Coteau. By the 1990s, the most popular Cajun acts on the dancehall circuit included Jamie Bergeron and the Kickin' Cajun and Travis Matte and the Zydeco Kingpins. These newer groups perform music from across genres and often add popular tunes to their repertoire, usually in response to audience requests. Matte, for example, has covered versions of "La Bamba" and "Summer of '69." Younger artists have blurred lines between Cajun and zydeco. Horace

Trahan and the New Ossun Express exemplifies this trend with a funky music not quite Cajun nor zydeco. In many ways, Trahan's sound is a throwback to a sparer rural sound. His hit "That Butt Thing" was a risque number gained unexpected success in 2001 and inspired a series of off color tunes such as Matte's "Booty Call" and "Vibrator" and Rosie Ledet's zydeco tribute to Viagra, "Pick It Up."

Groups such as the Pine Leaf Boys and the Lost Bayou Ramblers have mined the history of Cajun music in recent years and revived the older dancehall and swing styles. The Pine Leaf Boys, led by Wilson Savoy, play in the dancehall style of Austin Pitre and Lawrence Walker. The Lost Bayou Ramblers, centered on brothers Louis and Andre Michot, explore the Cajun swing style of Leo Soileau and Harry Choates. These groups perform high energy shows and have attracted large crowds of young Cajuns to whom the old sounds are new. They represent the fusion of the academic explorations of the music and performance that bring a new relevance to the best music from the genre's history. Meanwhile, dancehall veterans such as Ray Abshire and Walter Mouton enjoy a popular following and have emerged as cultural heroes to young fans attracted to the genre by the Lost Bayou Ramblers and the Pine Leaf Boys.

Zydeco continues to evolve and has added elements of rap and hip hop to its repertoire. This is best seen in the work of such artists as Chris Ardoin and Keith Frank. Ardoin in particular has taken the fusion to new heights, often shocking old school zydeco purists with his modern style. He draws a large and diverse audience when he appears in venues such as the Mid City Bowling Lanes in New Orleans. Rosie Ledet is the most important female zydeco artist on the current scene. She has injected a smoldering sexuality to her performances, which had been previously lacking in zydeco. Ledet is also a sensitive and creative songwriter. Perhaps the brightest star on the zydeco circuit is Geno Delafosse, the son of zydeco legend John Delafosse. Geno's music stylistically rests somewhere in the nexus between rural zydeco, Cajun music, and the more uptown sounds. As a result, Delafosse's popularity crosses racial lines and points out the old connections between Creole and Cajun music.

Cajun and Creole music was never "pure." At its heart lies a deeply improvisational culture willing to experiment while maintaining traditional boundaries. The music is also participatory, with dance remaining the driving force. Musicians, Cajun, zydeco and Swamp Pop, all try to live up to an old adage: "You can't go wrong, if you play it right."

## BIBLIOGRAPHY

### Music Books

Allen, Johnnie. *Memories: A Pictorial History of South Louisiana Music 1920s -1980s.* Lafayette: JADFEL Publishing, 1988.

Allen, Johnnie, and Bernice Larson Webb. *Born to Be a Loser: The Jimmy Donley Story.* Lafayette: JADFEL Publishing, 1992.

Amedee, Patricia Juste. *Zachary Richard: Au large du cap Enrage.* Montreal: Les Intouchables, 2005.

Ancelet, Barry Jean. *Cajun and Creole Music Makers, Musiciens cadiens et reoles.* Jackson: University Press of Mississippi, 1999.

Ancelet, Barry Jean. *Cajun Music: Its Origins and Development.* Lafayette: Center for Louisiana Studies, 1989.

Ancelet, Barry Jean. *"Capitaine voyage ton flag" The Traditional Cajun Country Mardi Gras.* Lafayette: Center for Louisiana Studies, 1989.

Ancelet, Barry Jean. *Travailler, C'est Trop Dur: The Tools of Cajun Music.* Lafayette: Lafayette Natural History Museum Association, 1984.

Bernard, Shane. *Swamp Pop: Cajun and Creole Rhythm and Blues.* Jackson: University Press of Mississippi, 1996.

Brasseaux, Ryan A., and Kevin S. Fontenot. *Accordions, Fiddles, Two Step, and Swing: A Cajun Music Reader.* Lafayette: Center for Louisiana Studies, 2006.

Broven, John. *South To Louisiana: The Music of the Cajun Bayous.* Gretna, LA: Pelican Publishing, 1983.

Nyhan, Pat, Brian Rollins, and David Babb. *Let the Good Times Roll! A Guide to Cajun & Zydeco Music.* Portland: Upbeat Books, 1997.

Olivier, Rick and Ben Sandmel. *Zydeco!* Jackson: University Press of Mississippi, 1999.

Russell, Tony. *Country Music Records: A Discography. 1921–1942.* Oxford: Oxford University Press, 2004.

Tisserand, Michael. *The Kingdom of Zydeco.* New York: Arcade Publishing, 1998.

Veillon, Ching. *Creole Music Man: Bois Sec Ardoin.* Philadelphia: Xlibris Press, 2003.

Wood, Roger. *Texas Zydeco.* Austin, 2006.

Yule, Ron. *When the Fiddle Was King.* Natchitoches: Northwestern State University Press, 2006.

## History and Culture

Ancelet, Barry Jean, Jay Edward, and Glen Pitre. *Cajun Country.* Jackson: University Press of Mississippi, 1991.

Bernard, Shane. *The Cajuns: Americanization of a People.* Jackson: University Press of Mississippi, 2003.

Brasseaux, Carl A. *Acadian to Cajun: Transformation of a People.* Jackson: University Press of Mississippi, 1992.

Brasseaux, Carl A. *The Founding of New Acadia.* Baton Rouge: Louisiana State University Press, 1987.

Brasseaux, Carl A. *French, Cajun, Creole, Houma: A Primer on Francophone Louisiana.* Baton Rouge: Louisiana State University Press, 2005.

Brasseaux, Carl A., Keith P. Fontenot, and Claude F. Oubre. *Creoles of Color in the Bayou Country.* Jackson: University Press of Mississippi, 1994.

Dorman, James H., editor. *Creoles of Color of the Gulf South.* Knoxville, 1996.

Faragher, John Mack. *A Great and Noble Scheme: The Tragic Story of the Expulsion of the French Acadians from their American Homeland.* New York: W.W. Norton, 2005.

# RECORDINGS

## Individual Artists & Groups

August, Lynn. *Sauce Piquante*. Black Top 1092. 1993.
Joe Barry. *I'm A Fool To Care: The Complete Recordings*. Night Train NTI CD. 2003.
Bergeron, Shirley. *French Rocking Boogie*.Ace 353. 1993.
Bruce, Vin. *The Essential Collection*. Swallow 6163. 2000.
Coteau. *Highly Seasoned Cajun Music*. Rounder 6078. 1997.
Fontenot, Rodney. *Cajun Fiddle The Way It Was*. Sterling 2001. 2006.
Fruge, Wade. *Old Style Cajun Music*. Arhoolie 476. 1998.
Magnolia Sisters. *Prends Courage*. Arhoolie 439. 1995.
McGee, Dennis. *The Complete Early Recordings 1929–1930*. Yazoo 2012. 1994.
*Matte, Travis, and the Zydeco Kingpins*. Mhat MP-04002. 2005.
Pitre, Austin. *Opelousas Waltz*. Arhoolie 452. 1997.
Queen Ida. *Caught in the Act*. Crescendo 2181. 1990.
Rockin' Sidney. *My Toot Toot*. Maison de Soul 1009. 1995.
Roger, Aldus & the Lafayette Playboys. *King of the French Accordion*. Masterworks 5060–2.
Sam Brothers 5. SAM *(Get Down!)*. Arhoolie 9004.
Trahan, Horace. *That Butt Thing*. Zydeco Hound ZHR 1010. 2003.
Zydeco Force. *It's La La Time*. Maison de Soul 1054. 1995.

## Various artists

*Alligator Stomp: Cajun and Creole Classics*. Rhino 70946. 1990.
*Allons Cajun Rock 'n Roll*. Ace 367. 1993.
*Another Saturday Night*. Ace CDCH 288. 1993.
*Cajun Country: More Hits from the Swamp*. JSP 7749. 2006.
*Cajun Dance Hall Special*. Rounder 11570. 1992.
*Cajun Early Recordings*. JSP 7726. 2004.
*Cajun Honky Tonk: The Khoury Recordings, The Early 1950s*. Arhoolie 427. 1995.
*Cajun String Bands*. Arhoolie 7014. 1997.
*Early Jin Singles: Southland Rock'n' Roll*. Ace CDCHD 878. 2004.
*Floyd's Early Cajun Singles*. Ace CDCH 743. 1999.
*Folksongs of the Louisiana Cajuns*. Arhoolie 359. 1994.
*Historic Victor Bluebird Sessions, Vols. 1, 2, & 3*. CMF 013, 017, & 018. 1994.
*Louisiana Cajun French Music Volume 1*. Rounder 6001. 1994.
*Louisiana Recordings: Cajun & Creole Music 1934–1937, Vols. 1 & 2*. Rounder 1842 & 1843.
*Louisiana Saturday Night*. Ace CDCH 490. 1993.
*Swamp Gold Country*. Jin 9082. 2006.
*Zydeco Champs*. Arhoolie 328. 1993.
*Zydeco Vol. 1—The Early Years, 1961–62*. Arhoolie 307. 1993.

## FILMS

*Cajun Country: Don't Drop the Potato*, VHS, Vestapol 13077.

*Cajun Visits/Les Blues de Balfa*, VHS, Vestapol 13001.

*Dance for a Chicken: The Cajun Mardi Gras*, DVD, Attakapas Productions.

*Dry Wood*, DVD, Flower Films.

*From La La to Zydeco*, DVD, University of Louisiana at Lafayette.

*J'ai Ete au Bal: I Went to the Dance: The Cajun & Zydeco Music of Louisiana*, DVD, Brazos Films BF 103.

*Hot Pepper*, DVD, Flower Films.

*Pete Seeger's Rainbow Quest: The Clancy Brothers & Mamou Cajun Band*, DVD, Shanchie 609.

*Spend It All*, DVD, Flower Films.

# 2

# Irish Music in America

## *Paul F. Wells*

### INTRODUCTION

Shortly before 10:00 o'clock on the night of July 15, 2005, a group of seven Irish musicians and more than ten times that many ardent fans gather in The Wayside Inn, a tavern near the town of East Durham in the Catskill Mountains of upstate New York. East Durham itself is not exactly on the beaten path, and the Wayside is several miles and two or three back roads away, in the village of Oak Hill. The night is hot and muggy, and the presence of so many bodies in the relatively small interior of the inn taxes the ability of the air conditioning system to keep everyone cool. The bar does a brisk business, and the clink of glasses provides a percussive counterpoint to the smuddling of the crowd and the musical snippets that fill the air as the musicians tune up and warm up.

The players are seated within an oblong half-wall enclosure that is no more than 12 feet wide and perhaps twice as long. Listeners two and three deep crowd around the perimeter, the ones in front lucky enough to be able to rest their drinks and their elbows on top of the half-wall. Many are poised with cassette and mini-disc recorders at the ready, eager to capture what they hope will be an evening of memorable music in a medium that will let them revisit the experience many times in the future. Others simply chat amongst themselves, waiting for the music to begin. Latecomers and those who are content to listen from afar fill the tables in another section of the room.

Bits and pieces of as many different tunes as there are musicians create a cacophony akin to that of an orchestra tuning up, though it is not a Beethoven symphony or Mozart concerto that will be played tonight. Finally, harpist Michael Rooney calls out: "Alright Mike—off you go!" and 78-year-old flute player Mike Rafferty launches into "My Darling Asleep," a well-known jig. As he finishes the first four-beat phrase, he is joined by Edel Fox on concertina, then by June McCormack, another flute player. By the time the initial run-through of the tune is completed, fiddler Dana Lyn and uilleann pipers Benedict Koehler and Brian McNamara have jumped in as well. Rooney, distracted by a conversation with someone in the crowd, is the last to join, but when he finally does the chordal accompaniment he plays on the harp provides some much-needed bottom end to the sonic spectrum, and pulls everything together. As the sound of the music swells, the ambient noise from the crowd diminishes, and the attention of the bystanders is focused on the music.

After everyone plays the tune three times through, McCormack flows right into the opening phrase of a different one. The others hesitate just long enough to effectively give her a four-beat solo, but as soon as they all recognize the new tune they come right back in. After three times through the second tune Rafferty again leads the way in a change to a third one. Again, there is only the briefest hesitation on the part of the rest of the musicians, and they move seamlessly into "Behind the Haystack." When they approach the end of the third rendering of that tune, nearly-imperceptible cues pass from one musician to another and the music comes to a halt. Everyone stops playing at the same time as if it had been a rehearsed move. Listeners offer enthusiastic applause and whoops of approval. The musicians move their instruments to "at ease" positions, reach for their drink glasses, and begin to chat with their neighbors. After a few minutes of this downtime for socializing, Rafferty picks up his flute and kicks things into gear again. It is a set of two reels this time, the individual names for which nobody seems to know but that are known collectively as "Crowley's Reels."

The evening continues in this fashion—a set of two or three tunes strung together in a medley, followed by a brief break, followed by more tunes—for nearly three hours. During the course of the evening a few other musicians join the core group, including Gearóid Ó hAllmhuráin on concertina, and Willie and Siobhán Kelly, a terrific young husband-and-wife, fiddle-and-flute team.

When everyone senses that it is time to wind things up for the night, one of the players calls for a final set, and they launch into a group of three classic reels: "Rakish Paddy," "Spike Island Lassies," and "The Old Bush." By this time the crowd has thinned out somewhat, and many of those who remain are looking a bit bleary-eyed due to the lateness of the hour. Nevertheless, the applause at the end of the set is enthusiastic and heartfelt. The musicians pack up their instruments but then sit down for one last pint and one last visit with friends. A sense of bliss lingers in the room. Nobody really wants the night to end.

What has gone on here tonight was an Irish music "session" or, as it is spelled in Gaelic, *seisiún*, a combination of informal music-making and general socializing that has emerged in the past generation or two as one of the principal performance contexts for Irish traditional music. This session at the Wayside was typical in some ways but unusual in others. It occurred as a scheduled event in Catskill Irish Arts Week (CIAW), an annual festival and music school that is one of the most popular such events in the country.[1] While many sessions are open to all comers, this particular one at the Wayside was one of the festival's "listening sessions." Participation as a player was by invitation only, and most of the musicians were members of the CIAW faculty. This ensured not only a high level of musicianship, but commonality of repertoire as well. This night's session was centered around Mike Rafferty, a native of Galway who emigrated to the America in 1949 and who has long been a mainstay of the Irish music community in the northern New Jersey and New York City area. He is a highly respected tradition-bearer, and the other musicians joining him at the Wayside were all younger players who were familiar with his repertoire. "Rafferty-centric" is the way one person described the night's session.

While the session at the Wayside was going on, there were numerous open sessions happening at other pubs scattered around the hills in the region. Every summer for the duration of Catskill Irish Arts Week, East Durham and environs becomes one of the centers of Irish music in the United States, or, for that matter, in the world. The CIAW faculty changes from year to year but always includes many of today's finest Irish and Irish-American musicians. In 2005 students came from such distant states as California, Washington, and Tennessee, and there was even a small contingent who had traveled from France. The chance to study with master musicians is one of the main draws, but the late-night pub sessions are just as important for pulling outsiders to the Catskills. Indeed, many who come do not register for any classes, but are there simply for the music and the *craic*—an Irish word (pronounced "crack") meaning great fun or good times—of the sessions. In 2005 there were approximately 475 registered participants. When one takes into account the friends and family members who accompany the registrants, plus those who fly under the radar altogether and come just to hang out, it results in what CIAW Artistic Director Paul Keating terms a "swell factor" of two to three times that many. Keating estimates that by the final weekend of the 2005 festival, the total influx to the community was in the neighborhood of 1,500 people (Keating 2006).

East Durham itself was once the principal resort town and vacation destination for Irish émigrés living in the New York City area, but with the increased availability of affordable airfares to Ireland and general shifts in the culture, its heyday has long since passed. In spite of this, the town's connection to and identification with Irish-American culture remains strong, and it serves as a good location for an event such as CIAW. Pubs and hotels with names like Erin's Melody, the Shamrock House, McKenna's, the Blackthorn, and McGrath's offer lingering testimony to the area's heritage.

Catskill Irish Arts Week is but one of several music schools and camps that one can attend in the U.S. to learn, hear, and play Irish traditional music. Irish music sessions are held in communities throughout the country, often in areas with no appreciable Irish cultural presence. Professional or semi-pro Irish and Irish-American performers go on concert tours and perform in venues ranging from large performing arts centers to living rooms in private homes.

Clearly, Irish traditional music is a popular commodity in twenty-first century America, and is enjoyed by many with no Irish heritage themselves. This has by no means always been the case, however. Even within Irish-American communities, traditional music was often not valued much at all in the middle of the twentieth century. Many older musicians laid their instruments aside, and there were few younger ones interested in taking up the old, uncool music. A revival of interest kicked into gear in the 1970s, starting a movement that has yet to reach its peak. Folklorists and enthusiasts sought out older musicians to interview, and facilitated the process of getting them recorded, and otherwise bringing their music into the public arena. Irish-American artists began appearing at folk festivals alongside representatives of other cultural groups, and festivals devoted exclusively to Irish music were staged. Older tune collections and histories of the music were reprinted, and new ones began to be published. Some older traditional musicians began schools for teaching the music to younger members of the Irish-American community, and summer music schools, such as Catskill Irish Arts Week, arose and began to draw those with no Irish heritage.

This resurgence of popularity has brought about new challenges and directions for the music. Since many of today's fans and players of Irish music have no connection to the culture that produced it, they do not necessarily have a sense of the broad legacy of Irish traditional music. With ears that are filled with the sounds of many different musical genres, many younger musicians are moving the music in directions that are not always endorsed by older players. New media have aided in the global spread of music that once was largely confined to small rural villages. Methods have been developed of sharing tunes across the Internet, and audio and video clips of performances by professionals and amateurs alike are readily uploaded and downloaded. The mass popularity of stage shows such as *Riverdance* and *Lord of the Dance* have carried a form of Irish traditional music to vast audiences who might otherwise have had no exposure to it. Some within the music community embrace all these changes and new contexts, while others fear for the integrity of the music, and even of Irish identity.

Irish music has a long and complex history in the world of American music. There is an Irish layer in several streams of American music, ranging from comic operas enjoyed by urban sophisticates in the late eighteenth and early nineteenth centuries, to antebellum popular song, to instrumental music played by musically literate amateurs in the early nineteenth century, to popular stage music of the late nineteenth and early twentieth centuries. In addition, Irish-American music has existed as its own entity, as a form of ethnic music apart from the American musical mainstream. The latter will be the primary concern of this chapter, though all areas will be touched upon to some extent.

## BRIEF OVERVIEW OF IRISH IMMIGRATION

The history of Irish music in America parallels, and is closely tied to, the complex history of Irish immigration to America. Although the most well-known aspect of the history of Irish immigration to the United States is that relating to the waves of millions of people who came in the wake of the potato famines in Ireland of the 1840s and 1850s, Irish people had been coming to these shores since the earliest years of the colonial era. As the early immigrants were largely absorbed into the melting pot of American culture so, too, was their music absorbed into the mainstream of American music.

Scholars estimate that between 300,000 and 500,000 people left Ireland and headed for the American colonies prior to the outbreak of the Revolutionary War (Miller 1985, 137). Most of those who came in the early part of the seventeenth century were Irish Catholics from the southern part of the country, but by the end of the 1600s Protestants (primarily Presbyterians) from the province of Ulster in northern Ireland had begun to emigrate to

## SELECTED LIST OF IRISH FESTIVALS

Searching on "Irish festival" or "Irish music festival" using any of the major Internet search engines quickly reveals that there are many Irish festivals held throughout the United States every year. They range widely in size, target audience, and styles of music presented. The following list is only a small sampling of events. The emphasis is on those that seem to be fairly well-established, and that present at least some percentage of traditional Irish music rather than solely Celtic rock bands or more pop-oriented performers. Dates and line-ups vary from year to year; readers should consult the festival's website for current information.

Alaska Irish Music Festival
    Anchorage, AK
    http://www.akirishmusic.com/
Catskill Irish Arts Week & Traditional Festival
    East Durham, NY
    http://www.east-durham.org/irishartsweek/index.htm
Milwaukee Irish Fest
    Milwaukee, WI
    http://www.irishfest.com/
North Texas Irish Festival
    Dallas, TX
    http://www.ntif.org/
Savannah Irish Festival
    Savannah, GA
    http://www.savannahirish.org/
Kansas City Irish Fest
    Kansas City, MO
    http://www.kcirishfest.com/
Buffalo Irish Festival
    Buffalo, NY
    http://www.shannonpub.com/irishfestival.htm
Colorado Irish Festival
    Littleton, CO
    http://www.coloradoirishfestival.org/
Cleveland Irish Cultural Festival
    Cleveland, OH
    http://www.clevelandirish.org/
Southern Illinois Irish Festival
    Carbondale, IL
    http://www.silirishfest.org/
Eugene Irish Cultural Festival
    Eugene, OR
    http://www.eugeneirishfest.com/

these shores. These latter were the so-called "Scotch-Irish" or "Ulster Scots," descendants of people who had left the Scottish lowlands for plantations in Ulster early in the seventeenth century. The largest flow from Ulster to America came in the years between 1717 and 1775 (Daniels 1990, 78). Although they settled in various areas, most went to the middle colonies, especially Pennsylvania. From there the flow continued south into the Shenandoah Valley of Virginia, the Carolinas, and the Appalachian region.

The term "Scotch-Irish" did not come into common usage until the era of the Irish potato famines, when the earlier Protestant emigrants from Ulster felt the need to distinguish themselves from the incoming masses of Irish Catholics. Historians argue about the cultural identity of the Ulster Scots. They were in Northern Ireland for a few generations prior to relocating again to America. Culturally, they were neither quite Scottish nor quite Irish, but maintained a culture of their own that incorporated some elements of both. Little is known specifically about their music. They not only left Scotland long before the great flowering of Scottish fiddle music in the mid to late eighteenth century, but in turn left Ulster for North America during the period in which regional repertoires of instrumental music were developing throughout the English-speaking world (Jabbour 1996, 253–254). Thus, any fiddle music that might have been played by early Ulster Scots immigrants is as likely to have developed on these shores as in Ireland or Scotland.

Many of the Catholic Irish emigrants who arrived in North America prior to the American Revolution came as indentured servants. As such they were required to complete several years of labor in return for trans-Atlantic passage. This, plus the fact that the majority of these emigrants were males, mitigated against the formation of any strong Catholic Irish culture in America at the time.

Beginning in 1845 and continuing for most of the next decade, there were serious failures of the potato crop in Ireland due to a blight caused by a fungus. The subsequent lack of food, coupled with failed relief efforts, resulted in the death of between a million and a million and a half people, and the emigration of even more (Daniels 1990, 134–135). Most of the emigrants went to the United States, although many went to Canada, and some of those eventually moved to the United States as well. This wave of emigration was quite different from that which had occurred earlier. Entire villages were sometimes displaced, resulting in extensive cultural disruption. Whereas many of the pre-famine immigrants settled in rural areas, those who came in the wake of the famine and throughout the nineteenth century largely settled in cities such as Boston, New York, Philadelphia, Chicago, and San Francisco (Daniels 1990, 136). Here they formed distinct Irish-American communities where there was greater possibility for cultural continuity with the homeland. Certain aspects of Irish culture, such as music, were retained, apart from the mainstream of American life and culture. However, they also came into a country in which anti-Irish sentiment was firmly entrenched, and many felt pressured to lose their "Irishness" and join mainstream American culture.

## IRISH MUSIC IN EARLY AMERICA

Given this cultural situation it is not surprising that the Irish influence on music in the early days of the United States—the pre-famine era—came about via means that did not necessarily have any attachment to Irish culture. Rather, much of the "Irish" music known in America in the late eighteenth and early nineteenth centuries was music that had roots in oral tradition, but which had been processed by classically-trained composers and arrangers. It existed as a form of art music or popular entertainment, enjoyed by sophisticated, urban, and largely non-Irish audiences; what scholar Lawrence E. McCullough calls "derivative idioms" (McCullough 1978, xiv). This music constituted a layer of Irish influence in the emerging realm of American music, but it was Irish music as popular culture rather than oral tradition.

One example of this sort of processed music was that found in British comic operas, which were popular stage entertainment in major cities such as Boston, New York, Philadelphia, Baltimore, and Charleston. The music of these works typically consisted of melodies drawn from folk or popular tradition and adapted for use on the stage with new lyrics. One such piece was *The Poor Soldier*, the work of Irish playwright John O'Keeffe (1747–1833) and English composer William Shield (1748–1829). It premiered in Dublin in 1783 and was staged in America for the first time in New York in 1785. It remained popular well into the nineteenth century, and songs from it were printed in sheet music form and anthologized in songbooks and pocket songsters into the antebellum period (Porter 1991, 479, 529).

Contemporary scores of *The Poor Soldier* carried the attribution that the music was "arranged and composed" by Shield, but there was a good deal more of the former than there was of the latter. Of the 18 tunes that formed the most stable group of airs used in the work, all but two can be traced in Irish or Scottish folk and popular tradition prior to Shield's use of them in *The Poor Soldier*. Several of these had continued life in American folk and popular music long after the opera itself passed out of popularity. Since these were tunes that were already in circulation prior to their incorporation into the opera, their subsequent currency is not necessarily traceable directly to *The Poor Soldier*. Nevertheless, their appearance in the opera surely was a factor in keeping them popular, and in some cases the title that an air acquired through its use in the opera is the one that has remained attached to it.

Such is the case with "The Rose Tree," the most well-known and enduringly popular of all the melodies used in *The Poor Soldier*. Variants of the tune were known in both Ireland and Scotland long before William Shield adapted it, but in *The Poor Soldier* it was used for a song called "A Rose Tree in Full Bearing." This song was frequently printed in contemporary songbooks and sheet music, and the tune by itself, as "The Rose Tree," was printed in many instrumental tutors and tune books. The tune remains popular today in old-time string band and contradance circles, as well as among Irish musicians, in a form that differs little from the way it appears in the score for *The Poor Soldier*.

But the history of "The Rose Tree" in America has also taken some more complex turns. Variants of the melody were used in early nineteenth century shape-note tradition for hymns titled "The Christian's Conflicts," "Land of Pleasure," and even "The Rose Tree." Two other very large branches of the tune family owe their growth to later nineteenth century stage traditions. The melody of "Old Zip Coon," one of the most popular songs from the blackface minstrel tradition, is a variant of "The Rose Tree." "Zip Coon" has, in turn, spawned a complex of related fiddle tunes including "Turkey in the Straw," which is arguably the most widely-known American fiddle tune, and some lesser-known ones including "Sugar in the Gourd" and "Natchez under the Hill."

Another major offshoot from "The Rose Tree" is a song known variously as "My Grandma's Advice" or "My Grandmother Lives on Yonder Little Green." This song employs a variant of the first strain of the "Rose Tree" melody. It became popular in the late 1850s through performances by the Tremaine Family, one of numerous singing families who were part of the wave of imitators that followed the success of the Hutchinson Family of New Hampshire. The song was published in sheet music and broadside forms, and seems quickly to have acquired the status of an "old familiar song." It has been widely recovered as a folk song in North America, and its popularity has even carried it back to Ireland.

Thus, a single melody from a popular Irish musical theater piece has woven its way throughout the broad fabric of American music (McLucas and Wells 1999, 99–107).

## IRISH INFLUENCE IN NINETEENTH-CENTURY AMERICAN POPULAR SONG

The work of Thomas Moore was in a similar vein. Moore (1779–1852) was an Irish poet whose work, *Irish Melodies*, was issued in eight volumes over a period of several years, beginning in 1808. It was first published in Dublin and London, but American editions soon followed; Moore's work was immensely popular in the United States as well in Ireland and England. Popular music historian Charles Hamm notes that the songs in *Irish Melodies* rank with those of Stephen Foster as being "the most widely sung, best-loved, and most durable songs of the entire nineteenth century" (Hamm 1979, 44).

Moore set his lyrics to Irish melodies that were first notated by Edward Bunting and others in the late eighteenth century, mainly from the playing of traditional Irish harpists. Moore chose the melodies and at times edited them to suit his needs, but his colleague, John Stevenson (1761–1833), wrote "symphonies and accompaniments" for the airs in much the same manner as William Shield did for the melodies used in *The Poor Soldier*. Many different editions of *Irish Melodies* were published during the antebellum era, and individual songs from the work were also printed in sheet music form and anthologized in songbooks and pocket songsters. Some songs enjoyed a life in print into the early twentieth century. The single most popular song from *Irish Melodies* was "'Tis the Last Rose of Summer," with "Believe Me If All those Endearing Young Charms" not far behind.[2]

As popular as Moore's songs were, their larger importance is the influence, both musical and poetic, that they had on the work of American popular song-writers such as Stephen Foster (1826–1864). This is not to say that Foster and his contemporaries were simply imitating Moore and Stevenson. They were at the same time drawing on and synthesizing elements of other musical streams, particularly that of African-American music—or at least their conception of it —in their process of crafting and expressing a musical voice that was distinc-tively and uniquely American. Themes of nostalgia and sorrow run throughout many of Moore's songs, and these were echoed in the work of many American songwriters of the early nineteenth century. Certain characteristics of scale and melody, such as the use of pentatonic (five-note) scales, and wide melodic leaps upwards followed by descending patterns, also can be traced to the influ-ence of Moore and other Irish sources.

## IRISH MUSIC AS A DISTINCT ENTITY IN AMERICA IN THE PRE-FAMINE ERA

Apart from these instances of Irish influence on American musical genres, unprocessed Irish music had some limited presence of its own. A few tunes of Irish origin appear in printed and manuscript instrumental collections in the early nineteenth century. They usually comprise a small portion of tunes in these collections, somewhere between 5 and 15 percent of the total contents.[3] A collection such as *Riley's Flute Melodies*, published in New York in two vol-umes in the middle of the second decade of the nineteenth century, contains a smattering of Irish tunes in a miscellany that includes popular airs of the day, melodies from stage productions such as *The Poor Soldier*, some Scottish tunes, and a variety of tunes from other sources. The audience for these collec-tions was primarily among urban amateur musicians; they are not necessarily a gauge of what music was flourishing in oral tradition in the U.S. at the time.

At least one collection, however, consisted almost entirely of Irish melodies: *Gentleman's Musical Repository*, compiled and published by Charles P.F. O'Hara in New York in 1813. Little is known about O'Hara apart from the fact that he lived in New York around the time of the publication of his book. It is an extremely rare collection; only a handful of copies are known to exist in American libraries, and it seems to have been overlooked by all previous writ-ers on Irish music in America. In the subtitle to the book O'Hara makes refer-ence to the fact the music is adapted for use by several instruments including the "union pipes"—an Anglicized term formerly applied to the uilleann pipes, or Irish bagpipes. O'Hara apparently felt that there were enough Irish pipers in early nineteenth century New York to warrant the publication of a collection that might have some appeal to them.

O'Hara's collection includes twelve pieces that are attributed to Turlough O'Carolan (1670–1738), the last and most famous exponent of Ireland's once-flourishing tradition of harpist-composers. O'Carolan's work occupies a place somewhere between art and folk music. His pieces are structurally and melodically more complex than the jigs and reels that are at the heart of dance-based Irish instrumental forms, yet are still relatively short. His most famous piece, "Carolan's Concerto" (which is included in O'Hara's collection), evokes something of the nature of Italian baroque works, but is by no means as long and complex as a true concerto.

## BLACKFACE MINSTRELSY AND THE "STAGE IRISH" IN THE NINETEENTH CENTURY

In the 1840s a new form of popular entertainment arose in the United States: the blackface minstrel show. White performers blacked their faces with burnt cork makeup and offered stereotyped depictions of African Americans, while performing music that had some basis in African-American musical styles but which also drew on numerous other strains. This included a certain component of Irish music and musicians. Several of the most important early minstrel performers were of Irish ancestry. Joel Walker Sweeney (1810–1860), who did much to popularize the five-string banjo on the minstrel stage, was the son of an immigrant from County Mayo. Dan Emmett (1815–1904), leader of the first full-fledged minstrel troupe, the Virginia Minstrels, and putative composer of "I Wish I Was in Dixie's Land," or "Dixie," was the grandson of an Irish immigrant (Moloney 2002, 29).

It is ironic that, in addition to portraying stereotyped African-American characters, many of these Irish-American minstrel performers made their living portraying stereotyped Irishmen. The anti-immigrant "nativism" movement of the 1830s and 1840s, and the rise of the "Know-nothings" in the 1850s, included a great deal of anti-Irish Catholic sentiment in the U.S. One manifestation of this sentiment was the rise of the "stage Irishman": stereotyped portrayals of Irish figures in musical theater productions.

This carried over from minstrelsy into a parallel form of musical theater entertainment known as "variety theater." As its name implies, this featured a diverse range of acts that included much comic material. Irishmen were portrayed as ape-like figures who were hard drinkers, quick tempered brawlers, possessed of little education or refinement, and who occupied the low rungs of the economic ladder. Like the portrayals of African Americans on the minstrel stage, these negative images were deeply ingrained in much of American popular culture well into the twentieth century. The genre spawned thousands of songs about Clancy and McGinty, or Mick and Pat, or Sullivan and O'Houlihan, drinking and fighting with fists and shillelaghs, and getting hauled off to jail for their troubles.

A less negative but no less stereotyped thread of Irish music that emerged on the popular stage was that of the sentimental songs of mother and home in

"Dear Old Ireland." This genre was typified by performers such as Chauncey Olcott (1860–1932; born John Chancellor). Olcott helped create and define the role of the "Irish tenor." In addition to his performing abilities he also wrote, or co-wrote, some of the most enduring Irish sentimental songs, including "Mother Machree," "My Wild Irish Rose," and "When Irish Eyes are Smiling."

## FRANCIS O'NEILL AND THE COLLECTION OF IRISH TRADITIONAL INSTRUMENTAL MUSIC

One of the most important figures in the history of Irish-American music was not a professional performer—though he was a musician—but rather the chief of police in Chicago, the second largest city in the country. Daniel Francis O'Neill (1848–1936) was born in Tralibane, County Cork. There was music in his family and community, and Francis took up the flute as a young man. While still in his teens, O'Neill left Ireland. He spent some years at sea, and after a series of adventures he came to the United States. He lived for a while in San Francisco and elsewhere in California, taught school in

"Tim Flaherty." Baltimore, MD: Wm. J. Schmidt (1865–1885). From the Kenneth S. Goldstein Collection of American Song Broadsides, Center for Popular Music, Middle Tennessee State University.

Missouri, and eventually moved to Chicago, settling there for good in 1871. On one of his early voyages he had met a woman named Anna Rogers. They remained in contact in the intervening years and married in 1870. After working a series of jobs in and around Chicago, he joined the police force there in 1873.

At the time O'Neill settled in Chicago there were around 40,000 Irish-born people living in the city, comprising 13 percent of its population (Carolan 1997, 11). The number of Irish in Chicago continued to rise throughout the rest of the century and kept pace with the overall growth of the city's population. By the time O'Neill joined the Chicago police force, there was a

Chauncey Olcott

"THE IRISH TENOR."

Donovan     New York

Chauncey Olcott (1860-1932; born John Chancellor) helped create and define the role of the "Irish tenor." In addition to his performing abilities he also wrote, or co-wrote, some of the most enduring Irish sentimental songs including "Mother Machree," "My Wild Irish Rose," and "When Irish Eyes are Smiling." From the Center for Popular Music, Middle Tennessee State University.

significant number of his fellow countrymen in service with him. O'Neill earned a reputation as an honest and capable officer. He rose through the ranks of the force, securing a promotion to lieutenant in 1890 and to captain in 1894. In 1901 he was appointed as general superintendent, or chief. He was reappointed to this position in 1903 and 1905, but resigned of his own volition in July of 1905.

During his early years in Chicago, O'Neill conceived the idea of making a collection of all the Irish melodies that he knew, or that he could obtain from other sources. Chicago was an excellent location in which to undertake such a project, as within the Irish community there could be found musicians from all of the 32 counties of Ireland. Although O'Neill did not himself possess great skill in transcribing music, he formed a partnership with another young policeman, James O'Neill (no relation) who did. James O'Neill hailed from County Down and was a traditional fiddler (MacAoidh 2006).

Francis O'Neill's position within the police force helped him build a strong network of musicians and music lovers. Throughout the latter decades of the nineteenth century the two O'Neills amassed a large quantity of music. Much was noted down from the playing of other musicians in Chicago and elsewhere, but they also gathered tunes from earlier printed collections.

The result of their efforts was the publication of a series of printed collections of Irish music that stand as some of the most important works of their type. The first of these, *O'Neill's Music of Ireland*, appeared in 1903. This monumental work contained 1,850 melodies and included many song airs and pieces attributed to Turlough O'Carolan in addition to the jigs, reels, hornpipes, and other dance tunes that were most representative of the repertoire of the Chicago musical community. This was followed in 1907 by *The Dance*

*Music of Ireland: 1001 Gems*, a work that omitted the airs and the O'Carolan compositions, and, as its title indicates, focused solely on the dance music. This book was the most influential of O'Neill's works and became known to later generations of musicians as "the Bible" of Irish traditional music, or simply "the book."

Additional, smaller collections followed, as did two works of prose—*Irish Folk Music: A Fascinating Hobby* (1910) and *Irish Minstrels and Musicians* (1913). In the former, O'Neill wrote of his own life and work and delved into some historical studies, while the latter consists mainly of biographical profiles of the musicians from whom he gathered his music. Thanks to the enormous scope of O'Neill's collecting and publication efforts, Irish-American music has been more fully documented than any other form of American ethnic music prior to the era of sound recordings.


## EARLY RECORDED IRISH MUSIC

When Thomas Edison invented the phonograph in 1877 he conceived of it primarily as a device to be used in the business world for the purpose of dictation. It was left to others to see and exploit its capabilities for reproducing musical performances. Irish musicians were quick to do so. Francis O'Neill reportedly was introduced to Edison's invention at the World Columbian Exposition in Chicago in 1893, as was uilleann piper Patrick J. "Patsy" Touhey, who was a regular performer at the Irish exhibit on the fair's Midway Plaisance. O'Neill was then in the midst of his efforts to collect and compile Irish traditional music, and he was quick to grasp the potential that the phonograph held as an aid to documenting the tradition. For the first time it was possible for a particular performance to be fixed and heard by people at a later time. It also meant that one did not need to be present at the time of a performance in order to enjoy it.

O'Neill took advantage of these factors and, together with Sgt. James Early, one of his musician friends and collaborators, obtained an Edison cylinder recorder and began to preserve performances by some of the players whom he admired. Most of the cylinders that O'Neill recorded are now lost, but some that he sent to Rev. Dr. Richard Henebry in Waterford, Ireland, in 1907 survive, and today are preserved in the archives at University College, Cork (Carolan 1997, 76). They provide remarkable documentation of the playing of musicians, many of whom were from a generation before those who recorded during the heyday of the 78 rpm era.

Of the cylinders O'Neill sent to Henebry, he writes: "As a Christmas present...I forwarded in 1907 to Rev. Dr. Henebry, at Waterford, Ireland, a box of Edison phonograph records which Sergeant Early generously permitted me to select from his treasures" (O'Neill 1913/1973, 113). Henebry, who earlier had taught at the Catholic University of America in Washington, D.C., was himself a scholar of Irish music and an avid supporter of O'Neill's work. Henebry was impressed with the playing on the cylinders and in particular with the music of piper Patsy Touhey, of whom O'Neill was also a great admirer. Henebry expressed his opinion of Touhey's playing in a letter to O'Neill, in what must be one of the first "record reviews" in the history of Irish music. Of Touhey's playing Henebry said: "The five by Touhey are the superior limit of Irish pipering. One of his, especially 'The Shaskeen Reel,' is so supreme that I am utterly without words to express my opinion of it." Henebry continued his effusive praise of Touhey's musicianship: "The Homeric ballads and the new Brooklyn Bridge are great, but Patsy Touhey's rendering of 'The Shaskeen Reel' is a far bigger human achievement" (O'Neill 1913/1973, 114).

Perhaps because of this response to a recording of his playing, or perhaps as a result of his own insight, Patsy Touhey (1865–1923) was able to see the commercial potential inherent in making sound recordings. Touhey, who was born in Loughrea, County Galway, but moved to Boston at age three, had been a professional piper since around 1890. He enjoyed a successful career on the vaudeville stage and performed at both the 1893 Columbian Exposition in Chicago and the 1904 Louisiana Purchase Exposition in St. Louis. He had an opportunity to make commercial recordings for the Edison company but turned it down for economic reasons (Mitchell and Small 1986, 9). Instead, he bought an Edison recorder, and around 1901 he began to advertise in the Irish-American press that he would make recordings on demand, for the price of one dollar per recording, or a dozen for ten dollars. He furnished his potential customers with a list of 150 tunes that he was willing to perform. Since there was not any means of reproducing these home-recorded cylinders, each one was a unique document of a particular performance, made for a particular customer. As with the recordings that O'Neill made, most of Touhey's private recordings have been lost, but some have been located and re-issued on compact disc.[4] Touhey did make some recordings for Victor in 1919. These are widely regarded as classics of Irish traditional music and have frequently been re-issued.

The first Irish-American traditional musician known to have made commercially-issued recordings was James C. McAuliffe (1859–?), another uilleann piper. McAuliffe recorded at least 19 selections on cylinder for Edison and Columbia, during the period 1899–1903 (Spottswood 1990, 2804).[5] Little is known about McAuliffe other than that he apparently lived in New York City at the time he made the recordings, and that he is buried upstate, in Hoosick Falls, New York, where he had lived earlier in his life ("James C. McAuliffe," accessed January 11, 2007). These recordings are quite obscure, however, and led to no further development of a market for recordings of Irish traditional music. McAuliffe was not nearly as skilled a piper as was Touhey. In commenting on the beginnings of recorded Irish music Francis O'Neill said: "He [Touhey] could not get enough money for his time from the record people. His theatrical business was more profitable. They found a cheaper man, McAuliffe, and cheaper work, of course" (Mitchell and Small 1986, 9).

The earliest commercial records of Irish music that did have lasting impact were those made by accordionist John J. Kimmel (1866–1942). Kimmel is something of an anomaly in that he was a superb performer of Irish traditional music but was himself of German extraction. He was born in Brooklyn on December 13, 1866, to German immigrant parents, and lived in Brooklyn all his life. He had a career on the vaudeville stage, playing in a group known as "The Elite Musical Four" in which he played saxophone, cornet, and xylophone in addition to accordion. All of his recordings were done on accordion or, more precisely, the melodeon (Walsh 1958, 31–32).

Kimmel is credited with being the first accordion player in any genre of music to make records. His first recordings were made in 1904 for the Zon-O-Phone company, and he recorded for many of the other early companies off and on until 1929. His recorded repertoire was a mixture of standard popular fare of the times, such as marches, rags, and cakewalks, and medleys of Irish reels and jigs. He was a virtuoso player, and his recorded performances reveal a solid mastery of the style and repertoire of Irish traditional music. Where and how he acquired this knowledge is a mystery. Presumably he was in contact with Irish traditional musicians in Brooklyn or elsewhere in New York City and was able to learn from them.

Another fact that makes Kimmel's skill at playing Irish music on the accordion so remarkable is that there is little record of the accordion's use in Irish music prior to Kimmel's recordings. Francis O'Neill, for example, focused solely on pipers, fiddlers, and flute players, and makes no mention of accordions or accordion players in any of his work on Irish music. Whether there were none, or whether O'Neill simply did not accept them as valid instruments for the tradition he was documenting, is unknown. Accordions, along with concertinas, harmonicas, and parlor organs, are a type of free-reed instrument. This class of instrument came to popularity in the 1840s, and at least a few jigs and reels were included in early printed tutors for the instrument.[6] It seems likely that some Irish musicians had begun to use the accordion for Irish traditional music by the middle of the nineteenth century, but this is an area that has received virtually no research.[7] For all practical purposes the history of accordion playing in Irish music begins with the era of sound recordings, and thus with John J. Kimmel and his contemporaries. Paul Brock, one of Ireland's leading accordionists of the late twentieth and early twenty-first centuries, is a great admirer of Kimmel and has learned much of Kimmel's repertoire. He credits Kimmel with having developed "extraordinary technique," but notes: "where he got it from, I don't know." Brock says that he "can only assume" that Kimmel must have come in contact with Irish immigrant musicians in New York City (Brock 2006).

Brock was unaware of Kimmel until the appearance of some modern reissues of Kimmel's recordings. In spite of Kimmel's exceptional ability to play Irish music and the seeming popularity of his recordings, he had surprisingly little influence on other Irish musicians of his era, at least not to the extent of some of the later recording artists whose work we will discuss in more detail later.[8] In general his recordings were not well-known in the Irish musical community until the 1980s when some were reissued on LP (Labbé and Carlin 1980).

One probable cause of this is the fact that they were not marketed specifically to the Irish-American community, but were part of the general offerings of the early record companies. The business of recording Irish traditional music explicitly to cater to a perceived market for it has its beginnings in New York City in 1916. In that year Justus O'Byrne DeWitt, whose family ran a record store in Manhattan, began actively to seek out Irish traditional musicians to record in response to their customers' demand for Irish records. He met accordion player Eddie Herborn and banjoist John Wheeler playing in Celtic Park on Long Island and convinced Columbia to record and issue their music. Columbia agreed on the condition that DeWitt's store purchase at least 500 copies (Moloney 1992, 522–523; Spottswood 1990, 2784). Herborn and Wheeler recorded for Columbia for the first time in September of 1916, and the records were announced among Columbia's new releases in February 1917.[9] The records sold well enough that Herborn and Wheeler recorded again on two other occasions, and in 1917 Columbia also recorded piper Patrick Fitzpatrick. Fitzpatrick also recorded for Edison and Victor that same year.

By the 1920s Columbia and other companies had begun separate catalog series targeted specifically to the Irish market.[10] They drew primarily on the Irish-American musical community in New York City, where most of the record companies were based, but reached into Chicago, Philadelphia, and Boston as well. An impressive wealth and variety of performers and musical styles were recorded. There was quasi-art music recorded by trained singers such as tenor John McCormack that was essentially a continuation of the tradition in which Thomas Moore had worked a century earlier and Chauncey Olcott in the latter part of the nineteenth century. In contrast to this was the "stage Irish" music that had its roots in the late nineteenth century and that has already been discussed. A third major category was the music that we have been discussing thus far in terms of recording, that is, traditional instrumental dance music played by fiddlers, pipers, flutists, accordionists, and others, either solo or in groups ranging in size from duos to full bands.

It is a curious twist of cultural history that the recording of Irish traditional music began in America rather than in Ireland. The American recordings were exported to Ireland and exerted an enormous influence there, as they did in this country. For the first time it was possible for a musician to be heard without being present in the same room as his audience. This was a profound change in a culture in which traditional music had largely been sustained in small, rural villages that were relatively isolated from one another. Travel was generally quite circumscribed, and musicians were exposed only to others within their own locales, or to those musicians who belonged to the itinerant "traveling people" of Ireland. Knowledge of tunes and styles was similarly limited. All of this changed with the advent of recording. Instead of musicians in a particular village or region looking up only to the top local players for inspiration, people all over Ireland and in Irish-American communities within the United States now had the opportunity to listen to, and learn from, recordings of the same players. The early recordings done by O'Neill and Patsy Touhey gave some indication of the possibilities of the changes that might be caused by the new medium, and once the commercial recording and distribution of Irish music began in earnest, change came swiftly and broadly.

The big stars of early recorded Irish music were a trio of fiddlers: Michael Coleman (1891–1945), James Morrison (1893–1947), and Paddy Killoran (1904–1965). All of these men happened to have emigrated to New York City from County Sligo, Ireland. All three were masters of Irish traditional fiddling, and their recordings remain influential to the present day.

Michael Coleman is perhaps the most highly regarded and most influential of the three. He was born in 1891 at Knockgrania in south Sligo into a musical family in a rich musical area (Bradshaw 1991). He began to play fiddle when he was only five or six years old and also learned how to step-dance. His older brother, Jim, was also a fiddler and apparently exerted a strong influence on Michael.

Michael Coleman left Ireland for America in 1914 and settled in New York City. Here he found work as a musician that was much more lucrative than what had been possible back home in Sligo. He began to play the vaudeville circuit and toured extensively, playing in the Keith chain of theaters. He made his first phonograph records in 1921, when he was 30 years old, for the small Shannon label, and shortly thereafter also recorded for the nationally distributed Vocalion label. Over the course of the next 15 years he went on to record for many different labels.

Coleman was an extraordinarily gifted and accomplished player and his recordings had a tremendous impact on Irish fiddlers on both sides of the Atlantic. Even today some of the sets (medleys) of tunes that he recorded are still played. Although Coleman died in 1945, his legacy continues to the present. It passed first through Coleman's pupil Andy McGann (1928–2004), who was known as one of New York's finest Irish fiddlers in the late twentieth century, and then to McGann disciple Brian Conway (1961- ), and is being carried into yet another generation by Conway's prize student Patrick Mangan.

James Morrison was virtually on a par with Coleman in terms both of skill on the instrument and in influence on subsequent players. Morrison also came from Sligo, from the town of Drumfin (Bradshaw 1989). In 1915 he sailed for America, using money that he had earned as a prize in a musical competition to pay part of his passage. He went first to the Boston area, where other members of his family had already settled, but he moved to New York in 1918. There was a rich community of Irish traditional musicians in the city at the time. In addition to Michael Coleman, this included pipers Patsy Touhey and Tom Ennis, accordion player P. J. Conlon, and flute player John McKenna. All of these men would have important careers in the early days of recording.

Morrison also made his first recordings in 1921. Like Coleman, he recorded for a variety of labels, but the majority of his work was for Columbia. Whereas most of Coleman's recorded output consisted of fiddle solos (with piano or guitar accompaniment), plus a few duet recordings, Morrison recorded with a variety of ensembles and groupings. Although the Great Depression brought an end to much of the recording of Irish music (and other genres) that had flourished in the 1920s, Morrison had enough appeal as a recording artist that he continued to make records until 1936. He died in Knickerbocker Hospital in Manhattan in 1947, the same hospital where Coleman had passed away two years earlier.

The third member of the triumvirate of great Sligo fiddlers, and the only one to make recordings in the LP era, was Paddy Killoran. Born in 1904 in Bally-mote, in County Sligo, Killoran emigrated to the United States in 1925. Like Morrison and Coleman, he settled in New York City (O'Neill 1977; Varlet 1996). He was able to make his living as a musician for at least part of his life. Like James Morrison, Killoran organized and led dance bands that worked in the then-flourishing dancehall scene in New York. His most famous band was his Pride of Erin Orchestra, whose home base was the Pride of Erin dance hall. During the 1930s Killoran and his band performed on ships that sailed between the U.S. and Ireland.

Killoran's recording career began in 1931, a decade after that of Coleman and Morrison. Much of his recorded output is in the context of a dance ensem-ble, although he made many fine and influential solo recordings as well. He also recorded numerous fiddle duets with fellow Sligoman Paddy Sweeny. Although most of his recorded output is from the decade of the 1930s, he recorded approximately half of a long-playing album around 1960. He is joined on some of the tracks on this album by another Sligo émigré, flute player Mike Flynn.

Killoran was among the musicians who played at the resorts in East Durham, in the Catskills of upstate New York. Mike Rafferty recalls hearing him there in the late 1950s or early 1960s. Killoran passed away in 1965.

In spite of the dominance and strong impact of Sligo fiddlers in the early days of recorded Irish-American music, there was really a great diversity of music recorded. Not all the performers who made records were virtuosos, but even those who were of only average ability contributed to a body of material that serves as important documentation of the vitality of Irish traditional music as it survived in the cities of the United States in the second quarter of the twentieth century.

There were numerous other fiddlers besides Coleman, Morrison, and Kill-oran who left extensive recorded legacies. Donegal native Hugh Gillespie (1906–1986) came to this country in 1928 and quickly met Michael Coleman. The two formed a relationship and played together on numerous radio broad-casts. Gillespie did not record as extensively as his mentor, but did a series of fine recordings in the late 1930s. These are notable not only for Gillespie's excellent playing, but also because they feature guitar as the accompanying instrument rather than the more typical piano.

Patrick "Packie" Dolan (1904–1932) was a fiddler from County Longford who left Ireland for New York in 1919. In addition to many recordings as leader of "Packie Dolan's Melody Boys," he recorded some fiddle duets with Michael Coleman. Hugh Gillespie was a member of the Melody Boys for a period of time. Dolan died tragically in a ferryboat explosion at the age of 28.

Frank Quinn (1893–?) was another emigrant from County Longford. A member of the New York police force, some of his records were issued under the name "Paltrolman Frank Quinn." He was an all-around entertainer who played both accordion and fiddle, and who sang. His performances were rough-hewn but spirited, and his extensive recording career—which ran from 1921 to 1936 and consisted of nearly 200 selections–is testimony to the appeal he had with Irish-American audiences. Much of his repertoire consisted of comic songs, though he recorded a lot of instrumentals as well.

Recordings by flute players were few and far between in the 78 rpm era. The principal flute player of the period, at least in terms of recording, was John McKenna (1880–1947), a native of County Leitrim, near where it intersects with Sligo and Roscommon. This was near where James Morrison hailed from, so McKenna was working within much the same musical tradition as the Sligo fiddlers. McKenna emigrated to New York in 1909 and was making records by about 1921. Like those of Coleman and Morrison, McKenna's records were exported to Ireland, where they had a big impact on players "back home." His playing was marked by great drive and lift. He recorded some duets with James Morrison that are regarded as some of the finest recordings of Irish-American music from the 1920s.

Tom Morrison (c. 1888–?; no relation to James), from County Galway, was perhaps the second most extensively recorded flute player of the era. Some of his recordings feature the accompaniment of Mayo emigrant John Reynolds on bodhran, a handheld drum (credited as a "tambourine" on the record labels). Although the bodhran is often regarded as an instrument of some antiquity in Irish traditional music, this is the only known instance of its use on an early recording.

John Griffin was a flute player and singer who was in much the same mold as Frank Quinn. Decidedly unrefined as a player and singer, his music is nonetheless full of life and energy. Also like Quinn, he—or his record company—played on his regular career to promote his recordings, billing himself as "The Fifth Avenue Busman."

After John J. Kimmel, perhaps the finest accordion player of the era was Peter J. Conlon. Conlon was from Milltown, County Galway, near the border with County Mayo. His first recordings were remarkably early, in 1917. Modern accordionist Paul Brock feels that Conlon "embraced the pure, hard-core Irish traditional music the best of all the early box players," and that he was "a totally rounded player" (Brock 2006).

It is ironic that although uilleann pipers were the first Irish musicians to be recorded, relatively few ultimately did so, and for most of these their recorded output consisted of only a few sides. The exception was Tom Ennis, a Chicago-born piper whose father, John Ennis, was an associate of Francis O'Neill. Ennis moved to New York sometime in the 1910s and recorded over 60 sides for various companies. These included several pieces with fiddler James Morrison that were widely popular.

The lack of extensive recording of uilleann pipers can be attributed to the overall decline in popularity of the instrument within Irish-American communities. Francis O'Neill had earlier lamented the decline of interest in the pipes and noted a general lessening of interest in the older forms of Irish music. The Great Depression, which caused an abrupt downturn in record sales, also had an impact. No 78 rpm recordings of American uilleann pipers were made after 1929 until the modern era.

The late 1920s and 1930s saw the rise of groups with a more commercial (though sometimes still rough), urbane musical style that found favor in the dance halls or the professional stage. Groups such as McGettigan's Irish Minstrels, the Flanagan Brothers, and the McNulty Family, though with roots in older forms, downplayed the older instrumental music in favor of vocals and popular dances such as waltzes. Showmanship and meeting the expectations of the audience became of prime importance.

The World War II era is often seen as a benchmark in the history of many forms of American vernacular music, such as blues, jazz, and country music, and it is for Irish-American music as well. This is true both for the changes wrought in the record business during this time, and for the widespread cultural changes brought about by the war. The dual problems of shellac rationing during World War II and a recording ban imposed by the musicians' union in 1942 and that lasted to 1944 brought about significant changes in the recording industry in the United States. By the 1940s the major labels had ceased their activities with Irish music. To fill the gap, independent, specialty labels arose that catered directly to the Irish market.

Among these was the Copley label, which was founded in Boston in the late 1940s by Justus O'Byrne DeWitt. DeWitt was the same person who was responsible for getting Herborn and Wheeler to record for Columbia in 1916. The label featured popular singers such as tenor Connie Foley and the McNulty Family, and a good deal of dance music by the ceili bands that had become popular in post-WWII Irish communities. Ceili bands of the era met the need for more volume in large, urban dance halls. They usually consisted of four or more musicians and tended to feature piano accordion as the lead instrument. They often included a saxophone player, while fiddlers and flute players were either not present or very much in the background.

However, Copley also issued a series of outstanding records of traditional fiddling by Kerry native Paddy Cronin (1925- ), who had recently emigrated to Boston. Cronin, like so many other fiddlers of his generation, was greatly influenced by the playing of Michael Coleman and the other great Sligo fiddlers who recorded in the 1920s. Cronin recorded in the early 1950s, a time when very little other Irish-American fiddling was being issued on record.

Copley also recorded another virtuoso musician, accordion player Joe Derrane (1930– ). Derrane was a Boston native whose parents had both emigrated to this country. Only 18 when he first recorded for Copley, Derrane was a stunning technician. He had taken accordion lessons from an older man, Jerry O'Brien, but had also discovered the recordings of John Kimmel and was greatly influenced by them. Boston had a thriving dance-hall scene at the time, and Derrane found much work as a dance musician. He also played over the radio, and it was these broadcasts that brought him to the attention of O'Byrne DeWitt and led to the Copley recordings. In addition to a series of solo recordings, Derrane made some duets with his mentor, O'Brien, and the two of them also recorded with other musicians as part of the All-Star Ceilidhe Band (sometimes billed as the Irish All Stars).

The 1950s were a low period for Irish traditional music in America. The experience of flute player Mike Rafferty, who emigrated from East Galway to New Jersey in 1949, is typical. Unlike the bustling scene in New York in the 1920s when a young musician like Hugh Gillespie could arrive and almost immediately link up with a master musician like Michael Coleman, Rafferty had trouble connecting with other Irish musicians. He relates:

Irish American performers at the National Folk Festival, held in Chattanooga, Tennessee, October 8, 1994. Mick Moloney (tenor banjo), Eileen Ivers (fiddle), John Doyle (guitar). Center for Popular Music, Middle Tennessee State University. Photo by Paul F. Wells.

The only man I came across, actually, was [fellow Galway immigrant] Jack Coen. He was out here before me. I come across him, we'd have an odd tune together. I wasn't playing that [much]. Well, the old flute I had wasn't much. There was a guy that was from the same place too, but he was living in Chicago and he came to visit us once. I had a few tunes with him again. He played the melodeon. And, then in Englewood, New Jersey, there was a guy that had a ceili club there. He was a Mayo fellow. He used to play there, play the accordion. And another man from Limerick played the fiddle. And I used to play with them for the dances. And we had a drummer as well. It was a little band. Englewood Ceili Band they called us. So we used to play there once a month. And that kind of kept me going, sort of. Until that died out, then that was the end of me. I wasn't playing then for a long time. (Wells and Casey 2002)

It was around 1955 when the musical opportunities "died out" for Rafferty. As a flute player, Rafferty had the additional problem of lack of good instruments. Irish musicians favor simple-system wooden flutes over the complex, fully-keyed Boehm system flutes played by modern classical and jazz musicians. Although now there has been a renaissance in the hand-crafting of such instruments, in the 1950s they were very hard to come by. All these factors put together, plus the demands of raising and supporting a family, caused Rafferty to set aside his music for about 15 years.

Although relatively few commercial recordings of Irish traditional music were being made in America during the 1950s, the increased availability of tape recorders resulted in a great deal of music being preserved by people within the Irish community for their own enjoyment. In recent years some of this material has been issued by friends and families of the musicians. Collections by important musicians such as fiddlers John Vesey and Paddy Reynolds and accordion player Kevin Keegan allow today's audiences to hear the music of players who were in their prime during this era.

Another musician who was active during the 1940s and 1950s but whose contributions to Irish traditional music have become widely recognized only since the late 1970s is fiddler and tune composer Ed Reavy (1898–1988). Reavy was born in County Cavan and emigrated to Philadelphia in 1912. He was active in the Irish musical community in Philadelphia and did a bit of recording in the late 1920s. Although he was an accomplished fiddler, Reavy's most significant contribution to Irish music was the many tunes he wrote. He is known to have written close to 130 tunes, and many of these have entered into common circulation among Irish musicians. Most of these were composed from the 1940s to the 1960s (Moloney 1975, 18).

Several factors came together in the 1960s and 1970s that brought new interest in Irish music and caused musicians of Mike Rafferty's generation to take it up again. The first was the rise in popularity of the Clancy Brothers and Tommy Makem during the folk revival of the 1960s. Brothers Pat, Liam, and Tom Clancy, from County Waterford, and their friend from County Armagh, Tommy Makem, were struggling actors in New York City when they began performing Irish folk songs to try to earn additional money. Their popularity grew rapidly, and they were able to ride the bandwagon of the urban folk-song revival that brought performers such as Pete Seeger, Joan Baez, and Bob Dylan to national prominence.

The Clancys and Makem were something entirely new in the world of popularized Irish music. Their material consisted largely of older traditional songs of the sort that, by the 1960s, were largely unknown to urban Irish-American audiences. But their performance style was lively and polished, and was of a manner not practiced by rural folk in Ireland. They mostly sang in unison, with occasional ventures into harmony, and accompanied themselves with guitar and Makem's five-string banjo. All in all their delivery owed more to popular American folk groups such as the Kingston Trio and Peter, Paul, and Mary than it did to any precedents in Ireland. Their enormous popularity resulted in the spawning of numerous other "ballad groups" that brought attention to, and new respect for, Irish music both in the U.S. and in Ireland.

The second important development was the establishment in Ireland in 1951 of Comhaltas Ceoltóirí Éireann (CCE), an organization dedicated to the preservation and promotion of Irish music. CCE sponsors classes, competitions, performances, and other activities to carry out their mission. They have a system of branches throughout Ireland, the U.S., and in many other countries that promote their aims on a local level.[11] Activities of the local branches help give musicians opportunities to play, and also help them connect with other musicians. Mike Rafferty cites the rise of Comhaltas as one factor that led him back to the music.

A third factor in rekindling interest in Irish music in the U.S. also had its roots in the folk revival. Many people who received their first exposure to any sort of traditional music through the revival were ultimately led to probe more deeply into streams of tradition that interested them. The appeal of the Clancy Brothers and similar groups was not limited to those with an Irish cultural heritage, and more and more people from outside Irish-American communities began to take an interest in Irish music. As the revival moved into the 1970s, people began to seek out the older musicians, interview them, and, if they had set their music aside, encourage them to take it up again.

One key figure in promoting Irish traditional music in the 1970s was a young musician and scholar from Limerick, Mick Moloney. Moloney came to this

Irish American performers at the National Folk Festival, held in Chattanooga, Tennessee, October 8, 1994. Sheila Ryan (dancer) and Seamus Egan (flute). Center for Popular Music, Middle Tennessee State University. Photo by Paul F. Wells.

country as a member of the Johnstons, one of the many folk groups formed in Ireland in the wake of the popularity of the Clancy Brothers. While on tour with them he met folklorist Kenneth S. Goldstein, who was then teaching at the University of Pennsylvania in Philadelphia. Moloney eventually returned to Philadelphia to undertake folklore studies with Goldstein. Moloney began doing fieldwork with Irish-American musicians, including working for the Smithsonian Institution's 1976 Festival of American Folklife. This was a huge event, staged in honor of the nation's bicentennial, and celebrated our cultural diversity. Moloney's work in conjunction with the Irish-American component was of major importance in bringing together Irish musicians from different parts of the U.S. He notes that the festival was "a major turning point in the whole scene," as it afforded musicians "the chance to meet Irish musicians from other parts of the country, like the musicians from New York met the musicians from Chicago, and they met the ones from Boston. That had never really happened. There'd been some national conventions of the musicians association, but nothing like this. For a whole week, to be together, and then to meet the crowd coming over from Ireland, too" (Winick 1993, 38).

Moloney followed up his work with the festival by continuing to do extensive fieldwork. "I was going around, hell-for-leather bent, trying to find all the old-timers, before they kicked off. Going round and finding the legends that were still around. Finding the likes of Mike Flanagan, tracking down members of the Dan Sullivan Shamrock Band, and so on" (Winick 1993, 38). It was not just the surviving players from the 78 rpm era whom Moloney ferreted out, but men of Mike Rafferty's generation as well. Recordings of many of these "old-timers" were issued.

By the late 1970s a full-fledged revival of Irish music was underway in America. Not only were older players taking up their instruments again, but they were also passing along the tradition to young people in their families and communities, young people who a few years earlier might have had no interest at all in taking up an old form of music. New record companies specializing in Irish music, such as Shanachie and Green Linnet, emerged. Other independent labels that dealt with a wide variety of traditional music, such as Rounder, Flying Fish, and Folkways, issued numerous Irish titles as well. As noted at the beginning of this chapter, Irish music has achieved widespread popularity in America—and elsewhere in the world—on a level that would have seemed impossible less than a generation ago. As a result, Irish-American music is now widely understood less as an assimilated expression of a particular ethnic heritage and more as a uniquely American art form, with a history and tradition all its own.

**The author wishes to thank Sally K. Sommers Smith for reading and commenting on early drafts of this chapter. Her cogent criticism was invaluable and much appreciated.**

## NOTES

1. For more information on the festival visit the Web site for Catskill Irish Arts Week: http://www.east-durham.org/irishartsweek/.

2. As an indication of relative popularity, there are more than 50 copies of "'Tis the Last Rose of Summer" in the sheet music collection of the Center for Popular Music at Middle Tennessee State University, and over a dozen of "Believe Me If All those Endearing Young Charms."

3. By comparison, tunes of Scots origin are more numerous, accounting for approximately 20–25 percent of the tunes in the collections surveyed.

4. *The Piping of Patsy Touhey*, Na Piobairí Uilleann, NPU CD001, 2005. Insert notes by Pat Mitchell and Terry Moylan.

5. Spottswood, *Ethnic Recordings*, vol. 5, p. 2804. Spottswood notes that McAuliffe also recorded for Edison in 1909 but suggests that these were re-recordings of earlier titles done for the label.

6. See, for example, Elias Howe, Jr., *Complete Preceptor for the Accordeon*, 1843.

7. See, for example, Smith, 1997. Although he titles a section of his article "Irish Accordion Playing Styles: A History," and says, "Button accordions began to be used by Irish musicians towards the end of the nineteenth century" (436), he offers no evidence to support this statement.

8. Kimmel's recordings were, however, very influential among French-Canadian musicians in Quebec.

9. In Moloney, 1982, he gives 1913 as the year in which Columbia issued their first Irish recordings. Columbia catalogs bear out the 1917 initial release.

10. This was part of a general move to market recordings to different linguistic and cultural groups within the United States. See *Ethnic Recordings in America*, especially Gronow, "Ethnic Recordings: An Introduction."

11. See http://comhaltas.ie/.

## BIBLIOGRAPHY

Bradshaw, Harry. "Captain Francis O'Neill: Chicago Police Chief and Collector/Publisher of Irish Music." Paper read at the annual conference of the Association of Recorded Sound Collections, Chicago, 1993.

Bradshaw, Harry. Insert notes for *James Morrison: The Professor*. Viva Voce 001 (2 cassettes). 1989.

Bradshaw, Harry. Insert book for *Michael Coleman, 1981–1945: Ireland's Most Influential Traditional Musician of the 20th Century*. Viva Voce 004 (2 cassettes). 1991. Re-released, with additional tracks, as Gael-Linn CEFCD 161 92. 1992.

Bradshaw, Harry, and Jackie Small. "John McKenna: Leitrim's Master of the Concert Flute." *Musical Traditions* 7 (mid-1987): 4–11. Reprinted online: http://www.mustrad.org.uk/articles/mckenna.htm. Also available at: http://www.iol.ie/~jfflynn/kenna.htm. Latter posting includes three sound samples of McKenna's playing.

Brasmer, William, and William Osborne, ed. *The Poor Soldier (1783)*. Recent researches in American Music, volume 6. Madison, Wisconsin: A-R Editions, 1978.

Brock, Paul. Telephone interview, November 22, 2006.

Carolan, Nicholas. *A Harvest Saved: Francis O'Neill and Irish Music in Chicago*. Cork, Ireland: Ossian Publications, 1997

Clark, Dennis. *Hibernia America: The Irish and Regional Cultures*. Contributions in Ethnic Studies, No. 14. Westport, Connecticut: Greenwood Press, 1986.

"Comhaltas." http://www.comhaltas.com/.

Daniels, Roger. *Coming to America: A History of Immigration and Ethnicity in American Life*. New York: Harper Collins, 1990.

Doyle, David Noel and Owen Dudley Edwards, eds. *America and Ireland, 1776–1976: The American identity and the Irish connection*. Westport, Connecticut: Greenwood Press, 1980.

*Ethnic Recordings in America: A Neglected Heritage*. Washington, D.C.: American Folklife Center, the Library of Congress, 1982.

Gedutis, Susan. *See You at the Hall: Boston's Golden Era of Irish Music and Dance*. Boston: Northeastern University Press, 2004.

Graham, Ian Charles Cargill. *Colonists from Scotland: Emigration to North American, 1707–1783*. Ithaca, New York: Cornell University Press, 1956.

Gronow, Pekka. "Ethnic Recordings: An Introduction." In *Ethnic Recordings in America*. Washington, D.C: American Folklife Center, the Library of Congress, 1982.

Hamm, Charles. *Yesterdays: Popular Song in America*. New York: W.W. Norton, 1979.

Howe, Elias, Jr. *Complete Preceptor for the Accordeon*. Boston: Elias Howe, Jr., 1843.

Jabbour, Alan. "Fiddle Music." In *American Folklore: An Encyclopedia*, edited by Jan Harold Brunvand. New York and London: Garland Publishing, 1996.

"James C. McAuliffe." Online article, http://www.tinfoil.com/mcauliffe.htm.

Keating, Paul. Personal e-mail communication, November 21, 2006.

Labbé, Gabriel and Richard Carlin. Insert notes to *John Kimmel: Virtuoso of the Irish Accordion*. Folkways RF 112 (LP). 1980.

Malone, Bill C. "Neither Anglo-Saxon nor Celtic: The Music of the Southern Plain Folk." In *Plain Folk of the South Revisited*, edited by Samuel C. Hyde, Jr. Baton Rouge and London: Louisiana State University Press, 1997.

Mac Aoidh, Caoimhín. *The Scribe: The Life and Works of James O'Neill*. Nure, Manorhamilton, County Leitrim, Ireland: Durmlin Publications, 2006.

McCullough, Lawrence E. "Style in Taditional Irish Music." *Ethnomusicology* 21 (1977): 85–97.

McCullough, Lawrence Ervin. *Irish Music in Chicago: An Ethnomusicological Study*. Ph.D. dissertation, University of Pittsburgh. 1978.

McLucas, Anne Dhu, and Paul F. Wells. "Musical Theater as a Link between Folk and Popular Traditions." In *Vistas of American Music: Essays and Compositions in Honor of William K. Kearns*, edited by Susan L. Porter and John Graziano. Warren, Michigan: Harmonie Park Press, 1999.

Miller, Kirby. *Emigrants and Exiles: Ireland and the Irish Exodus to North America*. New York and Oxford: Oxford University Press, 1985.

Mitchell, Pat and Jackie Small. *The Piping of Patsy Touhey*. Dublin: Na Píobairí Uilleann, 1986.

Moloney, Michael. *Irish Music in America: Continuity and Change*. Ph.D. dissertation, University of Pennsylvania. 1992.

Moloney, Michael. "Medicine for Life: A Study of a Folk Composer and His Music." *Keystone Folklore* 20 (1975): 5–37.

Moloney, Mick. "Irish Ethnic Recordings and the Irish-American Imagination." In *Ethnic Recordings in America: A Neglected Heritage*. Washington, D.C.: American Folklife Center, Library of Congress, 1982.

Moloney, Mick. *Far from the Shamrock Shore: The Story of Irish-American Immigration through Song*. With accompanying compact disc. Wilton, Cork, Ireland: The Collins Press, 2002.

Nelligan, Tom. "Joe Derrane: Button Box Master." *Dirty Linen*, June/July 2005, 40–43.

O'Connor, Nuala. *Bringing It All Back Home: The Influence of Irish Music at Home and Overseas*. 2nd edition. Dublin: Merlin Publishing, 2001.

Ó Gráda, Cormac. "Irish Emigration to the United States in the Nineteenth Century." In *America and Ireland, 1776–1976: The American identity and the Irish connection*, edited by David Noel Doyle and Owen Dudley Edwards. Westport, Connecticut: Greenwood Press, 1980.

O'Neill, Barry. Sleeve notes to *Paddy Killoran's Back in Town*. Shanachie 3303 (LP). 1977.

O'Neill, Captain Francis. *Irish Minstrels and Musicians, with Numerous Dissertations on Related Subjects*. Chicago: Regan House, 1913. Reprint, with new introduction by Barry O'Neill. Darby, Pennsylvania: Norwood Editions, 1973.

Porter, Susan L. *With an Air Debonair: Musical Theater in America, 1785–1815*. Washington and London: Smithsonian Institution Press, 1991.

Smith, Graeme. "Modern-Style Irish Accordion Playing: History, Biography, and Class." *Ethnomusicology* 41 (1997): 433–463.

Spottswood, Richard K. *Ethnic Music on Records: A Discography of Ethnic Recordings Produced in the United States, 1893 to 1942*. 7 vols. Urbana and Chicago: University of Illinois Press, 1990.

Vallely, Fintan, ed. *The Companion to Irish Traditional Music*. Cork, Ireland: Cork University Press, 1999.

Varlet, Philippe. Insert notes to *Milestone at the Garden: Irish Fiddle Masters from the 78 rpm Era*. Rounder CD 1123 (CD). 1996.

Walsh, Jim. "John H. [sic] Kimmel, 'The Irish Scotchman [sic]'." *Hobbies, The Magazine for Collectors*, February 1958, 30–35.

Wells, Paul F. and Mike Casey. "An Interview with Mike Rafferty." http://www.firescribble.net/flute/rafferty.htm. 2002.

Williams, W.H.A. "From Lost Land to Emerald Isle; Ireland and the Irish in American Sheet Music, 1800–1920." *Éire-Ireland* 26 (Spring 1991): 19–45.

Williams, William H.A. *'Twas Only an Irishman's Dream: The Image of Ireland and the Irish in American Popular Song Lyrics, 1800–1920*. Urbana and Chicago: University of Illinois Press, 1996.

Winick, Steve. "From Limerick Rake to Solid Man: The Musical Life of Mick Moloney." *Dirty Linen*, October/November 1993, 36–39, 106. Reprinted online, http://www.dirtynelson.com/linen/feature/48mick.html.

## RECOMMENDED READING

Breathnach, Breandán. *Folkmusic and Dances of Ireland*. Dublin: Educational Company of Ireland, 1971.

Carson, Ciaran. *Last Night's Fun: In and Out of Time with Irish Music*. New York: Farrar, Straus and Giroux, 1996.

Foy, Barry. *Field Guide to the Irish Music Session*. Boulder, Colorado: Roberts Rinehart Publishers, 1999.

Ó Canainn, Tomás. *Traditional Music in Ireland*. London: Routledge & Kegan Paul, 1978.

Ó hAllmhuráin, Gearóid. *A Pocket History of Irish Traditional Music*. Boulder, Colorado: The Irish American Book Company, 1998.

O'Neill, Captain Francis. *Irish Music: A Fascinating Hobby*. Chicago: Regan House, 1910. Reprint, with new introduction by Barry O'Neill. Darby, Pennsylvania: Norwood Editions, 1973.

O'Neill, Captain Francis. *O'Neill's Music of Ireland: Eighteen Hundred and Fifty Melodies*. Chicago: Lyon & Healy, 1903. Available in various modern reprints.

O'Neill, Captain Francis. *The Dance Music of Ireland: One Thousand and One Gems*. Chicago: Lyon & Healy, 1907. Available in various modern reprints.

Vallely, Fintan and Charlie Piggott. *Blooming Meadows*. Dublin: Town House, 1998.

## RECORDINGS

All recordings in compact disc format except as noted.


### Reissues

Coleman, Michael. *Michael Coleman, 1891–1945: Ireland's Most Influential Traditional Musician of the 20th Century*. Booklet notes by Harry Bradshaw. Reissue of forty sides recorded 1921–1934. Viva Voce 004 (2-Cassette set), 1991. Re-release, with additional tracks, Gael-Linn CEFCD 161 (2-CD set). 1992

Derrane, Joe. *Irish Accordion*. Produced by Paddy Noonan and Philippe Varlet. Liner notes by Philippe Varlet. Reissue of sixteen sides recorded c. 1948. Copley COP-5008. 1993.

Derrane, Joe and Jerry O'Brien. *Irish Accordion Masters*. Liner notes by Philippe Varlet. Reissue of twenty-six sides recorded c. 1948–1953. Copley COP-5009. 1995.

Dolan, Patrick James "Packie." *The Forgotten Fiddle Player of the 1920s*. Liner notes by Harry Bradshaw. Reissue of twenty-two sides recorded 1927–1929. Viva Voce 006. 1994.

Flanagan Brothers. *The Tunes We Like to Play on Paddy's Day*. Liner notes by Harry Bradshaw. Reissue of 24 sides recorded 1926–1930. Viva Voce 007. 1996.

Gillespie, Hugh. *Classic Recordings of Irish Traditional Fiddle Music*. Reissue of sixteen tracks recorded 1937–1939. Topic 12TP364 (LP), 1978; re-release, Green Linnet GLCD 3066. 1992.

Killoran, Paddy. *Paddy Killoran's Back in Town*. Liner notes by Barry O'Neill. Reissue of fourteen sides recorded 1931–1939. Shanachie 33003 (LP). 1977.

Kimmel, John J. *John Kimmel: Virtuoso of the Irish Accordion*. Liner notes by Gabriel Labbé and Richard Carlin. Reissue of fourteen sides, recorded 1907–1920. Folkways RF 112 (LP). 1980.

McGettigan, John. *John McGettigan and his Irish Minstrels: Classic Recordings of Irish Traditional Music in America*. Liner notes by Mick Moloney and John Paddy Browne. Reissue of eighteen sides recorded 1928–1938. Topic 12T1367 (LP). 1978.

McKenna, John. *His Original Recordings*. Annotated by Jackie Small and others. Reissue of eighteen sides recorded 1921–1937. John McKenna Traditional Society, no number (Cassette). © 1987.

Morrison, James. *The Professor*. Liner notes by Harry Bradshaw. Reissue of thirty sides recorded 1921–1936. Viva Voce 001 (2-Cassette). 1989.

Quinn, Frank. *If You Are Irish*. Liner notes by Chris Strachwitz. Reissue of twenty-five sides recorded 1924–1932. Arhoolie/Folklyric CD 7033. 1997.

Touhey, Patrick J. "Patsy."*The Piping of Patsy Touhey*. Liner notes by Pat Mitchell and Terry Moylan. Reissue of thirty-six sides recorded 1901–1919. Na Píobairí Uilleann NPUCD 001. 2005.

## Various Artists

*Ballinasloe Fair: Early Recordings of Irish Music in America*. Liner notes by Mick Moloney. Traditional Crossroads CD 4284. 1998.

*Fluters of Old Erin*. Liner notes by Harry Bradshaw. Reissue of sixteen sides recorded 1925–1938; not all by American artists. Viva Voce 002 (Cassette). © 1987.

*From Galway to Dublin: Early Recordings of Traditional Irish Music*. Liner notes by Philippe Varlet and Dick Spottswood. Reissue of twenty-five sides recorded 1921–1959; not all by American artists. Rounder CD1087. 1993.

*Milestone at the Garden: Irish Fiddle Masters from the 78 rpm Era*. Liner notes by Philippe Varlet and Dick Spottswood. Reissue of twenty-five sides recorded 1922–1959; not all by American artists. Rounder CD1123. 1996.

*Wheels of the World: Early Irish-American Music*. Two volumes. Liner notes by Don Meade. Yazoo 7008 and 7009. 1997.

## New Recordings

Burke, Kevin. *In Concert*. Green Linnet GLCD 1196. 1999.

Carroll, Liz. *Liz Carroll*. Green Linnet GLCD 1092. 1988.

Carroll, Liz. *Lost in the Loop*. Green Linnet GLCD 1199. 2000.

Carrol, Liz. *Lake Effect*. Green Linnet GLCD 1220. 2002.

Cherish the Ladies. *Out and About*. Green Linnet GLCD 1134. 1993.

Chulrua. *Down the Back Lane*. Shanachie 22001. 2003.

Coen, Jack and Charlie. *The Branch Line*. Topic Records 12TS337(LP) 1977; re-release, Green Linnet GLCD 3067. 1992.

Coen, Father Charles. *Father Charlie*. Green Linnet SIF 1021 (LP). 1979.

Connolly, Seamus. *Notes from My Mind*. Green Linnet SIF 1087 (LP). 1988.

Connolly, Seamus. *Here and There*. Green Linnet SIF 1098. 1989.

Connolly, Seamus and Paddy O'Brien. *The Banks of the Shannon*. Green Linnet GLCD 3082. 1993.

Connolly, Seamus, Martin Mulhaire, and Jack Coen. *Warming Up*. Green Linnet GLCD 1135. 1993.

Conway, Brian. *First through the Gate*. Smithsonian Folkways SFW CD 40481. 2002.

Derrane, Joe. *Give Us Another*. With Felix Dolan (piano). Green Linnet GLCD 1149. 1995.

Derrane, Joe. *Return to Inis Mór*. With Carl Hession (piano). Green Linnet GLCD 1163. 1996.

Derrane, Joe, Seamus Connolly, and John McGann. *The Boston Edge*. Mapleshade 10332 . 2004.

Doon Ceili Band. *Around the World for Sport*. Shanachie 23001. 2006.

Egan, Seamus. *A Week in January*. Shanachie 65005. 1990.

Hayes, Martin. *Martin Hayes*. Green Linnet GLCD 1127. 1993

Hayes, Martin. *Live in Seattle*. Green Linnet GLCD 1195. 1999.

Henry, Kevin. *One's Own Place: A Family Tradition*. Bogfire 2001. 1998.

Ivers, Eileen. *Wild Blue*. Green Linnet GLCD 1166. 1996.

Ivers, Eileen. *Crossing the Bridge*. Sony 60746. 1999.

Keegan, Kevin. *The Music of Kevin Keegan*. Clo Lar-Chonnacta CICD 156. 2004.

Kelly, James. *Traditional Irish Music*. Capelhouse CD896012. 1996.

Kelly, James. *Melodic Journeys*. James Kelly Music JKM0147CD. 2004.

Martin, Laurel. *The Groves*. No label, LKM7876. 2006.

McGann, Andy and Paul Brady. *It's a Hard Road to Travel*. Shanachie 29009 (LP), 1977; Shanachie 34011 (CD). 1995.

McGann, Andy and Paddy Reynolds. *Traditional Music of Ireland*. Shanachie 29004 (LP), 1976; Shanachie 34008 (CD). 1994.

McGann, Andy, with Joe Burke and Felix Dolan. *A Tribute to Michael Coleman*. Shaskeen Records OS-360 (LP), 1966; re-release as Green Linnet GLCD 3097. 1994.

McGann, Andy, with Joe Burke and Felix Dolan. *The Funny Reel*. Shanachie 29012 (LP), [c. 1980]; Shanachie 34016 (CD). 1995.

McGreevy, John and Seamus Cooley. *McGreevy & Cooley*. Philo PH 2005 (LP). 1974.

McGreevy, Johnny and Joe Shannon. *The Noonday Feast*. Green Linnet SIF 1023 (LP). 1980.

Moloney, Mick, and others. *The Green Fields of America*. Green Linnet SIF 1096 (LP). 1989.

Moloney, Mick, Robbie O'Connell, and Jimmy Keane. *Kilkelly*. Green Linnet GLCD 1072. 1988.

Moloney, Mick, Eugene O'Donnell, and Seamus Egan. *Three Way Street*. Green Linnet GLCD 1129. 1993.

Moloney, Mick. *McNally's Row of Flats*. Compass 4426. 2006.

Noonan, Jimmy and others. *The Maple Leaf*. Windjam Records WJ20130. 2001.

O'Brien, Paddy. *Stranger at the Gate*. Green Linnet GLCD 1091. 1988.

O'Donnell, Eugene and James MacCafferty. *The Foggy Dew*. Green Linnet SIF 1084 (LP). 1988.

O'Sullivan, Jerry. *The Invasion*. Green Linnet GLCD 1074. 1987.

O'Sullivan, Jerry. *The Gift*. Shanachie 78017. 1998.

O'Sullivan, Jerry. *O'Sullivan Meets O'Farrell*. Jerry O'Sullivan Music, no number. 2005.

Ourceau, Patrick and others. *Live at Mona's*. No label, MR001. 2004.

Rafferty, Mike, and Mary Rafferty. *The Dangerous Reel*. Kells Music KM-9509. 1996.

Rafferty, Mike, and Mary Rafferty. *The Old Fireside Music*. Larraga Records LR093098. 1998.

Rafferty, Mike and Mary Rafferty. *The Road from Ballinakill*. Larraga Records MMR112000. 2001.

Rafferty, Mike. *Speed 78*. Larraga Records MOR1302. 2004.

Reavy, Ed, and others. *TheMusic of Ed Reavy*. Rounder 6008 (LP), 1979; Rounder 6008 (CD). 2001.

Reynolds, Paddy. *Classic Recordings of the Irish Fiddle Legend*. No label or number. 2005.

Skelton, John and Kieran O'Hare. *Double-Barrelled*. Barrel Music, no number. 2003.

Solas. *Sunny Spells and Scattered Showers*. Shanachie 78010. 1997.

Vesey, John. *Sligo Fiddler*. No label or number (2-CD). 1998.

Williams, John. *Steam*. Green Linnet GLCD 1215. 2001.

Various artists. *Irish Traditional Instrumental Music from Chicago*. Rounder 6006 (LP), 1978. Re-released as *Traditional Irish Music in America: Chicago*. Rounder 6006 (CD). 2001.

Various artists. *Irish Traditional Instrumental Music from the East Coast of America*. Rounder 6005 (LP), 1978. Re-released as *Traditional Irish Music in America: The East Coast*. Rounder 6005 (CD). 2001.

Various artists. *Irish Music from Cleveland [volume 1] with Tom Byrne and Tom McCaffrey*. Folkways FS 3517 (LP). 1977.

Various artists. *Irish Music from Cleveland, Volume 2: The Community Tradition*. Folkways FS 3521 (LP). 1977

Various artists. *Irish Music from Cleveland, Volume 3: The Continuing Tradition*. Folkways FS 3523 (LP). 1977.

Various artists. *Off to California: Traditional Irish Music in San Francisco*. Advent 3601 (LP). 1977.

## FILMS

*Did Your Mother Come from Ireland?* Produced by Roy Esmonde, Conrad Fischer, and Mick Moloney. Fifty minutes. VHS. New York: Ethnic Folk Arts Center, 1989.

*From Shore to Shore: Irish Traditional Music in New York City*. Produced by Patrick Mullins, Rebecca Miller, Marian R. Casey, and Nye Heron. Fifty-seven minutes. VHS. El Paso, Texas: Cherry Lane Productions. 1993. Re-released on DVD with additional features, 2006.

# 3

# Chicano/Latino Music, from the Southwest to the Northeast

*Steven Loza*

As statistics of the population of people of Latin American descent in the United States continue to hover in the range of 14 percent or more as of 2006, with 90 percent in urban areas, the musical culture of this sector continues to be as diverse as Latin American culture in general. In order to control the immense possibilities for review and discussion of the rapidly growing identity of this U.S.-based musical culture and its related scholarship, I will structure this chapter on the following general categories: I) sectors of Mexican derivation; II) centers of Spanish-speaking, Latin Caribbean development; III) contemporary international styles; and IV) the music industry and LARAS. It should be noted that this very limited framework implies much diversity within each of its categories, and that it cannot, in this limited space of one book chapter, possibly be comprehensive. I will, however, attempt to portray what I have seen as some of the dominant musical styles, movements, and traditions that encompass the general topic.

## SECTORS OF MEXICAN DERIVATION

### Early Historical Contexts

Music of Mexican and Spanish origin has existed since the turn of the seventeenth century in the area presently known as the U.S. southwest, and has developed in a diversity of contexts in the states of New Mexico, Texas, Arizona, and California. James K. Leger observes that New Mexicans "possess the longest historical presence of any nonnative people in the United States" (2001, 754). It should also be pointed out that the terms *Mexican* and *Spanish* are somewhat ambiguous, as much of the music must be described as *mestizo* music, signifying the mixture of race and culture involving three continents —Native America, Europe, and Africa, with diverse musical genres more reflective of specific origins than others.

With the appointment of Santa Fe as the capital center of "Nueva Ciudad de México" in 1610 by colonists who had arrived in 1598 from Mexico, then known as Nueva España and under the dominion of Spanish rule, music in the northern region reflected contemporary practices brought by the mestizo culture from the south in addition to a diversity of ecclesiastic music. The situations in Texas, Arizona, and California were similar to that of New Mexico, although not generally as early. Social institutions of music and dance that developed extensively included the populist eighteenth and nineteenth century *fandango* and the more formal *baile*. In his book on the Mexican American "orquesta," Manuel Peña (1999) presents extensive analysis on the class dichotomy of these two social dance contexts. Whereas the baile was organized by formal invitation, the informal and more class-free fandango gatherings featured a *tecolero*, or master of ceremonies of the dance, who called out each woman for her turn. Improvised song verses were also a feature at the fandangos (see Swan 1952, 92; Bryant 1936, 409; Loza 1993, 7).

The mission system in the Southwest is an area in which to observe the musical interaction of the various native Indian cultures of the area. In New Mexico, plain chant was sung in the early mission churches, and liturgical missals were being printed by the early seventeenth century (Leger 2001). In California the Beneme and Genigucchi Indians sang *alabados* (praise songs) and *benditos* (grace) at the San Gabriel Mission, where "until 1834 the singing of the mass was always accompanied by instruments (such as flutes, violins, and trumpets) that local Indians had been taught to play by missionaries" (Stevenson 1986, 107). Active in the teaching of Western music to the Indian neophytes of the California missions was the Franciscan Narciso Durán (1776–1846), who developed a basic pedagogy to teach church music. Mission choirs composed largely of Indians were developed throughout New Mexico, California, Arizona, and Texas. The mission choirs developed an extensive repertoire, performing an abundance of the plain chant for several masses in addition to the chant of the Proper of the Mass for Sundays and feast days.

A rich Spanish/Mexican tradition that continued into the second half of the nineteenth century throughout the Southwest was that of the *pastores* and *pastorelas*. Based on the birth of Christ, these musical dramas depicted the journey of the shepherds to the Nativity manger. Pastorelas were often enacted at churches or private homes in conjunction with the *posada*, a social, religious gathering where songs celebrating the Christmas season were sung.

The traditions of the pastorela and posada continue to the present, although sometimes in a more formal context. Another intensely rich tradition based on religious belief is that of *los matachines,* which Romero (2003, 81) describes as "a ritual morality dance drama brought by the Spanish, which survives in the southwestern United States and Mexico among Indo-Hispanos and indigenous populations." Romero notes that there are two versions of the Matachines dance in New Mexico, the "Spanish" version, accompanied by violin and guitar and performed in both Indo-Hispano and Pueblo Indian contexts, and a version performed in the Jemez and Santa Clara Pueblos, referred to by outsiders as the "drum" version, and featuring a male chorus accompanied by a drum. Romero (1993, 1) has also observed that

> while the dance originates in the Old World and was brought by way of the Spanish, perhaps as early as the sixteenth century, in the New World it has merged with traditional indigenous dances and ideologies in many settings, sometimes so much that it can equally be described as an indigenous dance with only a superficial underlay of the Old World Matachines.

In New Mexico a rich history of musical expression and dance dating from the seventeenth century has been documented by various scholars, including, among others, Aurelio Espinosa (1985), Arthur Campa (1979), John Donald Robb (1980), Rubén Cobos (1956), Vicente Mendoza and Virginia R.R. de Mendoza (1986), Jack Loeffler (1999), Enrique Lamadrid (1994, 2003), Sylvia Rodríguez (1996), Brenda Romero (1997, 2003), James K. Leger (2001), and Peter García (1990). Romero makes the following observation concerning the Mexican tradition in New Mexico:

> Much of the folk music of the Mejicanos was already old when the Spaniards settled New Mexico in the early seventeenth century. Some of the songs collected here from 1930 to 1960 date back to the twelfth century and some are still older. They represent many different genres, including narrative ballads (*romances*), topical songs (*canciones*), and children's game songs. For centuries, folk singers took out their *cancioneros* (song books) in the evening hours, after the day's farmwork. They entertained themselves and taught songs to their children and relatives in extended family structures. Among those who continue to perform the old music today, this style of musical transmission is much the same as it used to be. It is not unusual to find similar transmission, from parent to offspring or sibling to sibling, of such nontraditional music as rock and roll, and many local bands reflect kinship ties among members. While the prevalence of older Spanish/Mejicano music has declined since the advent of electricity and the availability of radio and television, traditional Spanish/Mejicano music is still the musical foundation for many contemporary styles. (1997, 166)

One of the unique elements to have occurred in New Mexico has been the interrelationships between the Mejicano culture and various Native American groups. Native American captives who assimilated the Mexican culture became known as *genízaros*, creating an eventual legacy of mixed and often conflictual identity. With Mexican independence from Spain in 1821, Native Americans were granted full citizenship. Nevertheless, on the level of musical culture, unique hybrid expressions and rituals began to take form, including the phenomenon of the Los Comanches ritual tradition shared by Pueblo and Mejicano groups in New Mexico. The Comanche, a Native American group of the southern plains traditionally called the *numunuh*, had contact, much of it conflictual, with Pueblo Native Americans and the Mexicans in the area of New Mexico. These conflicts and other relationships are enacted in the Comanches ritual dramas that incorporate substantial musical expression (see Lamadrid 2003: *Hermanitos Comachitos: Indo-Hispano Rituals of Captivity and Redemption*). Another form that represents the juxtaposition of Mexican and Native American culture is that of the *indita*, which developed significantly during the nineteenth century in Mexico, including New Mexico. The form is based on a *son* type of rhythm, alternating 2/4 and 3/4 meters and melodically imitating what Mexican musicians perceived as indigenous sounding songs. The texts also often referred to themes based on the indigenous population. The text below (Example 1) is a fragment of an indita, "La jeyana," sung for the San Luis Gonzaga dances of San Acacio, originally a Spanish settlement on the Rio Grande in central New Mexico. San Luis Gonzaga was the young seventeenth-century Italian Jesuit saint and patron of devotional and social dance. The indita is characterized by sung "vocables" common among Native American music and chant and devotional dances reminiscent of those of the Pueblo Indians (Lamadrid 2003, 88–9). Highlighting the contemporary stylization of the traditional melody, Lamadrid notes that "although there are many more lyrics sung for San Luis, the most poignant for this young singer is the verse 'Dicen que las golondrinas de un volido pasan el mar' (They say the swallows cross the ocean in one flight), a symbolic reference to the Iberian diaspora" (137–8).

## Example 1: "La jeyana"

Ana jeyana
Ana jeyana
Ana jeyana
Yo jeyana
Yo jeyana yo

Ana jeyana, jeyana
Ana jeyana, je yo
Ana jeyana, jeyana
Ana jeyana, je yo.

Dicen que las golondrinas de un volido
Pasan el mar.
Dicen que las golondrinas de un volido
Pasan el mar.

On yet another regional front in the Southwest, it was during the early twentieth century, between 1904 and 1912, that writer/photographer Charles F. Lummis produced a collection of sound recordings of Mexican folksongs. They were originally recorded on 340 wax cylinders but have been rerecorded on magnetic tape and are catalogued and housed at the Southwest Museum in Los Angeles. These may be the first sound recordings of Mexican-American folksongs in California. Although most of the collection was not widely disseminated, Lummis did publish 14 of the songs in 1923 (transcribed by Arthur Farwell) in *Spanish Songs of Old California*.

## The Border Context and Intercultural Conflict

Perhaps the musical forms that took strongest root throughout the Southwest, especially during the late nineteenth and early twentieth centuries, were the *cancíon mexicana* (eventually evolving as the *ranchera*) and the *corrido*. Numerous studies have been done on these genres, but the work of Américo Paredes (1958, 1995) stands out, especially in terms of his lucid observations of the issues of identity and conflict embodied in the song/ballad repertoire. His reference to this corpus of music as the "greater Mexican folk song" is especially significant in that it ties contemporary Mexican culture to the former Mexican territory taken by the U.S. in the Mexican American War of 1846-1848. Paredes determined that the most salient theme of the corridos that he studied was that of intercultural conflict, a theory that he nurtured throughout his analyses of the ballads of the Texas-Mexican border, the Southwest, and other sectors of the U.S. In Texas, he perceived the consistent theme of conflict between the two dominant groups, the Anglo-Americans and the Chicanos, and describes 66 folk songs of the lower Texas-Mexican border (Paredes 1995).

Manuel Peña, a student of Paredes who has perhaps written more on Chicano music than any other scholar, wrote seminal studies of the music of Texas-Mexicans, specifically that of the *conjunto* and *orquesta* ensemble styles (1985a; 1985b). Adapting a Marxist framework, Peña observed not only the class divisions between the Mexicans and Anglos, but the conflicts at work within the Texas-Mexican, or *tejano*, community itself. Among his many significant conclusions is that "the symbolic structure(s) of conjunto and orquesta reflect the state of flux in which Chicano society is maintained" (1999, 4).

Paredes and Peña both provide lucid musical examples and analysis in their various bodies of work. Paredes, in fact, wrote a complete book, *With His Pistol in His Hand*, based on a ballad inspired by the experience of a Texas-Mexican, Gregorio Cortez, whose experience with the Texas legal system became a legendary epic among Mexicans in the U.S. and was also made into a corrido.

In his *A Texas-Mexican Cancionero*, Paredes's notes that "Gregorio Cortez" (Example 2) is without a doubt the epitome of the Border corrido, with the hero betrayed into the hands of his enemies" (1995, 31). Paredes comments on the origin of the Mexican corrido, which in part evolved form the Spanish *romance*, speculating that the earliest corridos could have emerged in the northern border area of Mexico and the United States. He cites the "El Corrido de Kiansis" ("Kansas") as the "oldest Texas-Mexican corrido that we have in complete form" (25) and as having been sung since the 1860s. Even at this early date, Paredes notes that "there is intercultural conflict in "Kiansis," but it is expressed in professional rivalries rather than in violence between men (see Example 3).

**Example 2: "Gregorio Cortez"**

En el condado de El Carmen
miren lo que ha sucedido,
murió el Cherife Mayor,
quedando Román herido.

En el condado de El Carmen
tal desgracia sucedió
murió el Cherife Mayor,
no saben quién lo mató.

Se anduvieron informando
como media hora después
supieron que el malhechor
era Gregorio Cortez.

Ya insortaron a Cortez
por toditito el estado,
que vivo o muerto se aprehenda
porque a varios ha matado.

Decía Gregorio Cortez
con su pistola en la mano:
-No siento haberlo matado,
lo que siento es a mi hermano.-

Decía Gregorio Cortez
con su alma muy encendida:
-No siento haberlo matado,
la defensa es permitida.-

Venían los americanos
más blancos que una amapola,

de miedo que le tenían
a Cortez con su pistola.

Decían los americanos,
decían con timidez:
-Vamos a seguir la huella
que el malhechor es Cortez.-

Soltaron los perros jaunes
pa' que siguieran la huella,
pero alcanzar a Cortez
era seguir a una estrella.

Tiró con rumbo a Gonzales
sin ninguna timidez:
-Síganme, rinches cobardes,
yo soy Gregorio Cortez.-

Se fue de Belmont al rancho,
lo alcanzaron a rodear,
poquitos más de trescientos,
y alli les brincó el corral.

Cuando les brincó el corral,
según lo que aquí se dice,
se agarraron a balazos
y les mató otro cherife.

Decía Gregorio Cortez
con su pistola en la mano:
-No corran, rinches cobardes,
con un solo mexicano.-

Salió Gregorio Cortez,
salió con rumbo a Laredo,
no lo quisieron seguir
porque le tuvieron miedo.

Decía Gregorio Cortez:
-¿Pa' qué se valen de planes?
No me pueden agarrar
ni con esos perros jaunes.-

Decían los americanos:
-Si lo alcanzamos ¿qué hacemos?
Si le entramos por derecho
muy poquitos volveremos.-

Allá por El Encinal,
según lo que aquí se dice,
le formaron un corral
y les mató otro cherife.

Decía Gregorio Cortez
echando muchos balazos:
-Me he escapado de aguaceros,
contimás de nublinazos.-

Ya se encontró a un mexicano,
le dice con altivez:
-Platícame qué hay de nuevo,
yo soy Gregorio Cortez.

Dicen que por culpa mía
han matado mucha gente,
pues ya me voy a entregar
porque eso no es conveniente.-

Cortez le dice a Jesús:
-Ora sí lo vas a ver,
anda diles a los rinches
que me vengan a aprehender.-

Venían todos los rinches,
venían que hasta volaban,
porque se iban a ganar
diez mil pesos que les daban.

Cuando rodearon la casa
Cortez se les presentó:
-Por la buena sí me llevan
porque de otro modo no.-

Decía el Cherife Mayor
como queriendo llorar:
-Cortez, entrega tus armas,
no te vamos a matar.-

Decía Gregorio Cortez,
les gritaba en alta voz:
-Mis armas no las entrago
hasta estar en caraboz'.-

Decía Gregorio Cortez,
decía en su voz divina:

-Mis armas no las entrego
hasta estar en bartolina.-

Ya agarraron a Cortez,
ya terminó la cuestión,
la pobre de su familia
lo lleva en el corazón.

Ya con ésta me despido
a la sombra de un ciprés,
aquí se acaba el corrido
de don Gregorio Cortez.

## Gregorio Cortez – In English

In the county of El Carmen, look what has happened;
The Major Sheriff is dead, leaving Roman badly wounded.

In the county of El Carmen such a tragedy took place:
The Major Sheriff is dead; no one knows who killed him.

They went around asking questions about half an hour afterward;
They found out that the wrongdoer had been Gregorio Cortez.

Now they have outlawed Cortez throughout the whole of the state;
Let him be taken, dead or alive, he has killed several men.

Then said Gregorio Cortez, with his pistol in his hand,
"I don't regret having killed him; what I regret is my brother's death."

Then said Gregorio Cortez, with his soul aflame,
"I don't regret having killed him; self-defense is permitted."

The Americans were coming; they were whiter than a poppy
From the fear that they had of Cortez and his pistol.

Then the Americans said, and they said it fearfully,
"Come, let us follow the trail, for the wrongdoer is Cortez."

They let loose the bloodhounds so they could follow the trail,
But trying to overtake Cortez was like following a star.

He struck out for Gonzales, without showing fear;
"Follow me, cowardly rinches; I am Gregorio Cortez."

From Belmont he went to the ranch, where they succeeded in
surrounding him,
Quite a few more than three hundred, but he jumped out of their corral.

When he jumped out of their corral, according to what is said here,
They got into a gunfight, and he killed them another Sheriff.

Then said Gregorio Cortez, with his pistol in his hand,
"Don't run, you cowardly rinches, from a single Mexican."

Gregorio Cortez went out towards Laredo;
They would not follow him because they were afraid of him.

Then said Gregorio Cortez, "What is the use of your scheming?
You cannot catch me, even with those bloodhounds."

Then said the Americans, "If we catch up with him, what shall we do?
If we fight him man to man, very few of us will return."

Way over near El Encinal, according to what is said here,
they made him a corral, and he killed them another sheriff.

Then said Gregorio Cortez, shooting out a lot of bullets,
"I have weathered thunderstorms; this little mist doesn't bother me."

Now he has met a Mexican; he says to him haughtily.
"Tell me the news; I am Gregorio Cortez."

"They say this because of me many people have been killed;
so now I will surrender, because such things are not right."

Cortez says to Jesus, "At last you are going to see it;
Go and tell the rinches that they can come and arrest me,"

All of the rinches were coming, so fast that they almost flew,
Because they were going to get the ten thousand dollars that was offered.

When they surrounded the house, Cortez appeared before them:
"You will take me if I'm willing but not any other way."

Then said the Major Sheriff, as if he was going to cry,
"Cortez, hand over your weapons; we do not want to kill you."

Then said Gregorio Cortez, shouting to them in a loud voice,
"I won't surrender my weapons until I am in a cell."

Then said Gregorio Cortez, speaking in his godlike voice,
"I won't surrender my weapons until I'm inside a jail."

Now they have taken Cortez, and now the matter is ended;
His poor family are keeping him in their hearts.

Now with this I say farewell in the shades of a cypress;
This is the end of the ballad of Don Gregorio Cortez.

### Example 3: "El Corrido de Kiansis"

Cuando salimos pa' Kiansis
con una grande partida,
¡ah, qué camino tan largo!
no contaba con mi vida.

Nos decía el caporal,
como queriendo llorar:
-Allá va la novillada,
no me la dejen pasar.-

¡Ah, qué caballo tan bueno!
todo se le iba en correr,
¡y, ah, qué fuerte aguacerazo!
no contaba yo en volver.

Unos pedían cigarro,
otros pedían que comer,
y el caporal nos decía:
-Sea por Dios, qué hemos de hacer.-

En el charco de Palomas
se cortó un novillo bragado,
y el caporal lo lazó
en su caballo melado.

Avísenle al caporal
que un vaquero se mató,
en las trancas del corral
nomás la cuera dejó.

Llegamos al Río Salado
y nos tiramos a nado,
decía un americano:
-Esos hombres ya se ahogaron.-

Pues qué pensaría ese hombre
que venimos a esp'rimentar,
si somos del Río Grande,
de los buenos pa' nadar.

Y le dimos vista a Kiansis,
y nos dice el caporal:

-Ora sí somos de vida,
ya vamos a hacer corral.-

Y de vuelta en San Antonio
compramos buenos sombreros,
y aquí se acaban cantando
versos de los aventureros.

## Kansas – In English

When we left for Kansas with a great herd of cattle,
Ah, what a long trail it was! I was not sure I would survive.

The Caporal would tell us, as if he was going to cry,
"Watch out for that bunch of steers; don't let them get past you."

Ah, what a good horse I had! He did nothing but gallop.
And, Ah, what a violent cloudburst! I was not sure I would come back.

Some of us asked for cigarettes, others wanted something to eat;
And the caporal would tell us, "So be it, it can't be helped."

By the pond at Palomas a vicious steer left the heard,
And the caporal lassoed it on his honey-colored horse.

Go tell the caporal that a vaquero has been killed;
All he left was his leather jacket hanging on the rails of the corral.

We got to the Salado River, and we swam our horses across;
An American was saying, "Those men are as good as drowned."

I wonder what the man thought, that we came to learn, perhaps;
Why, we're for the Rio Grande, where the good swimmers are from.

And then Kansas came in sight, and the caporal tells us,
"We have finally made it, we'll soon have them in the corral."

Back again in San Antonio, we all bought ourselves good hats,
And this is the end of the singing of the stanzas about the trail drivers.

In his book *Música Tejana*, Peña presents diverse examples of both conjunto and orquesta contexts and artists. The instrumentation of the traditional *tejano* conjunto is largely characterized by the use of accordion and *bajo-sexto* (a double stringed guitar with both bass and upper register strings). Early conjunto innovators of South Texas included Narciso Martínez, Pedro Ayala, and Santiago Jiménez. Martínez, born in 1911, became known as "el huracán del valle" (the Valley Hurricane), and many consider him the "father" of conjunto music. Conjuntos of a later generations would include those of Valerio

Longoria, Tony de la Rosa, Paulino and Eloy Bernál, Mingo Saldívar, Steve Jordan, and Flaco Jiménez. A corrido representing a good portion of conjunto repertoire reflecting the theme of intercultural conflict is "Los rinches de Texas" ("The Texas Rangers"), composed as a result of a series of strikes organized by melon workers and the United Farm Workers in Starr County in South Texas during the summer of 1967.

The orquesta tejana, as defined by Peña (1999), can be traced to origins in the late nineteenth century, and evolved having "ready made" models ranging from full symphonic groups to brass bands to minimal string groups both in the United States and Mexico. Thus, the orquesta style was not tied to any particular indigenous innovation, as with the conjunto. Peña notes a particular *bimusical* identity in the orquesta, and remarks that "this identity mirrored, at the level of musical expression, the ideological structures underpinning the *bicultural* identity of middle-class Texas-Mexicans who forged the orquesta tejana" (119).

Beto Villa, considered by many as the "father" of the *orquesta tejana*, first recorded in 1947. His style inaugurated what Peña refers to as the "Tex-Mex ranchero" variant of the polca-ranchera, becoming "by far the most important stage in the evolution of a Texas-Mexican orquesta. More important, Villa exerted enormous influence over countless *epigones*, not only in Texas but throughout the Hispanic Southwest" (ibid.). Peña cites the final stage in the orquesta tejana evolution and its political aesthetic to be the style lauched during the late 1960s by Little Joe and the Latinaires, renamed Little Joe y La Familia in 1970. A bimusical style was forged thereafter, known as *La Onda Chicana*, and was imitated by musical groups throughout the Southwest. The style was also often referred to as Tex-Mex.

The conflict of the Mexican experience, as presented above in the case of the Texas-Mexican border area, was also being expressed in other regions of the United States. One example of many, relating to southern California, is the classic corrido "El Lavaplatos" (The Dishwasher), composed by Jesús Osorio, who recorded the song with Manuel "El Perro" Camacho on the Victor label in 1930. It was later recorded by Los Hermanos Bañuelos during the same year on the Brunswick/Vocalion label and again by Chávez y Lugo on Columbia. Incorporating satire into the expression of an immigrant's illusion and disillusion with the dreams and myths of Hollywood, the song is a tragicomic sociocultural commentary critiquing contemporary life of the era (Loza 1993). Peña cites this particular corrido as a thematically significant one because of its reference to "political and economic issues that were at the heart of the Mexican's subordination in the capitalist Anglo order that reigned over the Southwest by this time" (1989, 67).

## Urban Contexts of Tradition and Innovation

In the 1920s and 1930s musical activity among Mexicans in the Southwest was largely diffused through Spanish-language radio broadcasts. During the mid-1920s recording companies such as Victor, Brunswick, and Columbia "began to exploit for commercial gain the musical traditions of Mexicans in California and in the Southwest" (Peña 1989, 67). Genres recorded and marketed included the cancíon mexicana, the corrido, boleros, and *huapangos*, among others. Instrumentation was frequently based on ensembles such as the *trío* and the *mariachi*. The latter had evolved from its rural identity into a larger and more commercialized instrumental format in Mexico, incorporating, by the 1930s, violin, *vihuela*, guitar, and *guitarrón*, and later the trumpet.

It is the mariachi ensemble which has come to be more associated with Mexican music than any other type of musical group, and which has been extremely popular in the United States since it became the vogue of Mexican radio during the 1930s. As immigration from Mexico to the United States has continuously increased, so has the growth of mariachis. As the most international symbol of Mexican music, thousands of mariachis based in the United States perform at restaurants, clubs, weddings, civil functions, holiday celebrations, and a variety of other occasions. Because of the constant popularity of rancheras and the singers who interpret them, mariachis have been a mainstay of musical accompaniment for that genre in addition to performing the traditional Mexican *son*, a musical form associated with the origin of the mariachi in the Mexican regions of Jalisco and Michoacán. Artists from Mexico have constantly toured cities in the United States, catering especially to inhabitants of Mexican origin and performing in spectacular shows and venues. Mexican based artists accompanied by mariachis and appearing since the 1930s throughout the United Stateshave included such notables as Jorge Negrete, Lucha Reyes, Pedro Infante, José Alfredo Jiménez, Lola Beltrán, Miguel Aceves Mejía, Luís Aguilar, Lucha Villa, Vicente Fernández, Chelo Silva, Juan Gabriel, Rocío Dúrcal, Aida Cuevas, Pepe Aguilar, Alejandro Fernández, and Luís Miguel, among many others.

Highly successful mariachis in the Southwest attaining international recognition have included Mariachi Cobre of Tucson, Arizona, Los Reyes de Albuquerque of New Mexico, Mariachi Campanas de America of San Antonio, Texas, and three based in Los Angeles, California: Mariachi Los Camperos de Nati Cano, Mariachi Sol de México de José Hernández, and Mariachi Los Galleros de Pedro Rey. The latter three mariachis, along with the internationally renowned Mexico City-based Mariachi Vargas de Tecalitlán, recorded and performed extensively with Linda Ronstadt during the period when she was awarded two Grammy awards for her mariachi albums *Canciones de mi padre* (1988) and *Mas canciones* (1991). Ronstadt, born and raised in Tucson and the daughter of a Mexican American, recorded not only mariachi music in Spanish but other recordings of popular and topical styles. Her involvement in mariachi sparked new interest in the style since the late 1980s, especially among young Mexican American musicians and especially among women musicians, although it must be said that women were already entering the realm of mariachi music since the 1960s. Exclusively female mariachis have especially emerged since the 1990s, exemplified by groups such as Mariachi Las Reynas de Los Angeles, Mariachi Adelita, and Mariachi Feminil. Another highly popular phenomenon has been the great success of mariachi festivals, highlighted by both concerts and mariachi performance classes, in cities including San Antonio, Tucson, Fresno, Los Angeles, and Albuquerque, among numerous others, and school programs throughout the Southwest and other parts of the country have incorporated mariachi classes into their curricula. Daniel Sheehy (1997, 1999, 2005) and Candida Jáquez (2003) have conducted extensive fieldwork and published on the mariachi context in the United States.

There have consistently been numerous individual artists who became musical leaders and symbolic beacons of hope for the Mexican population throughout the United States. In Texas, Lydia Mendoza attained immense popularity not only in the context of música tejana, but throughout the United States and Mexico. Born in Houston in 1916, Mendoza would at times during her youth also live in Monterrey, Mexico and San Antonio and other Texas locales, and she learned from an early age with her family to sing and perform the guitar. Mendoza would eventually became a major innovator in the interpretation and extensive recording of the canción, corrido, bolero, huapango, and other musical forms. Her first solo hit, "Mal hombre," was recorded in 1933 on RCA's Bluebird label, and she eventually recorded on the Falcón, Ideal, RCA Victor, Columbia, and DLB labels, and had great success with the recordings of "Celosa," "Amor de madre," "Joaquin Murrieta," among many others. She is featured in the documentaries *Chulas Fronteras* by Les Blank and *Songs of the Homeland* by Hector Galán. In 1982 she received the National Endowment for the Arts National Heritage Award, and in 1999 she was awarded the National Medal of the Arts by President Bill Clinton. A bilingual book, *Lydia Mendoza's Life in Music/La historia de Lydia Mendoza,* was written by Yolanda Broyles González and published by Oxford University Press in 2001.

Another individual artist who demands mention is Lalo Guerrero. Born in Tucson in 1916 and raised there in the Mexican neighborhood known as Barrio Libre, he based himself in Los Angeles during his early twenties and established a dynamic musical career as a songwriter, singer/musician, recording artist, and music club owner. During World War II he performed for troops as part of a USO tour through different parts of the U.S., and composed songs that became standards in the Mexican repertoire, including "Canción mexicana," recorded by Lucha Reyes in 1940, and "Nunca jamás," recorded by both Trío Los Panchos and Javier Solís. His orchestra recorded extensively and toured throughout the Southwest, performing popular music forms such as boleros, danzones, mambos, and cumbias, and he also recorded his own material as a singer with trios, mariachis, and *conjuntos norteños*. During the 1940s he composed a number of songs related to the *pachuco* culture of young Chicanos in Los Angeles, adapting the *caló* slang of Spanish that was popular among them. A number of these songs, including "Vamos a bailar," "Chucos suaves," and "Marijuana Boogie," were adapted by playright and director Luis Valdez in his musical play *Zoot Suit*, which was also made into a major film through Universal Studios in 1982, starring Edward James Olmos and musician/actor Daniel Valdez. Guerrero became highly recognized as a musical satirist, and composed songs related to the United Farm Workers Movement, immigration, and Chicano culture. Humor is an essential component of his music (e.g., "Pancho López," "There's No Tortillas," "No Chicanos On TV," "No Way José"), and he inspired many younger artists, including Los Lobos, who recorded a children's music album, *Papa's Dream*, with Guerrero in 1995, which was later nominated for a Grammy award. In 1991 Guerrero was awarded a National Heritage Award by the National Endowment for the Arts, and in 1997 he was awarded the National Medal of the Arts by President Bill Clinton. Lalo Guerrero is extensively profiled in Steven Loza's *Barrio Rhythm: Mexican American Music in Los Angeles* (University of Illinois Press 1993) and he wrote, with Sherilyn Meece Mentes, his autobiography *Lalo: My Life and Music*, published by the University of Arizona Press (2002).

In the numerous and diverse urban settings of cities throughout the United States, musicians and their followers of Mexican descent have nurtured musical forms reflecting the contradictions of tradition, nationalism, assimilation, innovation, reinterpretation, and hybridization, the latter term reminiscent of the Mexican/Latin American notion of *mestizaje*, the mixing of race and culture, and the evolutionary process that emerges from such interaction. By the 1950s and 1960s, Chicanos began to both assimilate and change "mainstream American" styles, including rhythm and blues, rock, jazz, disco, punk, and hip-hop.

In an article titled "The View from the Sixth Street Bridge: The History of Chicano Rock," Ruben Guevara, an important contemporary figure in the "Eastside Renaissance" of music (in East Los Angeles), formulates various theories concerning the development and adaptation of different musical styles and preferences among Mexican Americans in Los Angeles. Guevara's historical perspective traces his own musical life and enculturation in Los Angeles since the 1940s: "In East L.A., as in so many other places, the link between swing and early rhythm and blues and rock and roll was jump blues. Jump evolved in the thirties from Harlem bands like those of Cab Calloway and the Kansas City groups of Count Basie and Louis Jordan. In Los Angeles the leading early practitioners were Roy Milton and the Solid Senders" (Guevara 1985, 115). By the end of World War II, Roy Milton had achieved national prominence with his hit "R.M. Blues," recorded on Specialty Records. He was among the many swing artists who became popular among Mexicans in Los Angeles.

The zoot suit era of the 1940s was characterized not only by the popularization of swing, but also by an assortment of Latin styles, including the mambo, rumba, and danzón, all Cuban imports, often via Mexico, and Mexican music was also popular among zoot suiters. Swing and tropical rhythms were more popular among the zoot suit "cult," which adopted particular styles of dress, language (the *caló* dialect of Spanish previously cited in the music of Lalo Guerrero), music, and dance. Zoot suiters patronized particular entertainment spots and formed social groups that eventually became known as gangs. Many speculate that the pachuco gang evolved as a defense mechanism in response to the Zoot Suit riots, confrontations between pachucos and enlisted military men during the period of World War II.

A growing number of blacks were settling in Los Angeles in search of better-paying war industry jobs. The availability of low-rent housing in the Mexican neighborhoods of east and south-central Los Angeles prompted many blacks to settle there. Conversely, as Anglos became economically mobile, they moved away from those neighborhoods: "Blacks and Chicanos, isolated together, began to interact and, in large numbers, they listened to the same radio stations. For instance, there was Hunter Hancock ('Ol' H.H.') on KFVD. He had a show on Sundays called 'Harlem Matinee' that featured records by Louis Jordan, Lionel Hampton, and locals Roy Milton, Joe and Jimmy Liggins, and Johnny Otis," the latter who, as also noted by Guevara, introduced jump blues to Chicanos in the Los Angeles Eastside at the Angeles Hall in 1948 (Guevara 1985, 116).

One of the Chicano bands to emulate the jump blues style was the Pachuco Boogie Boys, led by Don Tosti and featuring Raúl Díaz on vocals and drums, Eddie Cano on piano, and Bob Hernández on saxophone and flute. A local hit emerged form the group's various recordings titled "Pachuco Boogie," which Guevara describes as a "jump style shuffle with either Raul or Don rapping in Caló about getting ready to go out on a date. Very funny stuff" (ibid., 117). Tosti, whose real name is Edmundo Martínez Tostado, was originally from El Paso, Texas, coming to Los Angeles as a young boy. He performed with the bands of Tommy Dorsey, Charlie Barnett, Les Brown, and Jack Teagarten. He also worked extensively as an arranger for the popular Los Angeles-based Mexican singer Rubén Reyes. Eddie Cano would emerge as a leading exponent of Latin jazz, performing with Miguelito Valdés in New York and eventually leading and recording with his own Latin jazz groups in Los Angeles (profiled in Loza 1993). In the same vein of Latin jazz, another Chicano based in Los Angeles, Poncho Sánchez, who often worked with Cano, would eventually emerge as an internationally acclaimed artist.

In 1952 Hunter Hancock aired an instrumental single titled "Pachuco Hop" by African American saxophonist Chuck Higgins. Hancock later became a disc jockey at KGFJ, the first station to broadcast the music of black artists exclusively seven days per week. "A massive audience in East L.A. tuned in on each and every one of those days. At about the same time D.J.s like Art Laboe and Dick 'Huggy Boy' Hugg started playing jump and doo wap on the radio" (Guevara 1985, 118). Chicano saxophonists Li'l Bobby Rey and Chuck Rio (Danny Flores) emulated the styles of the black saxophonists (in addition to Higgins, Joe Houston and Big Jay McNeely), but also added their own particular Mexican- and Latin-based stylistic idioms. Rio, as a member of the Champs, achieved international attention with his own composition and instrumental hit "Tequila" in 1958. The record rose to the number one spot on the national rating charts and since then has become a world classic.

In his book *The Mexican American Orquesta* (1999), Peña conceptualizes the orquesta as a musical ensemble much like the orquesta tejana, but as a phenomenon throughout the Chicano Southwest. It should be noted that this conceptualization, especially in regards to the use of the term "orquesta," is not necessarily universal among Mexican-American musicians. Recognizing the influences of the big swing band styles of Duke Ellington and Stan Kenton, in addition to the heavy influx of Afro-Cuban styles of dance music by way of the mambo and cha cha cha, in addition to the constant demand for typical Mexican dance music, it is safe to say that there did exist a proliferation of such orquestas throughout the Mexican-American Southwest. Peña offers some cross-regional analysis in observing the historical routes of ensembles in Texas, California, and Arizona. In addition to critiquing the orquesta tejana's evolution and its various artists, he offers an ethnographic portrayal of bandleaders in California and Arizona, specifically Don Tosti, Lalo Guerrero, Chico Sesma, and Pedro Bugarin. Of interest are the issues of class and musical aesthetics as related to Tosti and Sesma, and their experience with ranchera music. Tosti and Sesma, both formally trained musicians, gravitated much more to the tropical styles of Afro-Cuban music in addition to jazz, while Guerrero represented a diversity that swung from ranchera to boogie to mambo. Other important musicians emerging from East Los Angeles and associated with big band or Latin jazz styles included Andy Russell (Andrés Rábago), Eddie Cano, Paul López, Johnny Martínez, and Rudy Macías (see Loza 1993; Peña 1999). Another, although younger, artist who emerged from this context is 1999 Grammy award-winning Poncho Sánchez, who performed as the conguero for Cal Tjader and his Latin jazz ensemble for seven years until Tjader's death in 1984. He was contracted to Discovery Records and recorded his first album as a leader in 1979, and to Concord Records in 1983, for which he continues to record. Sánchez has also experimented with the blend of Afro-Cuban jazz and rhythm and blues music, recording various interpretations of the music of one of his early idols, James Brown, and has invited artists such as Tito Puente, Mongo Santamaría, Freddie Hubbard, Diane Reeves, Chick Corea, and Ray Charles to record on his albums. For in-depth studies on Sánchez, refer to Loza (2001, 1999, 1993).

Much attention has been given to what has been referred to as the "Eastside Sound" of Los Angeles (Rodríguez 1980a, b, c; Loza 1993; Reyes and Waldman 1998), the multitude of bands that emerged in East Los Angeles from the early 1960s through the early 1980s, and the dynamic ambience and impact that these groups nurtured during a period of Chicano reawakening. Although these rhythm and blues, rock-influenced bands largely emulated the pop music of the day ranging from James Brown to the Beatles, and from the Supremes to disco music, it has been argued that there did exist a specific style in their music, and that the sound and experience reflected the bimusical, bicultural context of Mexican Americans, especially those living in large urban areas. Thus, the sound was not relegated to Los Angeles, but resonated in San

Francisco, San Diego, Phoenix, Tucson, Albuquerque, San Antonio, Houston, and Dallas.

Although not from the eastside of Los Angeles, Ritchie Valens (Richard Valenzuela), who was raised in the northside of Los Angeles in the Pacoima barrio of the San Fernando Valley, achieved major stardom in the rock and roll music industry. He was promoted by producer Bob Keane, who recorded Valens on his own Del-Fi Records. Certainly 17-year-old Valens' international hit recorded in Spanish of the Mexican folk *son jarocho* "La Bamba" represented a radical change in the Top 40 music industry. What could have had an even more sensational impact—a Chicano entering the mainstream recording industry—was cut short with the death of Valens in a 1959 plane crash along with rock and roll stars Buddy Holly and J.P. "Big Bopper" Richardson. Other hits by Valens included "Donna," "Come On, Let's Go," "That's My Little Suzie," and "Little Girl" (the latter two posthumously). Besides Valens, for many years the only other Chicano musical artist to achieve a comparable height of fame was Vikki Carr (Victoria Cardona), born in El Paso, Texas, and raised in the San Gabriel Valley of Los Angeles County, who had a string of international hits during the 1960s including "It Must Be Him" and "With Pen in Hand." She would later emerge as a major artist throughout Latin America and Spain, recording new material in Spanish on the CBS International label and receiving Grammy awards in 1986 and 1992. Another El Paso native who also eventually relocated to Southern California was singer-guitarist Trini López, who attained national and international attention with various recordings on major labels during the 1960s and 70s with his folk/blues/Mexican hybrid of interpretation.

It was in San Francisco that another dynamic and innovative context nurtured the emergence of bands, led by Carlos Santana in addition to others such as Malo, Azteca, Tower of Power, and Cold Blood. Santana literally led a musical revolution with his mixing of Afro-Cuban music, rock, and blues, now universally referred to as Latin rock. His recordings such as "Evil Ways," "Black Magic Woman," "Samba pa' ti," "Europa," and "Oye como va" (a Tito Puente composition) transformed the world of popular music. In 1998 Santana was still at the top of pop music radio charts, characterized by his album *Supernatural*, which was awarded a record-setting eight Grammys for that year. The LP sold over 25 million copies alone, forming part of Santana's career 80 million. Born in Jalisco, Mexico, raised in Tijuana and San Francisco, and inspired by blues artists such as John Lee Hooker, B.B. King, and Muddy Waters, Carlos Santana represents, along with the California bands in general, the bimusical, bicultural character that epitomizes so much of the musical expression described in this chapter.

In the east side of Los Angeles, this context was personified through groups such as The Premiers, Thee Midniters, Cannibal and the Headhunters, Lil' Ray Jiménez, El Chicano, and Tierra. Although there were hundreds more bands in the circuit through a 20-year span, only a few such as those just cited reached popularity beyond southern California. Cannibal and the

Headhunters had a major radio hit in 1965 with "Land of a Thousand Dances," while in 1970 El Chicano recorded the now-classic "Viva Tirado," composed by African American jazz bandleader Gerald Wilson, who was married to a Chicana and highly influenced by Mexican culture. Tierra, featuring brothers guitarist Rudy Salas and lead vocalist Steve Salas, reached unprecedented success among Eastside bands in 1980 with the group's rendition of the Intruders' "Together," which became a platinum record.

An interesting regional parallel to the Eastside Sound era of Los Angeles was that of San Antonio-bred Sunny Ozuna and the Sunglows, who in 1662–1963 recorded a major rhythm and blues style ballad which became a national hit. "Talk to Me" achieved gold record status, and the group appeared on Dick Clark's top forty television show *American Bandstand*. Ozuna would eventually return to contemporary tejano music and become a major figure in *la Onda Chicana* of the 1970s. Leading this movement was the aforementioned Little Joe (José María de León Hernández), who grew up picking cotton and attending school only through the seventh grade. Learning guitar from friends and relatives, he joined the group David Coronado (his cousin) and the Latinaires. The group recorded its first single, a rock tune, entitled "Safari," parts 1 and 2. According to Peña (1999a, 153), the recording "is an important milestone in tejano music, because it may very well have been the first rock-and-roll tune recorded by a tejano group." Peña adds that "it testifies to the intensive assimilation of popular American music taking place among Mexican American youth throughout the Southwest." In 1959 Little Joe assumed leadership of the Latinaires, which developed a stylistic feature—that of the polca-ranchera (a ranchera in polka tempo) with vocal duets sung in the traditional parallel third ranchera harmony. Johnny Hernández, Little Joe's brother, accompanied the latter's voice, and their harmonic blend began to personify the group sound and a new tejano direction. In 1969 Little Joe changed the name and concept of the band from the Latinaires to Little Joe y la Familia, and Peña notes that "by 1970 the aesthetic transformation was complete— new fashions and hairstyles (hippie/militant Chicano), a new name, a counter-cultural lifestyle that included drugs (principally marijuana), and for Little Joe at least a drift towards the ideology of Chicanismo (1999a, 164). Launching la Onda Chicana to its next stage, La Familia recorded the LP *Para la gente* on Little Joe's own Buena Suerte Record label. The album became a hit throughout the Chicano Southwest, and one of the tracks, "Las nubes," became a virtual anthem of the Chicano Generation (ibid., 167) Stylistically, the arrangement of "Las nubes" included a brass section, electric guitar, electric bass, Hammond organ, trap-drums, and a string section. Peña (168) notes that "the horn obbligato inserted between the vocal phrases maintains a steady barrage of jazz-oriented licks in what amounts to a constant code-switching between Mexican and an American musical 'language' (ranchero and swing-jazz)." Little Joe y la Familia continued to record LPs in a similar vein throughout the 1970s. In 1985 Little Joe signed a contract with CBS Records, and in 1991 he was awarded a Grammy Award for his album *16 de Septiembre*. In

1992 he incorporated another record label of his own, Tejano Records. His recordings, over a million sold, have been distributed throughout the United States, Latin America, Asia, and Europe.

La Onda Chicana was also represented in New Mexico through the music of Al Hurricane in a similar yet somewhat different style. Leger (2001, 765) refers to Al Hurricane (Alberto Sánchez) as "the most influential New Mexican Hispano musician of the second half of the twentieth century." Along with his brothers Tiny Morrie (Amador Sánchez) and Baby Gaby (Gabriel Sánchez), Al Hurricane began a rock and roll group in the 1950s and in the 1960s recorded the popular Mexican ranchera "La mula bronca," which became a hit in the Southwest and Mexico. His groups have since concentrated on a contemporary style of Spanish language music, especially arrangements of the ranchera and ensembles featuring guitar, electric bass, and a horn section. The style is similar to that of Little Joe y La Familia, Sonny Osuna, and other tejano groups of the La Onda Chicana.

## Contemporary Chicano Musical Expression

The short-lived story of Selena (Selena Quintanilla-Pérez) is not so different than that of the stardom/tragedy paradox of Ritchie Valens. Born in 1971, she began singing professionally at an early age and led her own group, Selena y Los Dinos, with her sister Suzette at the age of 11. Although she developed within the tejano musical tradition, she eventually began to record a more international style of pop and became highly successful internationally, winning several Tejano Music Awards and a Grammy. She was contracted by one of the major record labels, Capitol/EMI, in 1989. Her top selling album was *Amor prohibido*, released internationally in 1994. She also recorded extensively in English, also attaining great success, and was attempting to develop a larger crossover style and market when she was tragically murdered in 1995 by one of her business employees. A major film, *Selena* (1998), directed by Gregory Nava, was produced shortly after her death, starring actors Jennifer López and Edward James Olmos. In addition to Selena, other contemporary tejano artists representing a period that Peña (1999) refers to as the post-Chicano era include El Grupo Mazz, La Mafia, and Emilio Navaira.

Los Lobos is a group that defies category, yet in many ways has fit into most of the categories overviewed in this section on the musical culture of Mexican derivation in the United States. Originally organized as high school colleagues out of Garfield High School in East Los Angeles and named Los Lobos del Este de Los Angeles, the young group began by performing Mexican and other Latin American folk music, and developed a strong following in the eastside of Los Angeles during the early years of the Chicano movement. Their folk and traditional repertoire comprised their first album, produced by Luis Torres and released in 1978. With time, the group diversified its style, expanded into the rock and blues the members had learned even before their venture into Mexican music, and recorded a series of seven albums from 1983 to 1994 on Slash Records, a Warner Brothers affiliate. Notable among these were the first,

*And a Time to Dance* (1983), which was awarded a Grammy for its track "Anselma" (a norteno/tejano conjunto styled ranchera/polka); the 1988 *La pistola y el corazón*, comprising all Mexican folk songs and which was awarded yet another Grammy; and the highly acclaimed 1992 *Kiko*, which featured an eclectic mix of rock, blues, Mexican folk, and world music influences such as the use of Japanese taiko drums and North Indian sitar. In 1987 Los Lobos collaborated on the major portion of the commercial soundtrack of the highly successful film *La Bamba*, based on the life of Ritchie Valens and written and directed by Luis Valdez. The title track, "La Bamba" (a remake of the original Valens hit of 1959), achieved the number one spot on the national charts in 27 countries. In the United States it held that spot for three weeks and earned a double platinum record for selling over two million copies. It was also nominated for a Grammy in the Song of the Year category. In 1995 the group released the aforementioned Grammy nominated children's album *Papa's Dream* with Lalo Guerrero. Los Lobos consists of four Chicanos: Louis Perez, Cesar Rosas, Conrad Lozano, and David Hidalgo, and Steve Berlin, a Jewish American originally from Philadelphia. A drummer, Victor Bisetti, was added to the group in the early 1990s. Los Lobos perform on a variety of musical instruments ranging from the Mexican *jarana, requinto,* violin, vihuela, guitarrón, *hidalgarrón* (an innovation of David Hidalgo), bajo-sexto, the Bolivian *charango*, and the tejano-style Hohner accordian to electric guitars and bass, tenor and soprano saxophones, keyboards, drum set and congas. Frequently referred to as a postmodern ensemble, Los Lobos represents the hybrid, intercultural characteristics of popular music that emerged at the end of the twentieth century, and has been recognized as innovators in this artistic movement. During the late 1990s the group switched labels to the Disney affiliate Hollywood Records.

Yet another movement that has personified much of the Chicano musical affinity has been that of punk, and by evolution, new wave, especially in the dense urban contexts of Los Angeles, San Francisco, and even Chicago, the city of the second highest population of Mexican descent in the United States (Los Angeles has the highest such population). Groups that achieved major recognition in Los Angeles during the 1980s included The Brat, Los Illegals, the Undertakers, and Los Cruzados (also known as The Plugz). "El Lay" is an immigration-themed song recorded by Los Illegals, in which the dialectic of conflict persists in what can in some ways be construed as a corrido concept. Molded in a heterogeneous musical style incorporating nuances from punk and hard rock, reggae, Latin, and the Spanish language, the song reflects the urban diversity of a city such as Los Angeles and its various levels of urban "angst." Added to this cultural ambience is some explosive political thought directed toward the exploited urban immigrant: the undocumented worker, or the "illegal alien"; the song's title, "El Lay," refers both to Los Angeles and to the slang expression for sexual intercourse, "a lay." Hopelessness and exploitation are thus conveyed through a metaphor that connotes a casual, demeaning sexual lifestyle characterized by faceless, noncommittal sexual activity and promiscuity. The song describes the illegal alien's arrival in, employment in, and deportation from Los Angeles—to the song's authors, nothing more than "a lay" (Loza 1993, 230–3).

Political and ideological undertones have characterized the music of the Chicano United States, from the corridos of south Texas and 1920s Los Angeles previously noted to the more contemporary musical movement such of Los Illegals briefed above, among many others. There has also developed music in direct collaboration with the Chicano Movement and the Farm-workers Movement. Popular songs and tunes such as El Chicano's "Viva Tirado" and Little Joe y La Familia's "Las Nubes" (a traditional ranchera reset in "La Onda Chicana" tejana vein described earlier) became themes associated on the popular level—that of music receiving both radio play and evolving as part of a Chicano identity. At an even more political level of musical activism was the music of movements such as that of Mexican farmworkers throughout the Southwest, expressing the organizational and social issues of farmworkers, union strikes, and protests. Some of the recordings produced in California were ¡Huelga en general! produced by El Teatro Campesino, a collection of farm-worker songs recorded by the University of California, Los Angeles Center for the Study of Comparative Folklore and Mythology (Las voces de los campe-sinos), and the LP Corridos y canciones de Aztlán. Numerous artists in California have produced music relevant to both the farmworker movement and other social issues of cultural identity. Daniel Valdez, a veteran musician-actor of El Teatro Campesino, released an important album, Mestizo, during the 1970s on the A&M label (later reissued by El Teatro Campesino). Another musician-composer from northern California is Agustin Lira of Fresno, who also wrote songs of the farmworker movement. Also from Fresno is singer-guitarist Al Reyes, whose album California Corazon featured his compositions about farmworkers, Vietnam veterans, and Chicano culture in the San Joaquin Valley. From San Diego, Los Alacranes Mojados established themselves as important troubadours of the Chicano movement, incorporating both border conflict and farmworker themes in their music. The album Si se puede (1976) features a collection of various Chicano musicians from Los Angeles and is dedicated to the farmworker struggle. From the San Francisco area, Los Pelu-dos was another prolific group with a political message stemming from the Chi-cano Movement.

During the early 1990s a unique emergence of a Mexican style of music and ensemble exploded onto the music scene of Mexicans and Chicanos in Los Angeles and other cities in the Southwest and eventually in the Midwest and Northeast. It was the style of banda, and the movement became known as the "banda craze" in the English-speaking media, which gave the phenomenon much attention. This intense vogue in Los Angeles was one of a specific nationalist character—namely, a Mexican character. The banda ensemble for-mat can be traced historically and stylistically to the traditional banda sina-loense, originally developed at the turn of the twentieth century in the state of Sinaloa, Mexico. It is rightfully one of the long recognized and colorful styles in the ample variety of regional music in Mexico. Consisting primarily of woodwind and brass instruments, the distinctive instrumentation of the Sinaloa style became the standard of the contemporary banda. It did, of course, undergo major innovation. A lead vocalist became a standard element in the formerly traditional instrumental format, and electric bass often replaced the traditional tuba. A modern drum set and Cuban-style timbales also often became part of the percussion section, formerly characterized by a battery or *tamborazo* of marching band cymbals, bass drum, and snare drum (although timbales had already been in use in the Sinaloa style).

The dance aspect of banda, referred to as *la quebradita*, was in many ways the central focus of this socio-artistic experience. Although the quebradita and its tango-like "break" choreography executed at many of the banda night clubs and dances throughout Los Angeles and other cities became the symbol for discussion of banda in general, the essential dance steps conform somewhat to combinations of the genres performed by the banda, ranging from polka beat to tropical rhythms to traditional Mexican *sones*. A dance style emerged that at times was a hybrid of cumbia, norteno/Tex-Mex, and zapateado. At many dances the actual quebradita was never executed because of space limitations.

In assessing the factors of identity, nationalism, and the emergence of a collective aesthetic in the making of the banda phenomenon, it has been useful to think in terms of both the movement's social force and its artistic representation and regeneration. One of the principal reasons for the international media exposure of this style was the ascent of banda-ranchera-formatted radio station KLAX, known as "La X" and spearheaded by disc jockey Juan Carlos Hidalgo. In August 1992 KLAX moved into the number one spot according to the Arbitron ratings for the city of Los Angeles, surpassing the syndicated KLSX morning talk show hosted by Howard Stern, which had previously held the number one rating. The radio industry immediately reacted in an almost bewildered manner (the terms "shock waves" in the industry were used by *Music Connection* magazine), not only unable to explain this demographic "alarm clock," but also unable to develop immediate and competitive marketing strategies to regain top ratings. The Spanish-speaking public of Los Angeles was simply not part of the mainstream radio industry. In 2001, a historical and analytical book on banda both in Mexico and the United States was released, written by Helena Simonett.and titled *Banda: Mexican Musical Life Across Borders*.

Hip hop is a more recent context exhibited by young Chicano musicians, with artists such as Kid Frost (Arturo Molina), A Lighter Shade of Brown, Aztlan Underground, Cypress Hill (including Mexican, Cuban, and Italian Americans), ALT (Al Trivette), the Los Angeles-based Cuban American Mellow Man Ace, and Delinquent Habits. A highly successful 1990 recording by Kid Frost on his LP *Hispanic Causing Panic* sampled the musical theme of El Chicano's (and Gerald Wilson's) "Viva Tirado" on his "La Raza" track. Pérez-Torres makes the following note concerning the recording:

Kid Frost's use of the popular "Viva Tirado" evokes that moment of great political and social activism among Chicano populations in the late

1960s and early 1970s. From the affirmation of Brown Power to the Blow-outs (the school walkouts in East Los Angeles), the Chicano Movement formed a high-water mark of the struggle by Chicanos for civil rights and political engagement. The musical incorporation of El Chicano suggests a recollection of subaltern resistance. (2000, 212)

Kid Frost's creative work, however, cannot be assessed solely through "La Raza." On a subsequent album he collaborated with other Latino rappers in a project entitled *Latin Alliance*. One track from the album, "Latinos Unidos," laces a mosaic of Latin rhythm and blues musical texture and rhythmic flavor; bilingual historical referents and interpretations of the Mexican southwest, Puerto Rico, and Nicaragua; and direct commentary on issues related to minority politics and intercultural conflict. Other compositions on the album include themes based on reflections on American identity, lowrider/boulevard culture, the political wars of Central America, and gangsta raps imaging violence, discrimination, incarceration, immigration, the Border Patrol, and romance.

In assessing the issues of cultural identity and ethnic nationalism, the aesthetics of rap emerge as a highly charged vehicle among a constantly growing corps of young Chicano/Latino contemporary rap artists. Although the aesthetic of rap has webbed itself internationally as a preferred expression of youth culture in a variety of languages, its relationship to Latinos in the United States as part of African American music is not simply an artistic interaction, dialectic, or experiment. Rather, it is reflective of living quarters such as South Central Los Angeles, Chicago's Southside, or the Bronx of New York, spaces almost exclusively populated by Latinos and African Americans. Rap has been a point of synthesis and inevitable value to the young members of this geographic/cultural sector.

Pérez-Torres also notes the manner in which Chicano hip hop artists incorporate various expressive modes of mestizaje. He notes that "the multiracial rap group Delinquent Habits make it a point to highlight the hybrid nature of their cultural and racial identities. Employing caló, English, Spanish, and street slang, the rappers Ives, Kemo, and deejay O.G. Style employ code-switching and bilingualism as both their linguistic and personal identities are foregrounded" (2000, 218).

Other musical enterprises that have developed in recent years continue the eclectic mix of musical mestizaje that has been identified as an essential factor of culture and creativity throughout this essay. Incorporating diverse styles from hip-hop to Mexican folk forms, from rock to jazz, and from Afro-Cuban forms and cumbia to rhythm and blues, have been groups such as Rage Against the Machine, Goddess 13, Ozomatli, Quetzal, Akwid, and A.B. Quintanilla y Los Kumbia Kings, the latter from Texas and a Grammy winner. For some time the innovative, multiracial rock group Rage Against the Machine was fronted by lead singer Zak de la Rocha who wrote prolific hip-hop/rap styled lyrics with potent political and social messages.

Other Los Angeles-based groups such as Ozomatli and Quetzál also represent the musical mestizaje referred to by Pérez-Torres. The indigenous names of the groups, both of Aztec reference, are reinforced by the incorporation of a multitude of musical styles, reflecting a multicultural and multiracial world in which these multiracial group members live. Ozomatli makes use of forms including hip hop, cumbia, salsa, Afro-Cuban son, merengue, flamenco, tango, and Mexican genres such as son and ranchera. Quetzál juxtaposes compositions ranging from Latinized rhythm and blues to funkified Mexican *son jarocho*. Pérez-Torres makes a significant point in noting that "the face of Chicano music continues to undergo a profound transformation as the Latino population in the U.S.—and in traditionally Chicano communities—comes to be increasingly diverse. The great continued flows and fluxes of transnational movements signal an ever-shifting musical landscape" (225).

The musical duo Goddess 13 has received much attention in both the academic press and the media, although unfortunately not the record industry, as the group has never recorded on a major label. Two veteran songwriters who were formerly lead singers for the Los Angeles based punk bands The Brat and The Bags, Teresa Covarrubias and Alicia Armendariz epitomize what George Lipsitz has conceptualized as a postmodern musical enterprise. In place of the electric, raging punk ambience of their former years, they have recently composed and performed songs on acoustic guitars and intricate two part vocal harmonies flavored by rock, folk, jazz, and Latin styles, and backed up by a versatile rhythm section. Their songs are in both Spanish and English, and cope with the contemporary issues of romantic love, domestic violence, multicultural themes, and misogyny. In the following passage, Lipsitz (1994, 90) makes an eloquent observation concerning not only Goddess 13, but the musical culture of the Chicano people in the United States.

> In their insistence on being Chicanas in their own way, Armendariz and Covarrubias grapple with the historical invisibility of their community in the mass media as well as with their determination to avoid being reduced to their race to the point of erasing their experiences as women, as workers, and as citizens. Chicano artists have long grappled with these problems, and they have often found solutions by taking on unexpected identities in order to make visible the hybridity and heterogeneity of their own community.

## LATIN CARIBBEAN DEVELOPMENT

Since the latter part of the nineteenth century, musical styles from the Spanish speaking Caribbean have not only migrated in great volume to the United States, but have had a major impact on its music, including jazz, blues, rock, and classical. The dominant influences have come from Cuba, Puerto Rico, and the Dominican Republic. In cities such as New York, Latino *barrios* formed comprising immigrants from the latter three countries, although it should be noted that immigrants have arrived there and to other U.S. cities from all parts of Latin America. In New York during the 1920s through the 1950s, most of the Caribbean immigrants, driven by economic motives, were from Puerto Rico (technically not "immigrants" as Puerto Rico was and still is a U.S. "possession") and Cuba. Interestingly, there are now more Dominicans in New York City than the other two groups. Other cities with large Caribbean-derived populations include Miami, Chicago, Philadelphia, San Francisco, and Los Angeles.

Contemporary Afro-Cuban music has not only retained a profound and significant portion of its African tradition but has also influenced music internationally, especially within the Americas. The *habanera, danzón, son, rumba, guaracha, mambo, cha cha chá*, and *songo* all emanated from Cuba, spreading throughout Latin America and the Latin quarters of the United States, and eventually throughout Europe, Asia, and Africa. The habanera was the first Cuban style to strongly influence music in the United States and was probably the most influential style throughout the Americas. Calling the habanera "perhaps the most universal of our musical genres," Cuban musicologist Emilio Grenet cites the melody "La Paloma" as an example of its influence (Grenet 1939, in Roberts 1979, 5). Composed in the 1940s by a Spaniard stationed in Havana, Sebastian Yradier, it most likely came to the United States via Mexico, with which it identified strongly. The most salient rhythmic feature of the habanera is its bass configuration.

## Cuban Influences

The music of such early pianists as Scott Joplin ("Solace: A Mexican Serenade," 1909), Jesse Pickett ("The Dream"), and Jelly Roll Morton ("New Orleans Joys," recorded in 1923) attests to the presence of the early Cuban habanera form, which many believe was first brought to New Orleans by the Mexican Eighth Cavalry Band around 1884. Morton claimed that it was the "Spanish tinge" that differentiated jazz from the earlier ragtime style of New Orleans music (Roberts 1979). One of the most vivid examples of the impact of the habanera and other Afro-Cuban forms on music in the United States was the musical and musicological work of W.C. Handy, one of the early innovators and composers of the blues. Handy toured Cuba and absorbed many musical ideas and practices, which influenced many of his compositions. Notable was his "St. Louis Blues" (1914), which incorporated the habanera rhythm in the middle of its three sections. One of the most significant recordings of this landmark piece was made in 1929 by Louis Armstrong, and it became one of his signature vehicles. By the 1930s, another vein was being established in this Latin and jazz encounter. Juan Tizol, the Puerto Rican trombonist who was a member of the Duke Ellington orchestra, co-composed with Ellington a piece that would strongly impact the concept of American jazz: "Caravan" (1936), featuring an alternation of a rumba/habanera based on *clave*—the rhythmic, syncopated heartbeat of Afro-Cuban dance music.

The Cuban style that most influenced music in the United States has been the *son*, which was the basis of the rumba's popularity during the 1930s. The son utilized Afro-Cuban rhythmic concepts such as the anticipated bass, in which the bass line and drum *tumbao* precede the downbeat of a measure by a half-beat. Son does not refer to a specific, formal, or uniform musical structure, but describes a particular sound and instrumentation, characterized by a unique feel or, to use a jazz term, "groove." It originally emerged from the black population in the rural districts of Cuba as a vehicle for entertainment at informal gatherings. In the early 1900s, it migrated to urban centers, eventually molding the entire phenomenon of Cuban music from the dance hall to the concert hall. Although the son form was based on African concepts, son guitar (specifically, *tres*) playing also displayed a strong Spanish tradition. Most original sones incorporated the African tradition of call-response vocals and/or other instruments, accompanied by complex rhythmic patterns played on the *tumbadora* drums and *bongós*. During both its rural and urban development in Cuba, the son acquired distinctive musical and dance characteristics. Both the Cubans and Puerto Ricans who migrated to the United States sustained and intensified the popularity of the son, especially in New York.

Arsenio Rodríguez was a major innovator of the son and lived out his musical career in Cuba, New York, and Los Angeles. Rodríguez, who was blind and performed the guitar-type Cuban tres, expanded the son sound by returning to the African-derived elements found in the rural performances of the son that had been simplified or omitted in some of the earlier Cuban ensembles. Instrumentally, he added a campana (bell), a tumbadora (conga drum), a second trumpet, and a piano to the *son conjunto* (the son ensemble). The contemporary *conjunto* instrumentation, similar to that of salsa, thus took its initial form. Rodríguez also emphasized the *guajeo* (the tres and piano interlocking rhythmic patterns) and incorporated the tumbao, an ostinato pattern resulting from interlocking patterns played by the bass and conga. Additionally, he structured the horn arrangements and musical breaks around the clave pattern and integrated the rhythm section of bongós, congas, bass, campana, tres, and piano in such a way as to create a melodic-rhythmic unity also revolving around the clave. Rodríguez expanded the accompanying function of the tres to that of a solo instrument and re-emphasized the role of the *estribillo* refrain. More important, he introduced a solo section referred to as *montuno,* in which the tres, piano, and trumpet players demonstrated their improvisatory skills. Yet another of Rodríguez's major innovative contributions was his incorporation of the mambo, which had been introduced by Israel "Cachao" López and his brother Orestes López, members of the *charanga* ensemble of Antonio Arcaño, into the dance halls of Cuba by the late 1930s. Using son conjunto instrumentation and the mambo, the compositions of Arsenio Rodríguez greatly influenced the Latin popular music of New York, which eventually produced many great salsa musicians such as Machito, Tito Puente, and Tito Rodríguez, all of whom incorporated mambo into their big bands, and to this day salsa musicians continue to interpret Rodríguez's compositions. Dynamically, the range and energy of Rodríguez's conjuntos grew extensively, remolding, yet preserving, the traditional son form. In recent years, there has been a retroactive, international fascination with a number of traditional son groups from Cuba, notably the Buena Vista Social Club and groups led by Compay Segundo, Abraham Ferrer, and Rubén González.

Since the 1930s specific musicians and bandleaders have played a central role in the development of Afro-Cuban dance music in the United States through various cycles of style and innovation. One of the earliest examples is that of Don Azpiazú, who relocated to New York with his band from Cuba and released his recording of composer Moisés Simons' *El manisero* (The Peanut Vendor), shortly afterwards also recorded by Louis Armstrong among many others, and eventually becoming one of the most-played standards in American music. Also active in the United States was Cuban composer and bandleader Ernesto Lecuona, who composed standard songs such as "Siboney" and "María de la O" in addition to chamber and piano pieces such as the now universally performed "Malagueña" from his *Andalucía Suite*.

## Mambo, Latin Jazz, and Salsa

By the 1940s, musicians, especially those of Cuban and Puerto Rican heritage, were largely developing their music in Spanish Harlem and catering to audiences in the highly popular Palladium Dance Hall in New York City during the height of Latin music's (especially the mambo and cha cha chá) popularity in the 1950s. Many of these artists also achieved international acclaim, made highly successful recordings, and eventually received numerous prestigious awards ranging from Grammys (although mostly not until the 1980s) to governmental honors.

Machito (1908–1984), whose actual name was Frank Grillo, was, along with his musical cohort Mario Bauzá, perhaps the principal thrust of the New York Latin music movement. Machito emigrated from his native Cuba to New York in 1937, and by 1940 had organized his own orchestra, Machito and his Afro-Cubans. Machito fronted the orchestra and was lead vocalist, while the arrangements of Bauzá, a saxophonist-trumpeter originally from Cuba, and pianist René Hernández were crucial to the development of this big band-styled ensemble. One of the principal innovations of the Machito orchestra was its blending of Afro-Cuban dance forms such as rumba, guaracha, and mambo with the musical qualities of the big band jazz and bebop movements so active in New York at this time. Heavily exposed to the music of Duke Ellington, Count Basie, Chick Webb, Cab Calloway, Charlie Parker, and Dizzy Gillespie (Bauzá had played with both Webb and Calloway) in the Harlem district where they lived, Machito and Bauzá spearheaded the convergence of U.S. and Latin musical styles, specifically those that eventually evolved into both contemporary salsa and Latin jazz. Exemplary of the "marriage" of jazz and Cuban music was the Machito orchestra's "Tanga" (composed in 1943, recorded in 1948) with its mambo-based structure, Ellingtonian palette of orchestral colors, and Basie-like blues-inspired riffs, considered by many aficionados to be the recording that best defines the emergence of Latin jazz.

A number of other respected musicians in the progressive Latin and jazz waves of the late 1940s had experimented with fusions of the Afro-Cuban and Afro-North American styles, but it was the association of trumpeter Dizzy Gillespie and Cuban conguero/vocalist/dancer Chano Pozo (recommended to Gillespie by Mario Bauzá) that played the most prominent role in what would be referred to as "Cubop," the mixture of Afro-Cuban music and the progressive bebop style of Gillespie, Charlie Parker, Thelonius Monk, and others. Roberts (1972, 119) notes that "in Cubop, Latins and [North] Americans were trying to work together without losing any crucial elements of either style." This was in certain aspects challenging, because although there were Afro-based similarities between the rumba and the jazz "bop" styles, the Afro-Latin and Afro-North American musical traditions were at the same time quite different. Nevertheless, Pozo's impact on music in North America endured, symbolized through the fusion music known as Latin jazz. Prominent conguero bandleader Mongo Santamaría stressed that Pozo's essential contribution was the exposure he gave the conga drum that spearheaded its rise in popularity. Among the more important Pozo-Gillespie musical collaborations were the compositions "Algo-Bueno," "Afro-Cuban Suite," and the profound "Manteca," a basic conga riff inspired by Pozo that received wide acclaim as the successful blend of the two Afro-American styles. Among the many artists who continued the school of Latin jazz have been Mongo Santamaría, Chico O'Farrill, Cal Tjader, Willie Bobo, Tito Puente, Jerry González and Fort Apache, Paquito D'Rivera, Arturo Sandoval, and Poncho Sánchez. A jazz big band that produced highly creative and experimental interpretations of Afro-Cuban music was that of Stan Kenton, which during the 1940s and 50s recorded classics such as the suite *Cuban Fire*, "Machito," "Viva Prado," and "28 N-82 W." An excellent documentary on Latin jazz artists, *Calle 54*, was directed by Spanish filmmaker Fernando Trueba and released in 2001.

The exact origin of the mambo is the subject of much conjecture. As noted above, the music and dance of the mambo originated in Cuba, especially in the innovations of Cachao and Orestes López and Arsenio Rodríguez. The height of the mambo's popularity spanned the first half of the 1950s, and Pérez Prado was perhaps the most widely acclaimed mambo bandleader. Originally form Cuba, he went to Mexico in the late 1940s and established a highly successful orchestra, even backing up the Cuban sonero Benny Moré on a number of recordings. In 1955, Perez Prado released a recording he had done in Hollywood, California for a film—the song was called "Cherry Pink and Apple Blossom White," which became the highest selling record worldwide in that year. As Roberts (1972) points out, Pérez Prado's mambo was not as popular among the Latin population in New York as were the mambo styles of Machito, José Curbelo, Tito Puente, or Tito Rodríguez. Internationally, however, Pérez Prado's success was unprecedented, and his musicianship should not be underestimated.

The cha cha chá, which also became highly popular in the United States, had originally been popularized in Cuba by Orquesta Aragón in 1953. A product of the Cuban *charanga* ensemble, the cha cha chá was an adaptation of the second section of the original *danzón*, and the crisp texture of flute, violins, and timbales contributed to its mass appeal. In New York, the Dominican-born flutist and bandleader Johnny Pacheco emerged during the 1950s leading a charanga.

As the son still largely defined the musical concept of this developing Latin music movement, vocalists were among the major stylists of Afro-Cuban dance music in the United States, especially in the growing Latin community of New York. Three of the most influential (besides Machito) have been Miguelito Valdés, Tito Rodríguez, and Celia Cruz.

Miguelito Valdés, a sonero ("singer of son"), became a major influence among audiences in the United States by the early 1940s. Originally

Carlos Santana. Courtesy of Photofest.

from Cuba but based in New York for a number of years, Valdés sang with the orchestras of Machito and Xavier Cugat, and by 1947 had formed his own band. As with Cugat, he also enjoyed substantial success in Hollywood movies, which during the period of his popularity included many films incorporating popular Latin styles such as rumba and mambo.

Singer-bandleader Tito Rodríguez (1923–1973), one of the first of many Puerto Ricans to achieve major status in Latin music in New York, represents one of the most important periods of the famous Palladium Dance Hall era and the international popularization of Latin dance music. After performing and/or recording with Xavier Cugat, Noro Morales, José Curbelo, Chano Pozo, Arsenio Rodríguez, and Machito, Rodríguez developed his own big band and by 1949 had achieved major success. The 1950s became the apex of Latin dance music at the Palladium, and Rodríguez, Machito, and Tito Puente became the dominant symbols of the movement. Some of his most popular recordings included "Vuela la paloma," "Cuando, cuando," "Cara de payaso," "Mama guela," and "Inolvidable," the latter selling over a million copies.

Celia Cruz emigrated from her native Cuba to Mexico in 1959, where she remained until 1961 with the Cuban conjunto Sonora Matancera, an ensemble that had highly popularized Cuban dance music throughout the Americas. Ultimately Cruz would establish herself as the most popular vocalist in the era of the development of salsa in the 1960s through the early 1990s, a tenure of unparalleled success among singers of the style. She continued to record not only with Sonora Matancera but with bandleaders Tito Puente, Johnny Pacheco, Ray Barretto, and Willie Colón, among many others. She also concertized and recorded with her own orchestras, directed by her long time husband Pedro Knight. Cruz was awarded a National Medal of the Arts by President Bill Clinton in 1994. Her death in 2003 was covered extensively by the Latin American and world news agencies, in addition to being a deeply sentimental moment for millions of aficionados.

In the estimation of many experts, the artist who became the major stylist and innovator following the early career of Machito was bandleader Tito Puente (1923–2000). Of Puerto Rican heritage and a virtuoso musician on timbales and vibraphone, Puente began his dynamic career in his native New York, performing by the early 1940s with various artists, including his principal mentor, Machito. After serving in the Navy during World War II, Puente returned to New York, studied music composition and arranging at the Juilliard School of Music, and played with the Picadilly Boys, a group that never recorded. It was during this period that Puente first brought the percussion section of his orchestra to the front of the bandstand, an innovation that became a permanent standard for Latin dance bands into the 1990s. In 1948 Puente formed his own band and in 1949 recorded one of his early hits, "Abanico," featuring Cuban sonero Vicentico Valdés. During the 1950s Puente's band became internationally associated with the mambo and cha cha chá eras with arrangements of tunes such as "Ran-Kan-Kán" and "Pa' los Rumberos." His *Dancemania* album on RCA became a classic. With the advent of the 1960s and the beginning of the salsa era, Puente continued as one of the principal stylists of Latin music, becoming popularized as El Rey del Timbal, "The King of the Timbales." Original tunes such as "Que será mi china?" and "Oye como va," the latter made into an international radio hit by Carlos Santana's recording in 1971, became standard arrangements in the Latin music repertoire. Puente also led an important Latin jazz ensemble that featured many of the top Latin jazz artists of the 1980s and 90s. Puente received the National Medal of the Arts in 1997 from President Bill Clinton, and six Grammy awards, the last posthumously for an album he recorded with Eddie Palmieri months before his death on June 1, 2000, which was mourned worldwide.

Another bandleader of Puerto Rican background who became one of the major contemporary artists of Latin music based in New York City is Eddie Palmieri (b. 1936). Although he was highly active prior to the 1970s, including the period of his innovative charanga styled group Conjunto la Perfecta, it was during that decade that Palmieri made a great impact on the salsa and Latin jazz scenes, emerging as an innovative pianist-composer-arranger who dynamically experimented with the blending of progressive Latin Caribbean forms and contemporary jazz shadings. Palmieri's piano style, for example, often reflected the style of the then highly influential McCoy Tyner, associated primarily with the progressive jazz styles of the period. Classic albums recorded by Palmieri and featuring numerous first-rate Latin and jazz musicians have included *The Sun of Latin Music* (1974), *Unfinished Masterpiece* (1975), and *Arete* (1995). As of 2004 he had been awarded six Grammys.

A popular trend that evolved from the salsa movement in New York during the 1960s was *bugalú*. A blend of Latin rhythms and African American rhythm and blues or soul, the style represented the close cultural and musical association of Latin and black music in the United States, and what Juan Flores (1988) has referred to as a unique cultural "complimentarity." There was also an ideological tie that developed between African Americans and Puerto Ricans in spaces such as the Bronx and other sectors of New York City, where the two cultures lived side by side and began to consolidate their common roots and political causes and goals during what was perhaps the most active national mobilization era of the Civil Rights Movement. Leading bandleaders of bugalú included Joe Cuba, whose 1966 recording of "Bang Bang" sold over a million copies, Joe Bataan (of Afro-Filipino heritage and raised in New York), Ray Barretto, who recorded the 1963 hit "El Watusi," and Hector Rivera, who recorded one of the most popular bugalú hits in 1967, "At the Party." George Lipsitz (1994, 83–4) notes that Latin Bugalú and salsa musicians played an important part in the disco craze of the 1970s, and late in the decade began to play a crucial part as well in the rise of hip hop in New York.

The many Puerto Ricans in New York and the East Coast who have so closely identified with both Cuban and U.S. jazz have played an important role in the crystallization of the hybrid salsa movement internationally, but especially in the Latin quarters of the United States. Lyrics sung in Spanish verse with a strong dance base have been fostered by a significantly growing U.S. population whose Caribbean, Chicano/Mexican, Central and South American composition continually enhances the Latino nature of the music. Additionally, as articulated by Max Salazar in so many of his writings, Latin music had served as a catalyst for racial integration, the Palladium era in New York being a metaphor for the interaction of not only diverse Latinos, but dancers and musicians of Italian, Jewish, African American, Anglo-American, and so many other heritages. With the constantly growing multicultural awareness and hybrid expressions within the United States, salsa has for many provided a mode of cultural expression that bridges and cures many intercultural conflicts and barriers. Its growth continues internationally.

An important artist who emerged from the salsa movement during the 1970s was Rubén Blades. Originally from Panama and trained in law, Blades ventured to New York where he worked for Fania Records and eventually established himself as a lead vocalist and prolific composer. His album *Siembra* with arranger-trombonist Willie Colón, released in 1980, sold a record volume of units, and two of its tracks, "Pedro Navaja" and "Plástico," became known throughout Latin America, the United States, Europe, and Japan. Blade's song texts that addressed social and political issues of Latin American and the Latino sector in the United States gained him special recognition. The 1980s witnessed a rather different mode of expression and new breed of salsa adapted to a

Los Lobos, circa 1992. Shown from left: Steve Berlin, David Hidalgo, Louis Perez, Conrad Lozano, Cesar Rosas. Courtesy of Photofest.

more international pop sound, that of *salsa romántica*. Exponents included Luis Enrique (Nicaragua/United States), José Alberto (Dominican Republic), Eddie Santiago (Puerto Rico), and Marc Anthony (New York). Some singers of the older school—Lalo Rodríguez for example, who recorded with Eddie Palmieri in the early 1970s at the age of 17—successfully adapted to the new trend. Another phenomenon was the international success of Grammy-nominated Orquesta de la Luz, a salsa group from Japan influenced by the New York style and whose recordings were originally produced in New York by Sergio George.

Afro-Cuban musical styles have become increasingly popular throughout the Untied Sates, with salsa and Latin jazz bands proliferating in cities such as Miami, Chicago, Phoenix, Philadelphia, Tucson, Houston, Dallas, and Albuquerque. In California, major exponents of the style have emerged since the 1940s, with the aforementioned Stan Kenton in addition to Cal Tjader (1925–1982), who was raised and learned to play music in the San Francisco area, eventually performing with the original jazz groups of Dave Brubeck. Inspired by the music of Machito and Tito Puente, he proceeded to form his own Afro-Cuban ensemble, and in 1957 Mongo Santamaría and Willie Bobo left Tito Puente's orchestra to join Tjader's ensemble. Tjader recorded prolifically on the Fantasy and Verve labels, including his classic *Soul Sauce* LP of 1964, which sold over 100,000 copies and helped popularize the word "salsa." In 1966 he recorded an LP with Eddie Palmieri, *El Sonido Nuevo*. Among the many musicians to work with him were Armando Peraza, Al McKibbon,

Jerome Richardson, Vince Guaraldi, Clare Fisher (composer of the cha cha standard "Morning"), Mark Levine, and Poncho Sánchez.

## Puerto Rican Musical Traditions

In addition to playing a major role in the development of salsa and other styles in the United States, musicians of Puerto Rican heritage have also been important to the popularization of Puerto Rican musical genres. In New York, in particular, Puerto Ricans perform *plena, bomba,* and the *jíbaro* forms of *seis, aguinaldo, and danza.* Plena and bomba music and dance originally developed along the coastal towns of Puerto Rico, and derive largely from African influence. Active interpreters of plena and bomba have included Victor Montáñez, Manuel "Canario" Jiménez, and the highly successful Rafael Cortijo and Ismael Rivera (the last three artists were based in Puerto Rico, but New York was a constant reference point). A highly influential bomba and plena group in New York during the 1990s was Los Pleneros de la 21, led by musician, teacher, and bandleader Juan Gutiérrez. The group innovated the percussive instrumentation of the plena and bomba ensemble by adding electric bass, piano, *cuatro,* and additional percussion. Los Pleneros were widely imitated throughout the United States and Puerto Rico.

The jíbaro styles, especially popular during the Christmas season, have also played an essential role in the transplantation of Puerto Rican traditional music culture into the United States. These in great part Hispanic-derived folk forms especially make use of the Puerto Rican *cuatro,* with ten strings grouped in five courses, in addition to the standard Spanish guitar and the *guiro* ("gourd scraper"). Influential in the formation of the contemporary *conjunto jíbaro* ("jíbaro ensemble") was the Puerto Rican *cuatrista* ("cuatro player") Estanislao Landí, especially during the 1930s. He increased the popularity of the jíbaro style by incorporating a diversity of musical genres into the cuatro repertoire and enhancing the instrumentation to include two cuatros, bongós, bass, and congas. Several conjuntos jíbaros exist in the United States, especially in the larger cities of the Northeast and Midwest. Virtuosos on the cuatro include Yomo Toro (New York) and Edwin Colón Zayas (Puerto Rico). A major contemporary vocalist of the style is Andrés Jiménez.

## Music of Dominicanos

The Dominican Republic has also had a major impact on the musical culture in the United States. The *merengue,* which originated there, is along with the Colombian *cumbia* one of the most popular dance rhythms throughout Latin American and the Latin quarters of the United States. The merengue that became internationally popular emerged from the *merengue cibaeño* ("regional merengue from Cibao"). Based on a fast tempo, the typical merengue ensemble included a button accordion, a metal rasp called *güira,* a two headed drum called *tambora,* and often a saxophone or marimba bass type instrument. Austerlitz (1997, 126) notes that the accordion-driven merengue, known as *perico ripiao*, became associated with Dominican national identity and also became an important symbol of and link to the Dominican culture and homeland in the United States, that is, New York City and other northeastern urban industrial areas, where immigration from the Dominican Republic escalated dramatically following the political and social upheaval after the death of dictator Rafael Trujillo in 1961. Dominicans especially settled in the Washington Heights district in New York City, which they began to refer to as *Quisiqueya*, the indigenous name for the Dominican/Haiti Island.

The first merengue bandleader to settle in the United States was accordionist Primitivo Santos. Santos, along with Joseito Mateo, who worked extensively in the United States, made merengue available to Dominicans and other aficionados and helped increase its popularity there. By the 1970s, merengue had become one of the most popular dance styles in New York and other cities. New York-based merengue bands included the group Millie and Jocelyn y los Vecinos, both of which developed a local and international audience (Austerlitz 1997, 125–6). Artists from the Dominican Republic who have attained immense popularity in the United States and internationally include Wilfredo Vargas, Johnny Ventura, and Elvis Crespo, among many others. During the 1990s, another Dominican style, the *bachata*, became highly popular throughout Latin America and the Latin quarters of the United States, and was internationalized largely through the recordings and performances of Juan Luís Guerra, who was awarded a Grammy in 1991, and whose group interpreted both the bachata and merengue, in addition to ballads and other types of arrangements. In 1996 Paul Austerlitz wrote an informative book titled *Merengue: Dominican Music and Dominican Identity*. Also of great significance is the 1995 book *Bachata: A Social History of a Dominican Popular Music*, written by Deborah Pacini Hernández.

## CONTEMPORARY INTERNATIONAL STYLES

As the scope of this chapter has focused on the musics of Mexican Americans (Chicanos) and Latin Caribbean cultures in the United States, the obvious note should be made that there certainly exist in the United States many other Latin American and Spanish or Portuguese genres and their associated makers and audiences, for example, Afro-Cuban folkloric *rumba*, the music of *santería* and other Afro-Cuban, Afro-Brazilian, and other religious traditions, the Argentine *tango*, Brazilian *samba* and *bossa nova*, *flamenco*, Central American forms, and contemporary/classical music from Latin America. In addition to Mexicans/Chicanos, Cubans, Puerto Ricans, and Dominicans, there are many Latinos in the United States of heritages originating in Colombia, Argentina, Brazil, Nicaragua, El Salvador, and all the other countries of Latin America.

With that in mind, however, I will stress here that this chapter has primarily focused on the popular musical expression of the U.S. "border" areas, that is, music related to the Mexican/Chicano Southwest and the Caribbean (Puerto Rican, Cuban, Dominican) Northeast. In a sense, music of these areas, on a geographical and historical basis, represents the concept of the U.S. "border," and given the fact that their geographic locations became the basis of two major bloody conflicts, the Mexican-American War (1846–8) and the Spanish-American War (1898), it is not surprising that the cultures of these spaces and their related time would have had so much impact on and penetration into the musical life of the United States.

We should also remind ourselves that the interaction has been both negative and positive, and with much "grey" in between; thus, the music reflects both sides and even more in between, especially in a contemporary society where cultural and social hybridity, or to return to the spirit of this chapter, the "mestizaje of it all," both melts and infiltrates creative blends and identities of both daily life and lifelong values.

There have been, in addition to the border blends, however, other international musics on both sides of the border that have been heavily consumed by constantly changing values and their corresponding aesthetics. International styles have emerged in the United States on both an external and internal market of trade, and have thus been either heavily imported or exported by means of airwaves, recordings, cyberspace, and the "video" explosion of the 1980s to the present. Prime examples from the United States would be artists such as Gloria Estefan, Tito Puente, Celia Cruz, Carlos Santana, and Christina Aguilera, not to mention Madonna, Britney Spears, and NSync. And there are the actual crossborder paradoxes, such as Los Tigres del Norte, who are from Sinaloa, Mexico, but live in San José, California. And then there are also the "grey" areas where artists such as Plácido Domingo, Wynton Marsalis, and Ravi Shankar concertize throughout the world, including Latin America.

Two of the examples above, Gloria Estefan and Los Tigres del Norte, might shed some insight into the state of contemporary international styles that have enjoyed the highest ranks of popularity simultaneously in both the United States and Latin America, without even citing other sectors of the world market. Vocalist Gloria Estefan has made a major impact on both the mainstream and Latino markets. Born in Cuba in 1957, Gloria Fajardo immigrated to Miami, Florida, as a young child in 1960 with her family, leaving the island after the 1959 Cuban Revolution. Eventually she and her husband Emilio Estefan organized a Miami-based group called Miami Sound Machine, which achieved international recognition with its 1985 hit "Conga." The recording remained on the Top 10 charts in the United States for 16 weeks. Gloria Estefan had numerous other international hits, in both English and Spanish, and for some time became the most popular artist in Latin America. Her album *Mi Tierra*, released in 1993, was awarded a Grammy and established unprecedented record sales. Other singers that developed a "crossover" style in some ways similar to that of Estefan, but during the late 1990s, were Ricky Martin and Marc Anthony. Martin created a sensational response in the international market with his recording of "Livin' La Vida Loca" in 1999 and was featured on the cover of *Time Magazine*.

The other example, Los Tigres del Norte, represents not only the phenomenal growth of the Mexican music industry in the United States, but also the constantly growing penetration of Mexican culture, often referred to in California as the Mexicanization of the state. Los Tigres del Norte interpret the norteño style of Northern Mexico, highly related to the South Texas conjunto style previously critiqued here. However, Los Tigres del Norte have achieved a massive cross-national audience composed of four distinct categories of aficionados: Mexicans living throughout Mexico; Mexican and other Latin American immigrants to the United States and other countries; native residents of other, especially Spanish speaking, countries in Latin America in addition to Spain; and Chicanos and other Latinos born and living in the United States. One of the most attractive features of the group, especially among immigrants to the United States, are the many immigration-themed corridos, rancheras, polkas, and cumbias included in its repertoire, as well as texts based on the drug world (e.g., the CD *Corridos prohibidos*, 1988), corrupt Mexican politics ("El circo" and *Jefe de Jefe*, 1997), and romance. In his book *Narcocorrido*, Elijah Wald offers the following perspective:

> Los Tigres are the kings of norteño, the Mexican country music that is one of the most popular styles in the United States and Central America. Though the Anglo media act as if the current Latin music boom were driven by Afro-Caribbean styles like salsa and merengue, Mexicans and Mexican Americans are by far the largest group of Spanish speakers in the United States, and Mexican bands account for roughly two-thirds of domestic Latin record sales. In this world, Los Tigres are like Willie Nelson and the Rolling Stones combined, the enduring superstars of down-to-earth, working-class pop. Their records sell in the millions, their concerts pack halls throughout the North American continent, and their songs have become part of the Mexican cultural heritage. They have never crossed over to Anglo fans for several reasons: First, their style is based on accordion-driven polkas and waltzes - not generally considered a sexy sound. Second, their music is old-fashioned and rurally rooted, a style disrespected by most trendsetting intellectuals and hipsters. Third, their most popular hits are narcocorridos, ballads of the drug traffic. (Wald 2001, 1–2)

It might be pointed out here that the narcocorrido, a topic that has received much recent attention (see also Simonett 2001a-b), is not so much a glorification of drug culture as a critique dressed in metaphor, satire, tragic drama, and historical tales of reality.

There are, of course, other dimensions to "contemporary international styles" germane to the concept of a U.S./Latin American "border" musical culture. Styles ranging from ballad, mariachi, rock, and other styles such as those promoted by Julio Iglesias (Spain), Vicente Fernández (Mexico), Juan Gabriel

(Mexico), Luis Miguel (Mexico), Jose Feliciano (Puerto Rico/New York), José Luis Rodríguez (Venezuela), Pepe Aguilar (Mexico), Shakira (Colombia), Los Fabulosos Cadillacs (Argentina), Maná (Mexico), Juanes (Colombia), Alejandro Fernández (Mexico), and Alejandro Saenz (Spain), among hundreds of other international artists, illustrate the volume and diversity of contemporary popular styles marketed in a multibillion dollar industry in Latin America, the United States, and other sectors of the globe.

## THE MUSIC INDUSTRY AND LARAS

As noted by Wald above, about two-thirds of the Latin American music recording product sold in the United States is that of Mexican regional styles including norteno, ranchera, and banda, among others. Other statistics confirm the impressive sales of Latin American musics; for example, recent statistics confirm the tremendous growth in the Latin music industry at about 25 percent during 1999, a rate of growth more rapid than that of non-Latin American recordings. Such statistics and interest in the U.S. Latino sector and Latin America have certainly had effect on the executive heads of the music industry in the United States. It is no coincidence that the National Academy of Recording Arts and Sciences (NARAS) established the Latin Academy of Recording Arts and Sciences in 1997, with its first annual Latin Grammy Awards, an internationally televised show, in September 2000. Still thriving as of 2005, LARAS awards 43 Latin Grammys annually, encompassing 16 fields among the 43 categories. These fields are organized as follows:

General Field (4 categories): Record, Album, Song, and Best New Artist of the Year.

Field 1—Pop (3 categories): Best Female Vocal Album, Male Vocal Album, Pop Album by a Duo or Group with Vocal

Field 2—Urban (1): Best Urban Music Album

Field 3—Rock (4): Best Rock Solo Vocal Album, Rock Album by a Duo or Group with Vocal, Alternative Music Album, Rock Song

Field 4—Tropical (5): Best Salsa Album, Merengue Album, Contemporary Tropical Album, Traditional Tropical Album, Tropical Song

Field 5—Singer-Songwriter (1): Best Singer-Songwriter Album

Field 6—Regional—Mexican (6): Best Ranchero Album, Banda Album, Grupero Album, Tejano Album, Norteño Album, Regional Mexican Song

Field 7—Instrumental (1): Best Instrumental Album

Field 8—Traditional (3): Best Folk Album, Tango Album, Flamenco Album

Field 9—Jazz (1): Best Latin Jazz Album

Field 10—Christian (2): Best Christian Album (Spanish Language), Christian Album (Portuguese Language)

Field 11—Brazilian (7): Best Brazilian Contemporary Pop Album, Brazilian Rock Album, Samba/Pagode Album, Música Popular Brasileira Album, Romantic Music Album, Brazilian Roots/Regional Album, Brazilian Song (Portuguese Language)

Field 12—Children's (1): Best Latin Children's Album

Field 13—Classical (1): Best Classical Album

Field 14—Production (2): Best Engineered Album, Producer of the Year
Field 15—Music Video (1): Best Music Video (1 song only)

In addition to these awards, LARAS has honored a "Person of the Year" annually since its initial awards year of 2001, including vocalist Julio Iglesias, producer Emilio Estefan, vocalist Vicente Fernández, songwriter/musician Caetano Veloso, and guitarist/bandleader Carlos Santana.

The diversity and magnitude of categories in the LARAS Grammy process is self-evident, so that the music's cultural impact and proximity to the United States in conjunction with its global popularity and high record sales prompted NARAS to form LARAS. In addition to the awarding of Grammys at an annual televised broadcast, which itself generates millions of dollars for the organization, LARAS also included as its agenda the promotion of "creative freedom, music education, copyright protection, health insurance, and human services to promote the free flow of musical ideas across borders" (Greene 2003, 241). One of LARAS's principal goals in recent years has been to challenge the dominant practice of music piracy in Latin America (primarily the selling of illicitly copied recordings). It has been estimated that as much as 50 percent of music recordings purchased in Latin America is pirated (Greene 2003, 243). From a critical perspective, however, the goals of LARAS on this issue must also be assessed from an equitable set of perspectives. How, for example, can one expect a Latin American citizen, whose average wages might be less than 75 dollars a week, to pay the same price for a CD (12–20 dollars) that a U.S. citizen pays and who makes a salary four or many more times greater? Yet the system has basically operated in this manner. Although considered "illegal" according to international law, is such piracy moral or not? That is a very good and important question—one not so different from the issue of immigration.

The members of LARAS are primarily from Latin America, the United States, and Spain (although it is open to anyone anywhere who fulfills the required professional credits). The main offices of LARAS are located in Miami (although NARAS is based in Los Angeles). Thus far, all the televised awards shows have been produced in Los Angeles and Miami.

## Conclusions

The concept and realities of Latino culture and "border" in the United States are constantly expanding and changing. With these political and social reconfigurations, the role of musical and artistic culture in general maintains a direct, relevant, and indelible effect on society in both the United States and Latin America. In a globalizing economy and world culture, the expanding, intercultural interface of music will hopefully play a major role in opening the borders of conflict, a theme frequently prevalent yet transcendental in working class Latino music. It is safe and wise to say that by the early twenty-first century, Latino music in the United States, from ranchera to Latin jazz to hip hop, has reached heights never before imagined by a quickly changing music industry and American society.

# BIBLIOGRAPHY

Aparicio, Frances. *Listening to Salsa: Gender, Latin Popular Music and Puerto Rican Cultures*. Hanover: Wesleyan University Press, 1998.

Austerlitz, Paul. *Merengue: Dominican Music and Dominican Identity*. Philadelphia: Temple University Press, 1996.

Barth, Fredrick. *Ethnic Groups and Boundaries*. Boston: Little, Brown, 1969.

Bateson, Gregory. "Culture Contact and Schismo Genesis." In *Steps to an Ecology of Mind*. San Francisco: Chandler, 1972.

Broyles-Gonzalez, Yolanda. *Lydia Mendoza's Life in Music/La historia de Lydia Mendoza*. New York: Oxford University Press, 2001.

Campa, Arthur L. *Spanish Folk-Poetry in New Mexico*. Albuquerque: University of New Mexico Press, 1946.

Campa, Arthur L. *The Spanish Folksong in New Mexico*. Language Series Bulletin 4:1. Albuquerque: University of New Mexico Press, 1933.

Cornelius, Steven. "Afro-Cuban Music." *Garland Encyclopedia of World Music* 3, 2001: 783–9.

Crespo, Francisco. "The Globalization of Cuban Music through Mexican Film." *Selected Reports in Ethnomusicology Vol. XI: Musical Cultures of Latin America: Global Effects, Past and Present*, 2003, 225–32.

Delgado, Kevin. "A Diaspora Reconnected: Cuba, Brazil, Scholarship, and Identity in the Music of Bata Ketu." *Selected Reports in Ethnomsucicology Vol. XI: Musical Cultures of Latin America: Global Effects, Past and Present*, 2003, 219–24.

Duany, Jorge. "Popular Music in Puerto Rico: Toward an Anthropology of Salsa." *Latin American Music Review* 5 (2, 1985): 187–216.

Espinosa, Aurelio M. *The Folklore of Spain in the American Southwest: Traditional Spanish Folk Literature in Northern New Mexico and Southern Colorado*. J. Manuel Espinosa, ed. Norman: University of Oklahoma Press, 1985.

Fernández, Raúl. *Latin Jazz: The Perfect Combination/La Combinación Perfecta*. San Francisco: Chronicle Books, 2002.

Fernández, Raúl. "On the Road to Latin Jazz." *Selected Reports in Ethnomusicology Vol. XI: Musical Cultures of Latin America: Global Effects, Past and Present*, 2003, 233–40.

Flores, Juan. "Bumbún and the Beginnings of Plena." *Centro* II (3, 1988): 16–25.

Flores, Juan. "Que Assimilated, Brother, Yo Soy Assimilao: The Structure of Puerto Rican Identity in the U.S." *Journal of Ethnic Studies* 13 (3, 2002): 1–16.

Flores, Juan. 1 "'Rappin', Writin', and Breakin'." *Centro* II (3, 1988): 34- 41.

García, Peter J. "The New Mexico Early Ballad Tradition: Reconsidering the New Mexican Folklorists' Contribution to Songs of Intercultural Conflict." *Latin American Music Review* 17 (2, 1996): 150–171.

Greene, Michael. "Building Bridges with Music: Spanning Latin Music's Diversity of Culture, Geography, Art, and Science." *Selected Reports in Ethnomusicology Vol. X: Global Effects, Past and Present*, 2003, 241–4.

Grenet, Emilio. *Popular Cuban Music: Eighty Revised and Corrected Compositions, Together with an Essay on the Evolution of Music in Cuba*. Havana: Carasa, 1939.

Haro, Carlos Manuel and Steven Loza. "The Evolution of Banda Music and the Current Banda Movement in Los Angeles". *Selected Reports in Ethnomusicology Vol. X: Musical Aesthetics and Multiculturalism in Los Angeles*, 1994, 59–72.

Jáquez, Candida. "*El Mariachi*: Musical Repertoire as Sociocultural Investment." In *Musical Migrations: Transnationalism and Cultural Hybridity in Latin/o America, Volume I*. New York: Palgrave Macmillan, 2003.

Koegel, John. "Crossing Borders: Mexicana, Tejana, and Chicana Musicians in the United States". In Clark, Walter Aaron, *From Tejano to Tango*. New York: Routledge, 2003, 97–125.

Lamadrid, Enrique. *Hermanitos Comanchitos: Indo-Hispano Rituals of Captivity and Redemption* (with CD). Albuquerque: University of New Mexico Press, 2003.

Lipsitz, George. *Dangerous Crossroads: Popular Music, Postmodernism and the Poetics of Place*. London and New York: Verso, 1994.

Loeffler, Jack. *La Música de los Viejitos: Hispanic Folk Music of the Rio Grande del Norte*. Albuquerque: University of New Mexico Press, 1999.

Loza, Steven. *Barrio Rhythm: Mexican American Music in Los Angeles*. Urbana and Chicago: University of Illinois Press, 1993.

Loza, Steven. "From Veracruz to Los Angeles: The Reinterpretation of the *Son Jarocho*." *Latin American Music Review* 13, 1992: 179–94.

Loza, Steven. "Hispanic California." *Garland Encyclopedia of World Music*, Vol. 3: 734–53. New York: Routledge, 2001.

Loza, Steven. "Identity, Nationalism, and Aesthetics Among Chicano/Mexicano Musicians in Los Angeles. *Selected Reports in Ethnomusicology Vol. X: Musical Aesthetics and Multiculturalism in Los Angeles*, 1994, 51–8.

Loza, Steven. "Introduction: Latin America, Mestizaje, and the Myth of Development." *Selected Reports in Ethnomusicology Vol. XI: Musical Cultures of Latin America: Global Effects, Past and Present*, 2003: 5–18.

Loza, Steven. "Latin Caribbean Music." In *Garland Encyclopedia of World Music*, Vol. 3: 790–801. New York: Routledge, 2001.

Loza, Steven. "Latin Jazz." In *Jazz: The First Century*. Jogn Edwards Hasset, ed. New York: Harper-Collins Publishers, Inc., 2000.

Loza, Steven and Milo Alvarez, Josefina Santiago, and Charles Moore. "Los Angeles Gansta Rap and the Aesthetics of Violence." *Selected Reports in Ethnomusicology Vol. X: Musical Aesthetics and Multiculturalism in Los Angeles*, 1994, 149–62.

Loza, Steven. "The Origins of the *Son*." *Aztlán* 15 (1, 1984): 105–22.

Loza, Steven. "Poncho Sánchez, Latin Jazz, and the Cuban Son: A Stylistic and Social Analysis. In *Situating Salsa: Global Markets and Local Meanings*. Lise Waxer, ed. New York: Routledge, 2002.

Loza, Steven. *Tito Puente and the Making of Latin Music*. Urban and Chicago: University of Illinois Press, 1999.

Lozano, Danilo. "*La Charanga* Tradition in Cuba: History, Style, and Ideology." Master's thesis, University of California, Los Angeles, 1990.

Lummis, Charles F. *Spanish Songs of Old California*. New York: Schirmer, 1923.

Manuel, Peter, with Kenneth Bilby and Michael Largey. *Caribbean Currents: Caribbean Music from Rumba to Reggae*. Philadelphia: Temple University Press, 1990.

Manuel, Peter. "Latin Music in the United States: Salsa and the Mass Media." *Journal of Communication* 41 (1, 1991): 104–16.

Pacheco, Javier Barrales. "A Chicano in a Cuban Band: Okan Ise and Songo in Los Angeles." In Clark, Walter Aaron, ed., *From Tejano to Tango*. New York: Routledge, 2003, 126–50.

Pacheco, Javier Barrales. "Salsa in San Francisco, 1974–1985: The Latin Music Experience." Master's thesis, University of California, Los Angeles, 1986.

Paredes, Américo. A *Texas-Mexican Cancionero: Folksongs of the Lower Border*. Austin: Universtiy of Texas Press, 1995.

Paredes, Américo. *"With His Pistol in His Hand": A Border Ballad and Its Hero*. Austin: University of Texas Press, 1958.

Peña, Manuel. "From Ranchero to Jaitón: Ethnicity and Class in Texas-Mexican Music (Two Styles in the Form of a Pair)." *Ethnomusicology* 29 (1, 1985): 29–55

Peña, Manuel. *The Mexican American Orchestra: Music, Culture, and the Dialectic of Conflict*. Austin: University of Texas Press, 1999.

Peña, Manuel. *Música Tejana: The Cultural Economy of Artistic Transformation*. College Station: Texas A & M University Press, 1999.

Peña, Manuel. "Notes Toward an Interpretive History of California-Mexican Music." In *From the Inside Out: Perspectives on Mexican and Mexican American Folk Art*. eds., Karana Hattersly-Drayton, Joyce M. Bishop, and Tomas Ibarra-Frausto, 64–75. San Francisco: The Mexican Museum, 1989.

Peña, Manuel. *The Texas-Mexican Conjunto: History of a Working Class Music*. Austin: University of Texas Press, 1985.

Pérez-Torres, Rafael. "Mestizaje in the Mix: Chicano Identity, Cultural Politics, and Postmodern Music. In *Music and the Racial Imagination*. Radano, Ronald and Philip V. Bohlman, eds. Chicago and London: University of Chicago Press, 2000.

Reyes, David and Tom Waldman. *Land of a Thousand Dances: Chicano Rock 'n' Roll from Southern California*. Albuquerque: University of New Mexico Press, 1998.

Robb, John D. *Hispanic Folk Music of New Mexico and the Southwest: A Self-Portrait of a People*. Norman: University of Oklahoma Press, 1980.

Roberts, John Storm. *Latin Jazz: The First of the Fusions, 1880s to Today*. New York: Schirmer Books, 1999.

Roberts, John Storm. *The Latin Tinge: The Impact of Latin American Music on the United States*. New York: Oxford University Press, 1979.

Rodríguez, Luis. "Eastside Story, Part II." *L.A. Weekly*, 15–21 August 1980a.

Rodríguez, Luis. "The History of the Eastside Sound." *L.A. Weekly*, 1–7 August 1980b.

Romero, Brenda M. "Cultural Interaction in New Mexico as Illustrated in the Matachines Dance." In *Musics of Multicultural America: A Study of Twelve Musical Communities*. Kip Lornell and Anne K. Rasmussen, eds. New York: Schirmer Books, 1997, 155–86.

Romero, Brenda M. "The Matachines Music and Dance in San Juan Pueblo and Alcalde, New Mexico: Contexts and Meanings." Ph.D. dissertation, University of California, Los Angeles, 1993.

Romero, Brenda M. "The New Mexico, Texas, and Mexico Borderlands, and the Concept of Indio in the Matachines Dance." In *Selected Reports in Ethnomusicology, Vol XI: Musical Cultures of Latin America: Global Effects, Past and Present*, 81-88.

Salazar, Max. *Mambo Kingdom: Latin Music in New York*. New York: Schirmer Trade Books, 2002

Sheehy, Daniel. "Mexican Mariachi Music: Made in the U.S.A." In *Musics of Multicultural America: A Study of Twelve Musical Communities*. Lornell, Kip and Anne K. Rasmussen, eds., 131–54. New York: Schirmer Books, 1997.

Sheehy, Daniel. "Popular Mexican Musical Traditions: The *Mariachi* of West Mexico and the *Conjunto Jarocho* of Veracruz." In *Music in Latin American Culture: Regional Traditions*. John M. Schecter, ed. New York: Schirmer Books, 1999, 34–79.

Sheehy, Daniel. *Mariachi Music in America: Experiencing Music, Expressing Culture*. New York/Oxford: Oxford University Press, 2005.

Sheehy, Daniel and Steven Loza. "Overview (South American, Central American, Mexican, and Caribbean Musics." *Garland Encyclopedia of World Music* 3, 2004: 718–33.

Simonett, Helen. *Banda: Mexican Musical Life Across Borders.* Hanover and London: Wesleyan University Press, 2001.

Simonett, Helen. "*Narcocorridos*: An Emerging Micromusic of Nuevo L.A. *Ethnomusicology* 45 (2, 2001) :315–37.

Wald, Elijah. *Narcocorrido: A Journey into the Music of Drugs, Guns, and Guerrillas.* New York: Harper Collins Publishers Inc., 2001

Yanow, Scott. *Afro-Cuban Jazz.* San Francisco: Miller Freeman Books, 2001.

# RECORDINGS

*The Afro-Latin Groove: Sabroso!* 1998. Rhino R2 75209. 1998.

Los Alegres de Terán. *Corridos famosos.* Falcon FLP 4001 (LP).

*Los Angelinos: The Eastside Ranaissance.* Zyanya, 1983; distributed by Rhino.

Aztlán Underground. *Sub-Verses.* Xican@Records 40003–2. 1999.

*La Bamba: Original Motion Picture Soundtrack.* 1987. Slash/Warner Brothers 9–25605–1.

Barretto, Ray. *La Cuna.* 1981. CTI Records. CTI 9002.

Barretto, Ray. *Ray Barretto y su orquesta.* 1983. Fania JM 623.

Batacumbele. *Afro Caribbean Jazz.*1987. MLP 525.Montieno Records.

Bernal, Conjunto. *Música tejana.* Bernal BELP-2035 (LP).

*Caliente=Hot: Puerto Rican and Cuban Musical Expression in New York.* 1977. Notes by Robert Friedman and Roberta Singer. New World Records NW 244.

Cano, Eddie. *His Piano and His Rhythm.* 1962. RCA Victor LPM/LSP-2636.

El Chicano. *Viva! El Chicano: Their Very Best.* 1988. MCA.

El Chicano. *Viva el Tirado.* 1970. Kapp MCA-548.

El Chicano. *Revolución.* 1971. MCA (Kap) KS-3640.

Colón, Edwin. *El Cuatro...Más allá de lo imaginable.* EC 001.

Cruz, Celia. *The "Brillante" Best.* 1978. Vaya SD 15.

Cruz, Celia. 1983. *Con la Sonora Matancera.* Peerless.

Cruz, Celia and Willie Colon. *Celia y Willie.* 1981. Vaya JMUS 93.

Colón, Wille. *El baquiné de angelitos negros.* 1977. Fania SLP 00506.

Cuarteto Coculense. *Mexico's Pioneer Mariachis, Vol. 4. Cuarteto Coculense: The Very First Mariachi Recordings. 1908–1909.* 1998 Arhoolie Folklyric CD 7036. Liner notes by Jonathan Clark and Hermés Rafael. www.arhoolie.com.

Delinquent Habits. *Delinquent Habits.* 1996. RCA 66929.

D'Rivera, Paquito. *Celebration.* 1988. Columbia Records AL 44077.

*East Side Revue: 40 Hits by East Los Angeles' Most Popular Groups.* 1966 [1969]. Rampart; distributed by American Pie as LP 3303.

*Golden Treasures, vol. 1: West Coast East Side Revue.* 1966. Rampart 3303.

*Golden Treasures, vol. 2: West Coast East Side Revue.* 1969. Rampart 3305.

González. Jerry. *Rumba para Monk.* 1989. Sunnyside Communications. SSC 1036D.

Grupo Mono Blanco y Stone Lips. *El mundo se va a acabar.* Urtext Digital Classics, S.A. de C.V. UL 3004.

Guerrero, Lalo. *Las Ardillitas de Lalo Guerrero*. Discos Odeón; distributed by Alhambra as OMS-73186.

*The History of Latino Rock, vol. 1: 1956–1965: The Eastside Sound*. 1983. Zyanya; distributed by Rhino.

Jiménez, Andrés. *Jíbaro romántico y algo más*. 1988. Nuevo Arte NA 100.

Kid Frost. *Hispanic Causing Panic*. 1990. Virgin Records 91377.

Los Illegals. *Internal Exile*. 1983. A&M 7502–14925–1.

Jordán, Steve. *Soy de Tejas*. Hacienda LP-7905 (LP).

*Latin Jazz: La Combinación Perfecta*. Smithsonian Folkways Recordings LC 9628, 2002.

Little Joe and the Latinaires. *Amor bonito*. El Zarape ZLP 1008 (LP).

Little Joe y la Familia. *Para la gente*. BSR 1038 (LP).

Little Joe y la Familia. *La voz de Aztlán*. Leona Record Corporation LRC 019 (LP).

Los Lobos. *How Will the Wolf Survive?* 1985. Slash, distributed by Warner brothers as 7599–25177–1.

Los Lobos. *Just Another Band From East L.A.* 1978. New Vista (re-released on Hollywood Records).

Los Lobos. *Kiko*. 1992. Slash/Warner Brothers.

Los Lobos. *Papa's Dream: Los Lobos with Lalo Guerrero*. Music for Little People 9 42562–2, 1995.

Los Lobos. *La Pistola y El Corazon*. 1988. Slash/Warner Brothers.

López, Isidro, y su Orquesta. *Isidro López: El indio*. Arhoolie CD 363 (CD).

Machito. *Machito and His Salsa big Band*. 1982. Timeless Records SJF 161.

Machito. Machito y sus Afro-Cubanos. *Tremendo cumban*. Tropical Records. TRLP 5063.

Mafia, La. *Un millón de rosas*. Sony CDZ 81722/469800–2 (CD).

*Mambo: Pérez Prado, Machito, Xavier Cugat, Tito Puente*. 1994. La Mejor Musica/Sarabandas SRL, CD 50318 AAD.

Mariachi Los Camperos de Nati Cano. *Viva el Mariachi! Nati Cano's Mariachi Los Camperos*. Smithsonian Folkways Recordings SF 40459. Liner notes by Daniel Sheehy. www.folkways.si.edu.

Mariachi Mujer Dos Mil. *La Nueva Imagen del Milenio*. Self-published recording. www.mariachimujer2000.com.

Mariachi Sol de México de José Hernández. *Sentimiento ranchero*. Serenata Records. www.mariachi-sol.com.

Mendoza, Lydia. Border Music Vol. 15, Part 1. *Lydia Mendoza: First Recordings, 1928–1938*. Folklyric Records 9023 (LP).

Mendoza, Lydia. *Mas exitos*. Falcon FLP 2029 (LP).

Moré, Benny. *15 Exitos de Benny Moré*. 1984. RCA-Victor MKS 2364.

*El Movimiento de Hip Hop en Español*. 2004. Univision Records 0883 10322 D.

*La Música de los Viejitos: Hispano Music of the Rio Grande del Norte*. University of New Mexico Press, 1999.

Navaira, Emilio. *Quedate*. EMI Latin H4 7243 8 37705 4 2 (CD).

Orquesta Broadway. *No tiene comparación*. 1979. Coco Records. CLP 158X.

Orquesta Harlow. *Tribute to Arsenio Rodríguez*. Fania Records. SLP 00404.

Ozomatli. *Ozomatli*. 1998. Alma Sounds, Inc. AMSD80020.

Pacheco, Johnny, y Melón. *Llegó Melón*. 1982. Fania 18.

*Pachuco Boogie featuring Don Tosti*. 2002. Arhoolie. CD 7040.

Palmieri, Eddie. *Unfinished Masterpiece*. 1975. Coco Rcords CLP 120.

Puente, Tito. *Dancemania*. 1958. RCA

Puente, Tito. *El Rey*. Concord Picante Records CJP 250.

Puente, Tito. *On Broadway*. 1987. Concord Picante Records CJP 207.

Quetzal. *Quetzal*. 1998. Son del Barrio Music, a division of Justice Matters, Inc. SDB 998–01.

*Hay Califas! Raza Rock in California*. Rhino Records.

Rage Against the Machine. *Evil Empire*. 1996. Epic 57523.

Rodríguez, Arsenio. *Arsenio Rodríguez: Su conjunto y Chano Pozo, Machito & His Orchestra*. Mln.

Rodríguez, Tito. *Palladium Memories*. 1988. TR Records TR 200.

Ronstadt, Linda. *Canciones de mi Padre*. 1987. Elektra/Asylum (Warner Communications) 9 60765-1.

Rivera, Ismael. *Esto si es lo mio*. 1978. Fania Records JMTS 1428.

Russell, Andy. *Ayer, Hoy, y Siempre*. 1982. Kim K-725.

Sánchez, Poncho. *Out of Sight*. 2003. Concord SACD 1031–6.

Sánchez, Poncho. *Papa Gato*. 1987. Concord (Picante) CJP-310.

Sánchez, Poncho. *Sonando*. 1983. Concord (Picante) CJP-201.

Santamaría, Mongo. *Afro Roots*. 1972. Prestige Records 24018.

Santamaría, Mongo. *Soy yo*. Concord Picante RecordsCJP 327.

Santana. *Santana*. 1969. Columbia Records. CS 9781.

Santana. *Santana's Greatest Hits*. Nd. PC 33050.

Selena y los Dinos. *Dreaming of You*. EMI Latin H2 72433 34123 2 7 (CD).

Selena y los Dinos. *Selena Live*.EMI Latin H4 07777 42770 4 4 (CD).

Silva, Chelo. *Mis favoritas*. Falcon. GLP 14 (LP).

*Sonora Matancera con Justo Betancourt*. 1981. Barbaro records. B 207.

Sonora Poncena. *Night Raider*. 1981. Inca Records. JMIS 1079.

Sunny and the Sunliners. *Amor de mis amores*. Key-Loc Records 3030 (LP)

Sunny and the Sunliners. *Yesterday – and Sunny Ozuna*. Teardrop TD-2054 (LP).

Texas-Mexican Border Music. *Orquestas típicas: The First Recordings (1926–1938)*. 1996. Arhoolie Records, CD 7017.

Texas-Mexican Border Music. *Tejano Roots: Orquestas tejanas*. 1992. Manuel Peña, ed. Arhoolie Records 368.

Texas-Mexican Border Music Volume 2. *Corridos, Part I: 1930–1934*. 1974. Arhoolie/Folklyric Records 9004 (LP).

Texas-Mexican Border Music. Volume 3. *Corridos, Part 2: 1929–1936*. Arhoolie/Folklyric Records 9005 (LP).

Texas-Mexican Border Music. Volume 4. *Norteño acordeón, Part 1: The First Recordings*. 1975. Arhoolie/Folklyric Records 9006 (LP).

Texas-Mexican Border Music. Volume 10. *Narciso Martínez: El hurucán del Valle*. Arhoolie/Folklyric Records 9017 (LP).

Texas-Mexican Border Music. Volume 14. *The Chicano Experience*. Guillermo Hernandez, ed. Arhoolie/Folklyric Records 9021 (LP).

Texas-Mexican Border Music. Volume 17. *The First Women Duets*. Philip Sonnichsen, ed. Arhoolie/Folklyric Records 9035 (LP).

Texas-Mexican Border Music. Volume 18. *Los Madrugadores*.Arhoolie/Folklyric Records. 9036.

Texas-Mexican Border Music. Volume 24. *The Texas-Mexican Conjunto*. Manuel Pena, ed. Arhoolie/Folklyric Records 9049 (LP).

Thee Midniters. *Best of the Thee Midniters*.1983. Zyanya; distributed by Rhino as RNLP 063.

Thee Midniters. *Giants*. Distributed by Marketing West as 1002-C.

Tigres del Norte. *El tahur*. Discos Fama 577 (LP).

Tierra. *City Nights*. 1980. Boardwalk 7912–36995–1.

Tierra. 1973. 20<sup>th</sup> Century T-412.

Valens, Ritchie. *The Best of Ritchie Valens. 1958, 1959*. Del-Fi; distributed by Rhino as RNDF 200.

Valens, Ritchie. *The History of Ritchie Valens*. Rhino RNBC 2798.

Valens, Ritchie. *Ritchie Valens*. Del-Fi; distributed by Rhino as RNLP 70231.

Valdés, Miguelito. *Mr. Babalú (with Noro Morales' Orchestra)*. Tumbao TCD 025, 1993.

Villa, Beto, y su Orquesta. *Father of the Orquesta Tejana*. Arhoolie Productions 364 (CD).

*Zootsuit: Music from the Original Motion Picture*. MCA 5267 (MCA 2757).

# 4

# Indigenous Music of North America

*Maria Williams*

## INTRODUCTION

This chapter is intended to introduce new listeners to Indigenous music of North America. The information includes a brief history and outline of the broad cultural groups complemented by more detailed specific music descriptions. This is a vast subject, and one chapter cannot do justice to the topic, however, it can provide some basic conceptual understanding of the music of Native North America. It is a brief overview and not a comprehensive representation. There are many ways to approach this topic; and I have relied upon the work of other Indigenous scholars such as Charlotte Heth (Cherokee), Ben Black Bear, Sr. (Lakota), Marilyn Help (Navajo), Ellen McCullough Brabson, Joe Sando (Jemez Pueblo), and Louis Ballard (Quapaw/Cherokee). The following chapter introduces some basic principles of North American Indian music, in addition to examples of the many different musical styles that exist.

In the study of music cultures of the Indigenous peoples of North America one quickly encounters certain ethical dilemmas, specifically in the area of sound recordings of religious music. I have included references to recorded materials that are commercially available, and the majority of these are what would be considered social or non-ceremonial in nature. For those recordings that are part of religious practices, such as the Sun Dance, Ghost Dance,

Native American Church, Apache *Gaan* songs, and Navajo *Yeibichai* chants, it must be acknowledged that these are sacred repertoires, and great care must be taken in presenting these materials. I have great respect for the deep spirituality that exists in all Native American music and therefore relied upon commercially available sound recordings, and trust the listeners and readers will be sensitive and aware of these issues.

## INDIGENOUS PEOPLES OF NORTH AMERICA

The Indigenous peoples of North and South America represent the first "nations" of the western hemisphere. There are many terms commonly associated with America's Indigenous people, including: Indian, Native American, Aboriginal, First Nations, etc.[1] In reality, there is no one monolithic Indigenous nation, but literally over 1,000 distinct languages and cultures, and even within same-language speaking groups, cultural differences can vary greatly. There was and still is a vibrant and wide range of Indigenous cultures, and an equally wide range of musical styles.

Where did the ancestors of these Indigenous people come from? This has been a hyper-focus of archaeologists and anthropologists, with theories ranging from the Bering Land Bridge—which could have been crossed by ancient Siberians between 15,000 and 30,000 years ago—to ancient Polynesian connections. Archaeological evidence indicates that the Americas have been inhabited 20,000-50,000 years. The ancestors of today's Native American population have been hunting on the North and South American continents since the Pleistocene age. From the Indigenous perspective, each tribe, and even individual clans within tribes, have their own unique origin stories that tie them to their environment and their place in both the physical and spiritual world. For example, the Tlingit (a Northwest Coast tribe) trace their origins back to a founding ancestor-spirit, and each clan has its own history of origin and associated body of songs/dances. The origin stories are almost always linked to music/dance practices. Most tribes have complex and lengthy origin histories. For example, according to Navajo cosmology, they are now in the fourth or "glittering" world, and their origin story encapsulates the first, second, and third worlds.[2] Their cosmology is the foundation of their social structure, their ceremonial practices, and the sacred chants used in ceremonies. Other examples are the tribes of Southern California, who have a genre of music called "Bird Songs"—this is a metaphoric reference to their migratory origins—as they believed they flew around the world—like birds—before they permanently settled in Southern California. The origin histories of tribes are prime examples of the differences between western and Indigenous perspectives—and ones that must be kept in mind when studying or learning about Indigenous cultures.

### Indigenous Perspective

Indigenous people have a holistic worldview that is often in direct contrast with western thought, which is more compartmentalized in approach. Western perspective isolates an idea or thought, in contrast with the Indigenous world-view, which is holistic and examines the physical world as an interconnected whole with the spiritual world. There is no separation between nature and people, between spirituality and secular everyday life. One of the vital aspects of studying music from other cultures, especially non-western and non-European societies, is the variety, depth, and complexity of how worldview is reflected through music. As one begins to study and learn about Indigenous musical cultures, this is a necessary component and also affords a greater understanding of music's role in society and that the music is inseparable from culture.

There is not always a separate word for music and dance in Indigenous languages, and almost all Indigenous people have one meta-word that means both music/dance, because they were completely interconnected. Sometimes the Indigenous term for music/dance is a metaphor. For example the Tewa Pueblo word for dance is "shadeh," which literally means "to be in the act of getting up, of waking up." (Swentzell & Warren 1992, 93). The great scholar of pre-Columbian music, Robert Stevenson, noted in his monumental research on Aztec musical culture that music was "...a twin to ritualistic dance..." (Stevenson 1968, 5). One could also add text/poetry to form a triumvirate, because in Aztec culture, music, dance, and the poetic text were not viewed as isolates but as one. This represents another example of how music/dance is defined in other Indigenous music cultures of the Americas.

In studying Native American music and culture it is helpful to have an idea of the number of different languages and tribes. Oftentimes the self-designative terms for Indigenous North Americans translate as "people," and also indicate the language spoken.[3] Because of the large number of different languages it is not always possible to understand the song texts. For anyone to pursue thorough study of Indigenous music, one must learn the language or have a basic working knowledge. In many cases, ethnomusicologists have worked in partnership with Indigenous speakers of the language, which has resulted in excellent publications and articles on Native American music and dance practices. Although it is not entirely realistic for the average American to learn an Indigenous language, it is advantageous to have an understanding of the important relationship between music and language (song text).

## Basic Commonalities in Native American Music

Although there is a diverse Indigenous population in North America, there are some commonalities, musically speaking. One of these is the use of vocables in almost all forms of music. Vocables are meaningful syllables, as opposed to words or text. Vocables are similar to the use of "la la la la" in English folk songs, or "yeah yeah yeah" used in contemporary rock and roll music. They are not words, but make up an important part of the melodic phrasing. Vocables are meaningful syllables and serve and important role in the song structure. In the past these were oftentimes called "nonsense syllables," which is not an acceptable definition because they are not nonsense—they do have meaning and are an important architectural device within songs. As one listens to Native American music and becomes more familiar with hearing vocables, their importance becomes obvious, especially in regards to how they are used in various genres as part of the overall form and structure of the piece. For example, specific patterns of vocables are used in King Island Inupiaq social dances, and in Stomp dances of the Cherokee, Seminole, and Choctaw. Other commonalities are the use of the human voice—singing is of primary importance among all Indigenous cultures in North America. There are few instrumental forms or genres, because most music is vocal music. Of course, as we study further we will learn about the different styles of vocal music, but the fact is that vocal music predominates.

Most Indigenous forms of music are learned orally, and Indigenous people do not use written techniques to learn or study music—this is in direct contrast to Western European classical traditions where learning to read music is of primary importance. Indigenous musicians must possess a gift for memorizing not only the melodic lines, but also the text and associated vocables. It is not unusual for Indigenous musicians to know 600 to 1,000 or more songs.

There are also a large variety of drums and percussion instruments, such as rattles, bells, whistles, and flutes. The North American Indigenous drum technique is one-handed; this changes in Central Mexico—where two-handed techniques become common.

## Terminology

Syncopation—accent on the weak beat or the up beat
Song Structure—the form or organization of music
Rhythm/meter—regular pulse in music; can be organized in duple or triple meters
Monophonic—single melodic line
Homophonic—two or three simultaneous sounding notes
Polyphonic—music in which three or more different melodic lines sound simultaneously
Vocable—meaningful syllables in a song
Text—meaningful words in a song
Push-up—repetition in Northern and Southern Plains style
Leader/Chorus—relationship between lead singer and chorus, usually alternating melodic lines

## BRIEF COLONIAL HISTORY

Although Indigenous people have experienced tremendous colonial pressures since 1492, there is also a great deal of resilience; many languages are still spoken, religious practices intact, as are music and dance repertoires. As Europeans arrived and established settlements in the sixteenth and seventeenth centuries, encounters with the Indigenous people varied from initial peaceful exchange to wars and struggle over land and resources. Most tribes in the North American continent have experienced relocation and harsh policies from European powers, and later the Canadian, U.S., and Mexican governments.

Indigenous reaction and adaptation varies from tribe to tribe because Europeans arrived at various times to different regions for different purposes. The Spanish were the first European power to begin a campaign of conquest in the sixteenth century.[4] The English, and later the French, Dutch, and other Western Europeans, arrived to North America with their families to carve out a new way of life and escape religious persecution. Europeans arrived at different times to North, Central, and South America for different purposes, but eventually long-term settlement and establishment of new colonial states were created.[5] Another devastating effect of the European presence was the introduction of unknown diseases, such as typhus, smallpox, measles, influenza, and tuberculosis. These diseases resulted in unprecedented population loss and major disruptions to social life in virtually every single Indigenous community in both North and South America.[6]

## Culture Areas/Cultural Map

One of the academic approaches in studying Native Americans is to link geographical regions to culture groups—in essence a cultural map. Anthropologists have linked the physical geography with culture groups and identified broad culture areas—these include the Northwest coast, Great Basin and Plateau, Sub-Arctic, Arctic, Eastern Woodlands, Southwest, California, and the Great Plains. This represents a taxonomic approach, and although it is not a dimensional model that would include additional cultural and historic contextual information, it is a useful tool. Indigenous peoples tend to adapt to their physical and geographic environment, incorporating them into their spiritual worldview and cultural practices such as music/dance. Although this is not an absolute rule, if one studies the physical geography of North America, one finds there is often a parallel to the cultural and musical practices. For example, the Tlingit, Haida, and Tsimshian tribes of southeastern Alaska all speak completely unrelated languages, yet have very similar cultural practices, including social structure, visual aesthetics, and how music is placed within their societies. Their rainforest and seafaring environment link them, resulting in shared cultural practices, even though they speak unrelated languages. The sense of place is heightened among Indigenous communities.

Some broad generalizations can be drawn from these cultural/geographic areas that can be helpful in identifying some of the unique musical qualities. Although there are exceptions to these overarching characteristics, they are helpful especially for the listener unfamiliar with Indigenous music. For example, music of the southwestern United States from the Rio Grande Pueblo, Hopi, and Zuni employ unique rhythmic changes, which are part of their aesthetics; music of the tribes in the Eastern Woodlands employs a call and response style that is particular to that region; tribes in the Northwest coast employed harmony and polyphony, etc. These "markers" assist the beginning student in identifying the various musical styles found in North American Indian music.

The following includes a brief outline of the culture area and one or two musical genres from each region—this is purely introductory in nature and should not be considered comprehensive information. Included are suggested listening materials and videotape sources as well that might prove useful in providing a more fully dimensional picture of each region.

## Eastern Woodlands

The Eastern Woodlands is the broad eastern portion of the North American continent that stretches north to south from present-day Nova Scotia to Florida, and west to east from the Appalachian Mountains to the Atlantic Ocean.[7] The region is sometimes interpreted as the Northeast and Southeast, with the dividing line around present-day North Carolina. There are many shared cultural characteristics and musical styles found among the hundreds of tribes that inhabited the region. The area was a thickly wooded forest, with rich land for agriculture, along with many rivers, lakes, and streams. There was no shortage of fresh game and fish; all the tribes practiced agriculture, growing corn, beans, squash, and various types of melons and potatoes. Their musical repertoire reflects their deep ties to the agricultural cycle and the primary crops of corn, beans, and squash (often referred to as the "three sisters") and the potato (yes, this is an American food). The Eastern Woodlands was densely populated with numerous tribes. The tribes from the northeastern part of the Eastern Woodlands are often called "People of the Longhouse," in reference to their religious and political organization that centered on gatherings in large dwellings or Long Houses. In the Southeast, the Cherokee, Choctaw, Chicka-saw, Seminole, and Creek of the Southeast are often called the "Five Civilized Tribes," in reference to one of the area's largest confederacies.

One of the primary political developments found in this region and other parts of Native North America was that of the confederacy. There were many confederacies that existed throughout the entire Eastern Woodland area, the most well known being the Iroquois Confederacy, which came into being sometime around 1,000 A.D. after a prophet and his orator (Deganawida and Hiawatha) began advocating for a new political and ideological concept of civilization.[8] The Iroquois Confederacy was established and included the Seneca, Oneida, Huron, Mohawk (Akwasasne), Onondaga, and later the Tuscarora, which minimized warfare among themselves and created a unified system of political hegemony that fended off potential enemies.

In 1607, 144 English Colonists arrived in what is now called Chesapeake Bay, Virginia. They were a group of mostly English Puritans who fled Europe because of religious persecution. They depended upon the Indians in their new homeland to learn about agriculture, weather, flora/fauna, and other sur-vival needs. In 1608 another 190 colonists arrived, led by Captain John Smith (this was one of the first colonies to actually survive past one year). In 1624, colonists settled New Netherlands on Manhattan Island. Soon conflict over land erupted as the colonies continued to grow, and other colonial interests, such as the fur trade, broadened the geopolitical landscape, making it difficult for peaceful relations to continue.[9]

The main commercial interest was fur, and major colonial enterprises included the French, Dutch, and English companies who vied for control of the lucrative fur market. As the fledgling Spanish, English, and Dutch colonies grew, they carved out a large area, oftentimes in conflict with the local Indigenous people. As the settlements increased in size and power they had an adverse effect on the Indigenous communities. This resulted in the French-Indian war (1756-1763), which was really a war of capital between French and British forces, who were vying for control of northeastern North America. These conflicts with European powers over control over regions in North America had a detrimental effect on the Indigenous population, and often resulted in divisions between tribes over which European power to ally with. The Iroquois Confederacy, members of which had maintained peace in the region since 1,000 c.e., was divided in their opinion of which European country to ally with, and their council fires were extinguished until the conflict ended.[10] During this period the great Iroquois Confederacy was divided, and after the American colonies won their freedom from Europe they began to model their new government and constitution on a new concept called "democracy." The basic tenets of the Iroquois Confederacy, or Great Law of Peace, were the model for American democracy and the Constitution of the United States because they provided a new approach or ideology for civilization for the Europeans and their descendents that was antithetical to the European theocratic and aristocratic models. The concepts of leaders being voted for, everyone having an equal voice, and arriving at consensus of the majority, rather than having power concentrated in a few hands, were key political practices of the Indigenous confederacies and so impressed Thomas Jefferson and Benjamin Franklin that the Indigenous model became the new model of democracy for the United States (Grinde and Johansen 1991).

Musically the Eastern Woodlands style employs the use of call and response or leader-chorus, meaning that a song leader would call or sing out a melodic line and a chorus or group of singers respond, either with a repetition of the leader's melodic line or with a formulaic response. This can be heard in the "Shake the Bush Dance," the "Corn Dance," and the "Stomp Dance" (Heth, New World Records 337, *Songs and Dances of the Eastern Indians from Medicine Spring & Allegany*, 1985). The "Shake the Bush" dance incorporates a water drum, hand rattles, and a song leader and chorus of singers as well as dancers. The water drum is a unique instrument to North America, found in the Northeast and Southeast as well as the Southwest. The drum is a hollow vessel that contains water, with the head or skin of the drum stretched over the top—it can be tuned by changing the level of water.

The leader plays the water drum, and the half-a-dozen or so singers use hand rattles. The "Shake the Bush" dance songs are a genre rather than a specific song. This genre typically opens with a leader-chorus introduction followed by a unison chorus in an AA BC song structure. The song leader starts out, calling out a melodic line, and is then joined by the rest of the singers, who sing a formulaic response. The melodic line is striking in its use of syncopation—another musical characteristic common throughout the Eastern Woodlands culture area. At the end of each song, which lasts several minutes, the tempo slows down and a tremolo rattle signal marks the time when the dancers must change places, and then the next song is introduced (Heth, CD Notes 1985).

The same relationship of leader/chorus or call and response is also heard with the Stomp Dance, another genre that is commonly practiced among the Cherokee, Choctaw, Seminole, and Creek tribes, formerly of the Southeast.[11] Stomp Dance season lasts from spring to fall and occurs as part of larger ceremonial and social gatherings. Dancing occurs from dusk to dawn, lasting all night. The Stomp Dance refers to both a particular genre of songs as well as a larger event that brings many people together. The music of the Stomp Dance opens with an introductory phrase by the Song Leader, who is joined by a chorus of singers who respond with a formulaic musical phrase. Long complex melodic phrases with syncopated accompaniment from the women shell shakers create a rich and unmistakable texture that is characteristic of the Stomp Dance. (Recorded musical examples in Heth, 1985; *Songs of the Muskogee Creek*, Parts 1 and 2, Indian House 3003, 1978.)

> Introductory formulas and songs vary from leader to leader, but some general observations can be made. The first call and response is followed by a shout from the men. A series of short responsorial (leader-chorus) introductory formulas follows, with minimal pitch or text changes. Just before the first song begins, the text and the melody change noticeably. The one or two pitches used in the introduction expand to three or more, and the flat-footed running step of the men and women begins, accompanied by the double shake of the shell shakers and the rhythmic pulse of the drum. (Heth, 1985 CD Notes)

Stomp Dance song texts are primarily vocable with minimal text, and it is not unusual to have many different tribes present and participating in the event. As mentioned earlier, vocables are meaningful syllables, rather than meaningful words, and are common to virtually every Indigenous singing style in North America. The main practitioners of the Stomp Dance are the Cherokee, Seminole, Creek, and other Southeastern tribes. When these tribes were forcibly removed from their homeland to Oklahoma in 1838-39, they transplanted their music there as well, and Stomp Dances are now commonly found in Oklahoma.

Rhythm is provided by a water drum and by the distinctive leg rattles worn by the female dancers, who are called the shell shakers; these are often made of turtle shells.[12] Once the song begins, after the initial opening phrase by the Leader, the dancers who are organized in an alternating male/female/male/female circle begin to move; the women's leg rattles create a syncopated rhythmic pulse. The singing and dancing lasts all night, and the stamina of the singers and dancers is remarkable. The dancers move around a fire—which is sacred—and the music and dance are a type of prayer. The Stomp Dance and other songs from the Southeast are considered songs of the sacred fire. Both social and ceremonial music of Southeastern tribes are performed around a sacred fire. The Fire Keeper usually starts the fire early in the day, before any of the events begin and after the area is blessed.

> The caller or organizer chooses the song-dance leaders, consulting with each in turn. He then moves to the east side of the fire and gives the call for the designated man and his helpers to come out. In a Stomp Dance the men enter from the west side of the ground and begin walking around the fire counterclockwise. The shell shakers and other women take their places alternately between the men, and the singing begins. (Heth, CD Notes, 1985)

An important ceremony to the tribes in the Southeast is the Green Corn Ceremony, which usually occurs in July and is centered on the agricultural practices important to these societies. Usually at the end of the Green Corn ceremony, after dusk, the Stomp Dancing begins and lasts until sunrise. (Suggested listening for Green Corn songs: *Caddo Tribal Dances*, Indian House, SC300, 1955.)

## The Great Plains

The most recognizable of all Native North American musics and cultures is that of the Plains. The Great Plains is a vast geographic span that is relatively flat and rich in grasses and that stretches south to north from present-day southern Texas to Alberta, Manitoba, and Saskatchewan, and west to east from the Rocky Mountains to the Mississippi River Valley. The mighty buffalo herds, formerly numbering in the tens of millions, roamed the entire area. The classic Plains horse culture arose only after the introduction of the European horse, which occurred in the late 1600s after the Pueblo Revolt in 1680; the Spanish horses were free to roam into the Plains where the Indigenous people quickly adopted the horse and radically changed their own lifestyles. Most of the Indigenous people in this region were semi-agriculturalists, but with the introduction of the horse their lifestyle became more mobile, and agriculture was no longer their primary method of food production. Music and dance styles of this area are dramatic—both visually and aurally. The Europeans and Americans who first saw Plains regalia, heard the music, and witnessed their dramatic dance styles must have been understandably awestruck.

Today the Northern and Southern Plains musical and dance styles are most visible at Powwows, which are inter-tribal gatherings that occur all over the United States and Canada. The Powwow as we know it today had its origins in the late nineteenth and early twentieth century; however, its roots are based on Plains intertribal gatherings.

During the late nineteenth century, as the U.S. government forcibly moved tribes onto reservations, the Plains people had more intense exchanges with the Cavalry as they fought for their survival. The destruction of the great buffalo herds and loss of traditional homeland, in addition to exposure to diseases for which they had no immunity, put into question their very survival. Many of

The Eagle Dancers (four Winnebago men) performing outdoors for the Stand Rock Indian ceremonial. Dells of the Wisconsin, Wisconsin © 1929. Courtesy Library of Congress.

the Plains tribes were large and powerful, such as the Lakota/Dakota, often-times called Sioux.[13] The Lakota/Dakota had a homeland that stretched from present-day Canada to North and South Dakota—many of the other Plains tribes needed vast territories for their hunting lifestyles. It was a difficult transition to move into smaller tracts of land where the U.S. Government could control them when they were forced onto reservations in the late nineteenth century. The tribes in the Plains survived the initial reservation period and continued to share their music and dance styles, and now these are found in almost all parts of the United States and Canada.

Musically the Plains can be divided into a Northern and Southern style. The large Plains-style drum and the musical forms are the basis of modern-day Powwow music. Typically, Plains-style music features a large drum placed on the ground, with drummers and singers stationed around it; each drummer also sings, and uses the one-handed playing technique that is found all over North America. Northern style usually features a much higher vocal pitch or falsetto, a quicker beat, and the beaters used on the drums are furry or fuzzy. Southern style does not have falsetto singing, the beat is slower, and the beaters are not furry or fuzzy. In terms of song structure, the Northern style often has 10 "push-ups" or more, while the Southern has six to seven ("push-up" refers to the number of repetitions of each phrase). The song leader is usually the lead drummer. The musical style and Northern Plains vocal style is best summed up by Ben Black Bear, Sr.

The Lakota way of producing the singing voice, the "Indian throat," results in a very unique sound that is difficult to describe fully. The higher parts of songs are sung by men called "li'oka wicasa" in falsetto ranging from piercing to mellow. As the melody descends, the voice gains energy and rhythm. The sound is produced at the back of an open mouth and throat with the volume and quality of the voice depending to a good part on development of abdominal muscles. The women called "wicaglata" sing an octave higher than the men usually joining in the latter parts of each rendition and trailing out songs a little longer at the endings. In addition to their singing, the women produce a unique trilling sound at special junctures in the song to indicate deep feelings, to express intensive joy or appreciation, such as when a relative, who is being honored, has his name mentioned. It is called [in Lakota] *"honnagicala hotun."* For both men and women the voice is not judged so much on sweetness or smoothness, but rather on its range, its volume, and its expressive quality. (Ben Black Bear, Sr. 1976, 11-12)

The structure of the social songs/dances of the Plains varies; however, the most common form is as follows. The lead singer usually starts and is then followed by a second singer and/or the rest of the singers. This type of leader/chorus structure is an earmark of Plains social songs/dances. The group of drummers/singers sings together to the end of the first section. For each repetition the lead singer starts each phrase—which is called a "push-up," is the highest part of the song, and usually employs vocables. Then the second and/or chorus again join the leader. The melodic line is usually monophonic, with all singers on the same pitch (with women an octave higher). The Leader starts on the highest pitch, when the second and/or Second/Chorus/Leader enter it is at succeeding lower pitches—this is commonly referred to as a "terraced descent." The songs can be all vocables, a combination or vocables and text, or all text and no vocables.

| Leader | | |
|---|---|---|
| | Second | |
| | | Second/Chorus |

| Leader | 2nd Push-up/Leader | 3rd Push-Up/Leader |
|---|---|---|
| Second | Second | Second |
| Second/Chorus | Second/Chorus | Second/Chorus |

There are variations in terms of how the leader/chorus song structure is used in Plains music. They can include first endings, second endings, and usually at the final end of the piece, the second ending is repeated. There are also special drumbeats or patterns used that are particular to each song. Upon first hearing Powwow or Plains music, the listener might have difficulty in hearing how the drum is employed, but it is specially composed for each song. The songs are not improvised, but are composed and learned in the many rehearsals necessary for the singers to learn the songs and the drumming. Sometimes the lead singer employs specialized individual drum beats in the songs that are accented—sometimes these are called "honor" beats. The steady tempo of the drumming, which is all in unison, is usually in divisions of two. Sometimes the one is emphasized, other times it is the two, or they receive equal emphasis.

ONE two ONE two ONE two One two
Or
One TWO one TWO one TWO one TWO
Or
ONE TWO ONE TWO ONE TWO ONE TWO

Special drum rolls can also be used for special changes or as commentary to what is occurring at a Powwow.

As mentioned earlier, the dance styles are many and varied. The music can hardly be separated from the various dance styles. The regalia of the dancer are specific to the type of dancing they do. Fancy Dancers wear elaborate head-dresses and bustles and move in dramatic and very quick motions, employing foot movements that show how light they are on their feet. Straight or Traditional Dancers usually only wear headdresses and no bustles, use a double step, and are more stately in their dance style. They emphasize head movements and body movements from the waist up. Women's Fancy Shawl dancing employs a similar style to the men's Fancy dancing. Women wear beautiful shawls and move around while employing special circular motions, also emphasizing light footwork. Women's Jingle Dress dancing is a contrast to Fancy Shawl dancing, and the women wear dresses that have hundreds of "jingles" or small metal-shaped cones that make a jingling sound—hence the name of the dance.[14] The women move only from the knee down with no upper body movement to emphasize the sound their dresses are making. This is just a brief summary of the many different types of dances that can be seen at a Powwow.

Contest dancing is a big part of a Powwow, and the dancers are judged by experts and then awarded prizes: First, Second, Third, and Honorable Mentions. Powwows have grown in recent years, and are quite popular. The Gathering of Nations, which occurs each April in Albuquerque, New Mexico, often attracts 20,000–30,000 audience members. There are a growing number of these large Powwows, in addition to the many smaller community Powwows that occur all over the United States and Canada. These events are open to the public, and all ages are present at these community-style gatherings.

The Plains area, especially the Northern Plains, is also known for the Sun Dance, a religious or ceremonial event. The musical style differs from the Pow-wow. The Sun Dance is also found among tribes in the Great Basin. It occurs usually during the summer solstice and is an event characterized by solemnity and intensity. The individuals that choose to pray and participate in a Sun

Dance must fast and participate in sweat baths to purify themselves and prepare themselves for the Sun Dance. The individuals who choose to participate must make a four-year commitment—meaning they must do this for four consecutive summer solstices. They are supported by their individual families and communities as well, as the purpose is to ensure continued survival, to bless the people, and to give thanks for life itself.

Before a dance begins, a medicine person or Sun Dance Chief identifies a Sun Dance area, and a select group of people erect a pole. Then, the grounds are blessed, and people follow specific protocols of behavior. Drummers and singers usually sit off to the southeast area of the grounds, and family supporters occupy the northeast area. The dancers move to and from the center of the pole for a period of three days and nights, with no water or food. Sometimes dancers go into a trance and receive visions, and are taken care of by the Sun Dance Chief and his assistants. There are slight variations of the Sun Dance from tribe to tribe, but the main focus, that of prayer, fasting, and intense inward meditation, does not change.

The music of Sun Dance uses a distinctive instrument—the eagle bone whistle. This is a sacred instrument blown during the course of the dancing, capable of producing two pitches—a standard pitch and an overblown pitch. The drum used is the large Plains style drum. Musically there is a regular pulse, with a hint of syncopation, and the song texts are primarily vocables with meaningful texts and are considered prayer. (Listening examples of Southern Plains style: Library of Congress AAFS L35 Kiowa; Northern Plains style: Library of Congress AFS L40 Sioux.)

## Alaska

Alaska is a vast sub-continent of North America—it is over 536,000 square miles and has more than 33,000 miles of coastline, thousands of islands, and the largest mountain in North America (Mt. McKinley/Denali), reaching almost 21,000 feet. It is home to seven broad cultural groups who speak 20 different languages and numerous dialects. These range from the circumpolar Inuit—called Inupiaq in Alaska—to the Unangan who occupy over 1,200 miles of the Aleutian archipelago. The musical cultures in Alaska reflect a wide array of styles and cultural contexts.

The seven broad culture groups in Alaska include: 1) the Iñupiaq who reside in and above the Arctic Circle; 2) the Yup'ik of mainland southwestern Alaska; 3) the Siberian Yupik, who live on St. Lawrence Island; 4) the Unanagan (Aleut) who live in the 1,500-mile-long Aleutian Island archipelago; 5) the Sugpiaq who live on Kodiak Island, the Alaska Peninsula, and Prince William Sound areas; 6) the Athabascan Indians, who live in the entire interior regions[15]; and 7) the Pacific Northwest culture tribes of the Tlingit, Haida, and Tsimshian.

The Inuit occupy the Arctic circumpolar regions in Alaska, Canada, Siberia, Scandinavia, and Greenland. The Inuit, called Iñupiaq in Alaska, live in and above the Arctic Circle and speak a wide array of dialects that are not all mutually intelligible. The word Iñupiaq means "people." The self-designative terms are now being used, rather than the pejorative terms such as "Eskimo." The Yup'ik people, along with the Iñupiaq, were formerly all grouped together and simply called "Eskimo." The term, although still used, is outdated and reflects the colonial history of Alaska and the Arctic. There are many differences between Yup'ik and Iñupiaq people, including different music/dance styles, different languages, and different social systems. When reading through material on these two Alaskan Native groups, one must recall that there is a clear distinction, and the term "Eskimo" does not reflect the cultural or linguistic differences between the Yup'ik and Iñupiaq.

There are three broad Iñupiaq regions in Alaska—the North Slope, Kobuk area, and Seward Peninsula. The dance and musical style of the Iñupiaq varies from village to village, although there is a definite stylistic similarity and shared cultural and social practices.[16] The social songs are bi-partite in structure and usually performed twice, lasting about three to four minutes in length. Music falls into several categories that include invitation dances, specifically choreographed fixed motion dances, and ceremonial dance complexes. Invitation dances are pre-composed musically and occur at the beginning and end of all musical events. Audience members are welcome to join in on these invitations, and the dance motions are improvised rather than choreographed. The choreographed motion dances usually tell stories, histories, legends, and also include social commentary. Some of these are also reflective of their kinship relationships and specifically composed for their teasing or cross cousins[17]. The ceremonial dance complexes have become increasingly rare due to the combination of a strong Christian missionary presence in the nineteenth century along with devastating epidemic diseases that resulted in 50 to 90 percent mortality rates. The ceremonial dance/music complexes that have survived include the Eagle/Wolf Dance or Kivgiq, and village-specific events that accompany whaling and Polar Bear hunting. The ceremonial activities are usually performed for special events and occasions, while social dancing can take place anytime.

The long and dark winter months were filled with the music, dance, and ceremonial activity. These took place indoors in community houses. The type of drum common to the Iñupiaq is a large single-headed handheld frame drum. The head is usually made from a marine mammal membrane (i.e. walrus stomach, whale heart or liver). The beater is usually quite long, and the drummers hit the frame of the drum, not the drumheads, as they play seated behind the dancers. The drummers are also the singers; the dancers do not sing. The dancers move in the same exact motion using hand, arm, and head gestures that reflect the song text. The male and female dance styles vary slightly; the men's style is more aggressive and uses more leg movement then the women's style, which emphasizes grace.

Iñupiaq songs almost always start with vocables and then meaningful text and are repeated twice. The drum patterns are unique to each song. All singing is monophonic, with women singing an octave higher then the male singers.

(Suggested listening example: "Ballard's Eskimo Ice Cream Song," *Native American Indian Songs*, 2004; *Oyate Ta Olowah*; Video: KYUK Camai Festival, 1995.)

The Yup'ik people that occupy the Bering Sea Coast, Yukon/Kuskokwim Delta, and Bristol Bay regions adapted to both marine and riverine environments. Their language has several dialects, including Cup'ik and Siberian Yupik, which are mutually intelligible. This is a populated area because of the abundance of food sources from rivers, the ocean, and a variety of land animals as well as flora. Yup'ik music/dance also uses a single-headed handheld frame drum; however, the drummers strike the drumheads rather than the frame, and the drums are slightly smaller then the Iñupiaq counterpart. The male dance style is unique, as men dance seated or on their knees while the female dancers stand behind them. Men and women use dance fans—different styles for male and female—and the women wear headdresses. The motions are choreographed, and all the dancers make the same motions using hand gestures that reflect the song text. There are codified hand gestures that are like sign language—certain motions that mean "walking," "far away," "paddling a kayak," etc.—and are understood by all. The songs are usually eight to ten minutes in length and have many verses. There is a lot of humor, especially in Yup'ik social dance and with each repetition of the verse; humor is often exaggerated, much to the enjoyment of the audience.

Chorus:
Cauyaqa nauwa, cauyaqa nauwa
mumqa-llu tamariayugaqa,
ililiranga iluaraurlluma wii
kingu'arqaralua, ye'ia-rri-ia-iaia

1st Verse:
Yugyaqa waniwa, apallumnek
tamariayug'aqua
ililiranga iluarauluma wii
kingu'arqaralua, ye'ia-rri-ia-rri-ia-rri-ia-ia-ia

[back to Chorus]

2nd Verse:
Yugyaqa waniwa, apallumnek
nunariyug'aqua
ililiranga iluaraurluma wii
kingu'arqaralua, ye'ia-rri-ia-rri-ia-ia-ia

Back to Chorus

Where is my drum, where is my drum,
and my drumstick, I keep on losing it.
My dear old friend/cousin dances with me,
after he teasingly makes fun of me and puts me down.

Here is my spirit/soul/life,
I keep on losing the lyrics to my songs.
My dear old frien/cousin dances with me,
after he teasingly makes fun of me and puts me down.

[Back to Chorus]

Here is my spirit/soul/life,
I am having a joyous time [my songs make me happy
My dear old friend/cousin dances with me,
after he teasingly makes fun of me and puts me down.

St. Lawrence Island is in the Bering Sea, and although the residents speak Siberian Yupik, which is mutually intelligible to Central Yup'ik spoken on the mainland, their dance and musical styles are more similar to Iñupiaq. Their island culture and remote location probably led to their unique cultural characteristics. They are very close to their Siberian counterparts and have trade and regular gatherings with them. During the Cold War (1945-1990) exchange was forbidden, but with the fall of the Soviet Union these are more commonplace again. Their language retention is quite high, and their music has a strong Siberian sound, including use of microtonal intervals. The St. Lawrence Island people use the single-headed handheld frame drum, and play it similarly to the Iñupiaq style. Their dance style is also very similar to the Iñupiaq style, although it has some stylistic differences that are unique to their culture.

There are 11 different Athabascan-speaking tribes that occupy most of the interior of Alaska. Their Indigenous music is varied and contains social songs and dances as well as ceremonial repertoires. During the nineteenth century the Hudsons Bay Company established a post in Fort Yukon in 1847. The French-Canadian traders brought with them fiddles, guitars, and a new style of music that the Athabascans quickly adopted.

This is one of the few cases in Alaska in which an entirely new set of instruments and repertoire were introduced and wholeheartedly loved by the Indigenous peoples. (Suggested listening: *The Wood that Sings*, National Museum of the American CD, 1998; *Folkways Music of the Alaskan Kutchin Indians*, 1974; *Gwich'in Athabascan Fiddle Music by Bill Stevens*, Sandcastle Studios, 1998)

## Northwest Coast

The Pacific Northwest Coast cultural area stretches from Northern California to Southeastern Alaska. It is a narrow strip of land that contains large areas of rainforest habitat. The tribes had abundant sources of food from the oceans, rivers, and from large and small game, in addition to quantities of large trees.

The Tlingit, Haida, and Tsimshian Indians live in the northernmost area of the Pacific rainforest that extends from northern California to Southeastern Alaska. There are three tribes or nations in Alaska that represent the northernmost tribes in the Pacific Northwest culture area. The Tlingit, Haida, and

Tsimshian speak completely unrelated languages; however, as mentioned earlier they have many shared cultural practices that include music, dance, visual images, and similar clan systems of social organization. The music in the Northwest Coast culture area often uses harmony, which is the earmark of this region.

During events that feature music and dance there is always an entrance song and an exit song in which the dancers, drummers, and singers enter together, and after the performance exit together. There is one lead drummer and song leader. There is a chorus of singers—usually the dancers sing as well—and other drummers that follow the song leader. The drum used is a single-headed handheld frame drum. The drums range in size from 12-15 inches in diameter and are usually made of deer hide with frames made of bentwood that are about three to four inches deep. The drumheads are emblazoned with symbols of the clan of the dance leader or group. Similarly, the regalia worn by the dancers are also decorated with the clan emblem of that individual. In the past, each clan had their own dance group; in most villages there were numerous clan houses, each with their own dance group, and distinct repertoire. Songs and dances were and still are viewed as cultural property rights of the particular clan that owns that song. The concept of song ownership is very strong. Before a song is performed, there is often a speech given that explains the history of the song, or recognizes the composer. Oratory is an important aspect of all Indigenous groups, but is especially important to Northwest Coast tribes. Song structures can vary greatly.

The tribes of Northern California are the southernmost tribes of the Pacific Northwest Coast Culture area. The Tolowa and Yurok share many musical and cultural practices even though they speak two unrelated languages. Because of their shared environment and long association with one another, they have similar musical practices. Their music features complex relationships between the leader singer(s) and the chorus that often employ harmony and polyphony. They have a genre of songs called Brush Dance Songs that are primarily for healing. The song structure features sung prayer and a chorus that employs a rhythmic ostinato response to the lead singer. This creates a rich and very full song texture. (Suggested Listening: *Oyate Ta Olowah, Northwest Coast CD*; *Sealaska Heritage Celebration Videos*; Heth, *Songs of Love, Luck, Animals and Magic: Music of the Tolowa and Yurok*, 1977; Suggested video: *Music in the World of the Yurok and Tolowa Indians*, 1978.)

## The Southwest: The Pueblo People

The entire American Southwest includes New Mexico, Arizona, Utah, and Southern California. It is a semi-arid to arid region that includes the Mojave Desert (hottest place on Earth), major mountain ranges, and the Rio Grande river. The area has been occupied since time immemorial, and there is a vast archaeological record that dates back thousands and thousands of years. It is home to many different tribes, ranging from the Pueblo people, the Yuman-speaking deep desert dwellers, and the Athabascan-speaking Apache and Navajo. There are a wide variety of musical cultures in this region.

The Indigenous Pueblo people include the 19 Rio Grande Pueblos, the Hopi, and Zuni, who are the descendents of the Anasazi or "ancient ones" who left magnificent architectural evidence of their culture at Chaco Canyon, Mesa Verde, Canyon de Chelley, and other sites. The Spanish first applied the term "Pueblo" to the Indigenous people in this area because they were village people. They live in villages and historically in city-states; with the arrival of the Spanish in 1540 their lifestyles changed due to harsh colonial activities of the Spanish and introduction of previously unknown diseases. The Pueblo people participated in a major coordinated rebellion in 1680 that effectively pushed the Spanish out. Perhaps because of their tenacity and early experience in protecting their way of life from colonial invasion, they have closed societies that have formed a protective wall around their languages, religion, and ceremonial practices from the non-Pueblo world.

The Pueblos share a religious and spiritual worldview based on ceremonials that revolve around a calendric cycle and are deeply reflected in dance and music practices. Their cultures emphasize spirituality and prayer and continuance of the people. Agriculture is the primary focus of their life ways, and corn, as well as chili, beans, squash, and pumpkins are their mainstay. Corn is especially significant, and each Pueblo has at least one annual Feast dance that is open to the public and celebrates their harvest.

There are many different languages spoken by the Pueblo people: the Hopi language is from the Uto-Aztecan language family; Zuni is a language isolate and is related to no other language in the world; the Pueblo of Jemez speak Towa; the Taos, Picuris, Sandia, and Isleta people speak Tiwa; the San Juan/Oke Owinge, Santa Clara, San Ildefonso, Nambe, Tesuque, and Pojoaque Pueblos speak Tewa; and the Acoma, Cochiti, Laguna, San Felipe, Santa Ana, Santo Domingo, and Zia Pueblos speak Keresan. What have united these diverse language speakers are their religion and their environment. Their religious practices are deeply tied to ceremonial music/dance, and there is little separation between the sacred and secular.

**Language Families in New Mexico and Arizona**
**Tanoan**

Tiwa (Taos, Picuris, Sandia, Isleta) NM
Tewa (San Juan/Oke Owinge, Santa Clara, San Ildefonso, Nambe, Tesuque, Pojoaque) NM
Towa (Jemez) NM

**Keresan** (Acoma, Cochiti, Laguna, San Felipe, Santa Ana, Santo Domingo, Zia) NM
**Zuni**—language isolate NM
**Uto Aztecan language family**

Hopi AZ
Pima [Tohono O'odam] AZ
Papago [Akimal O'odam] AZ

**Yuman language family**

Upland Yuman

- Hulapai
- Havasupai
- Yavapai (lower Colorado River) AZ

River Yuman

Mojave
Yuma
Cocopa
Maricopa

**Athabascan Language family**

- Dine/Navajo
- Apache (Jicarilla, Mescalero, Kiowa-Apache, Chiricahua)

In 1692 the Spanish returned to reconquer New Mexico, but the Pueblos were able to negotiate a more autonomous relationship and secured their religious freedom. Hence, the traditional religious practices are still very much a part of contemporary Pueblo life. In 1848, with the Treaty of Guadalupe Hidalgo, the United States claimed not only New Mexico, but Utah, California, and Arizona, and the Indigenous people had to learn a new European language (English) and deal with a new government (United States). The reaction of the Indigenous people in the southwest to colonial expansion has defined their cultural survival into the twenty-first century. Even through the

Jemez Pueblo Indians in a ceremonial dance, New Mexico. © 1908. Courtesy Library of Congress.

American period, Christian missionaries, and epidemic diseases, the Pueblo people live in their ancestral homeland and have not experienced the degree of relocation that many other tribes have been subject to.

Musically the 19 Rio Grande Pueblos, the Hopi, and Zuni employ intricate and complex rhythmic patterns and elaborate ceremonial dances with multi-faceted musical structures. The use of a shifting beat—or additive rhythm—is a marker of these cultures. In virtually every song there is a rhythmic shift that occurs in a specific part of the song—the dancers' movements reflect the rhythmic shift as well. It happens seamlessly and quickly—going from duple to triple to duple, or from 4/4 to 6/8 to 4/4, or 4/4 to 5/8, usually in one measure. (Suggested listening: *Turtle Dance Songs of San Juan Pueblo*, 1972, Indian House records IH 1101; *Ceremonial Music of San Juan Pueblo*, Music of the World, 1995; Video: *American Indian Dance: Dances for the New Generation*, 1996.)[18]

The *Oke Owinge* Turtle Dance or *Okushare* is performed on December 26 each year. It is an all-day ceremonial event that is open to the general public. The *Okushare* or Turtle Dance is a genre, and each year new music and text are specially composed for that particular year. It is generally in five sections with each section consisting of four parts (La Vigna 1980, 77-97). It is a complex musical structure. The Turtle Dance is a dance that traditionally occurred during the winter solstice, but with the introduction of the Catholic church the date of December 26 was adopted as the date of performance. It is not unusual to see accommodation for the Christian calendar.

The instruments used include the Pueblo-style gourd rattle and the turtle shell rattles that are tied behind the right knee of each of the dancers. The dancers also wear bells, and as they move, these add to the rich sound. The song consists of vocables as well as meaningful text and is sung in a monophonic fashion by the all-male singers. The songs of the *Okushare* always open up with a gourd rattle signal and introductory pattern that is specific to the genre. The dance lasts from morning until the sun sets around 5 p.m. There are usually between 30-60 dancers, along with the song leader and other singers. They practice in advance to learn the new song and new choreography. The choreography and regalia are specially designed for this genre. It is not unusual to have direction (north, east, south, west) play an important role in the choreography or movement of the dancers.

> ...the Turtle dancers file out of the practice kiva,[19] proceeding to the south plaza. After reaching this area, the dancers line up shoulder to shoulder, facing north, and begin the first song. When the first rendering of the initial song has been completed, the men file out to the north plaza. While still facing north they sing the first song again. This procedure is repeated in the east plaza, except that the dancers are now facing west. After the third rendition, the dancers file back into the practice kiva to give the fourth and final rendering of the first song. Only one verse however, is sung while in the kiva. The second, third, and fourth songs are presented in the same manner, and by late afternoon the songs

for the Okushare are concluded. The final song to be performed is the Ange'in and it employs the same plaza circuit pattern just described in connection with the Okushare. (LaVigna 1980, 82-83)

In virtually all Indigenous music and dance, the directions, the seasons, summer and winter solstice, and other considerations dictate the event. Each tribe has different interpretations, but the incorporation of these into the Indigenous ceremonial activities is undeniable. The *Okushare* is no different, as it occurs close to the winter solstice and is a prayer of thanks and protection. The song texts are newly composed and usually reference the deities, the importance of corn and rain, and the sacred geography of the people.

We're praying for the betterment of the people—that we have a better crop the following year, and any hunter that goes out in the field will have luck. It is the end-of-the-year dance, and the thanking of the deities that we had a good crop this year. Also, its protection in the old days, the people would pray for protection from the deities, because they might be attacked by somebody. The reason for the name of the dance is probably because the turtle has a lot of protection—his shell...(Emiliano Archuleta and Peter Garcia, 1972)

## The Navajo

The Navajo or Diné are Athabascan-speaking peoples that live in New Mexico, Arizona, Utah, and Colorado.[20] They are the second largest tribe in the United States, with over 200,000 tribal members. The Navajo and the Apache arrived in the American Southwest sometime before the Spanish came—perhaps 1,000 C.E. However, their cosmology and history link them to the Southwest because it is their spiritual place of origin.

The Navajo and Apache are distinct cultures and societies, but have a similar cosmology that differs from that of the Pueblo, Hopi, and Zuni. Musically they also have a unique sound and a rich ceremonial and social repertoire. The Navajo are known for an array of ceremonials that include Nightway, Enemyway, Beautyway, and others. These are lengthy ceremonials that can last from three to nine nights. These incorporate the deities or *Yeibichai* ("Grandfather-of-the-Gods" or "Gods-our-Grandfathers") and imbue the participants with protective and curing powers. The instrument used by the medicine person is the water drum. The event is led by the medicine person and his or her assistants. The ceremonial chants are one of the main components of these events, and contain hundreds of songs with thousands of lines of ritual poetry (McAllester and Mitchell, 1983). These are of course memorized and learned through long apprenticeships and rigorous initiations. There is an architectural organization for these Holy Way rites and a specific sequence of activities that includes blessing of the grounds, blessing of the Hogan (dwelling place where activity takes place), many special prayers and offerings to deities, in addition to the dancing and singing and use of sand paintings.

There is a complex poetic structure to each chant that contains an introductory formula, phrases that contain vocables and a refrain, and many lines of text with the refrain; these are a procession of ideas within a poetic framework (Help and McCullough-Brabson, 2001). These ceremonials contain the heart of Navajo identity and culture; the texts relate various aspects of the Navajo creation stories and tenets of their worldview. These are elaborate and not unlike the epics found in other world religions, such as those of the Greeks, the Hindus, and the Christian Bible.

> What is most distinctive and striking about the Navajo people and their culture is their aesthetic tradition. The woven rugs and silver jewelry, impressive as they are by themselves, ultimately have their roots in the traditional dry paintings of the Navajo religion. And the dry paintings, in their turn, are but concrete pictorial representations of the great songs or chants that comprise the living vitality of Navajo religion. Hence, the entire Navajo aesthetic tradition is inspired by what are at once prayers, myths, poetry, and sacred scripture rendered into song. (Ortiz 1979, 3)

Marilyn Help and Ellen McCullough-Brabson's book on Navajo music, *We'll Be in Your Mountains, We'll Be in Your Songs* (2001), includes cultural and historical information on the Navajo, as well as examples of their music. It includes 12 pieces of music that are analyzed in terms of scale patterns and rhythmic characteristics, in addition to the rich cultural meaning of each song/dance. General characteristics of Navajo music include a tendency for the melodic lines to start low, move higher in pitch, and then descend, with an emphasis on the tonic, third, and fifth scale degrees. Vocables play an important role in Navajo music and usually occur in the beginning and end of song; they also have some songs that consist entirely of vocables. The meter can be complex and subtle (Help & McCullough-Brabson 2001, 79).

It is not unusual during ceremonial activities to have social songs/dances incorporated into a larger ceremonial. For example, the social songs performed during prescribed times of an Enemyway ceremony include Circle Dance songs, Squaw Dance songs, and Sway songs. The Circle Dance songs are dances in which men and women dance together and are usually in triple meter. (Suggested listening: Help and McCullough-Brabson, CD 2001; Suggested Video: *Sam Yazzie, Navajo Singer,* 1989.)

> Squaw Dance songs are the social part of the Enemyway ceremony, and outsiders, non-Navajos, may observe and even join in the dancing. The Squaw Dance repertoire includes Sway, Gift, Circle, Two-step, and Skip songs. Even though the designation Squaw Dance suggests that each of these song types includes dancing, that is not the case. Singers perform the Sway and Gift songs without dancing to them. In addition, each category of songs has a set order of performance during the Enemyway ceremony. Sway songs precede the Two-step and Skip songs every time

the Dine sing them in the ceremony. (Help and McCullough-Brabson 2001, 9)

Navajo music also incorporates new forms and styles of music that include Powwow songs, Native American Church, and popular forms such as rock and roll, jazz, blues, rap, and heavy metal. A Navajo rap group called Tribe 2 is now receiving recent critical recognition, as is a Navajo metal group called Ethnic De Generation. (Suggested listening: Tribe2 Entertainment, *Tribal Scars*, 2004; Ethnic De Generation, *Rezerection*, 2003.)

## The Apache

Historically there were numerous bands of Apache. Some of the Apache tribes did not survive the nineteenth century due to American expansion into their territory after 1848. Today there are eight Apache tribes that include White Mountain, Cibecue, San Carlos, Chiricahua, Mescalero, Jicarilla, Lipan, and Kiowa-Apache. They speak different dialects of Apache, which are Athabascan languages. Historically the Apache people moved over large areas of land and were known to have raided neighboring Pueblo tribes. Despite some of their conflicts the Apaches did aid the Pueblos during the Pueblo Revolt of 1680 against a mutual enemy—the Spanish. In the nineteenth century the Apache fought encroachment onto their land by the Americans. Today there is no single Apache nation, but several sovereign Apache tribes and reservations in New Mexico, Texas, and Arizona that include the Mescalero, Jicarilla, White Mountain, Yavapai-Apache, Lipan, and San Carlos.

In 1848 the entire southwestern area of North America came under the jurisdiction of the United States—this included New Mexico, Arizona, Utah, Nevada, and California. The United States began to systematically move Indigenous populations into reservations. When the Navajo and Apache resisted they became military targets of Kit Carson's scorched earth campaign. This is a bitter history for the Navajo and Apache people, as they fought, lost, and were then forced to move hundreds of miles away from their traditional homelands. Many died during what became known as the Navajo Long Walk of 1864. Some Apaches and Navajo fled to northern Mexico to escape the brutality and extermination of Carson's campaign, while others refugeed to neighboring tribes and were protected. In 1868 the Apache and Navajo were allowed to leave Fort Sumner (the place of their four-year imprisonment). The Apache continued to resist reservation life until the mid 1870s.

The music and dance of the Apache focus on healing and their spiritual relationship with Changing Woman, one of the main deities in their belief system. The Mountain Spirits, or Gaan, are represented in some of their ceremonial dances. An examples is found in the Crown Dancers or Apache Mountain Spirit Dances.

The Apache Mountain Spirit, or Crown Dancers, come to the people during the Girl's Coming of Age Ceremony—these are also called Sunrise

Ceremonies because the Gaan come out right before sunrise during a 16-day ceremony. The Apaches believe that the Mountain Spirits, or Gaan, came into the world through the middle of the ocean to help the people. After a great flood, one of these beings survived (Changing Woman) and gave birth to two children, Monster/Enemy Slayer and Talking God. The Medicine person and his or her assistants direct the event, songs, and prayers. They invoke the power of the Gaan and call them from the Mountains. There are elaborate patterns of vocables in these songs, as well as song texts—again these are viewed as prayers. The number four is prominent in Apache cosmology—the songs are in repetitions of four, and the dancers move facing the four directions. There are 32 songs sung during an event—four songs for each of the four directions performed twice. Songs can come to certain individuals in dreams or are learned from older medicine men. The water drum is used, and all singing is monophonic. There are four dancers, the medicine man, and a clown. There are usually four drummers as well. The clown uses the bullroarer, which is whirled around to create the sound of the wind, one of the sources of the Gaan's power, which blesses the four directions.

The Gaan, or Spirit Dancers, wear elaborate regalia and body paint. Their faces are covered and they wear crowns made of yucca with designs and sacred symbols (stars, lightening, sun, direction symbols, etc.). They also have wands that they use as well. Rattle snake rattles are sometimes used, as well as eagle fluff, wild turkey feathers, and wooden pendants that symbolize rain. They are beautiful and dramatic, and music/prayers that accompany them are powerful. The dancers move counterclockwise around the fire. (Suggested listening: *Song of the Indian*, 197-, Canyon Records; *Traditional Apache Songs*, Canyon Records, 1970; Suggested Video: *American Indian Dance Theatre, Volume 1: Finding the Circle*, 1996.)

## California

California is often considered its own cultural area because of its size and diversity. The tribes in Southern California area have some shared musical and cultural characteristics with tribes in the Southwest, perhaps because of a similar habitat. Historically, there were over 60 tribes in California, 8 language families, and 100 languages. Pre-contact population estimates are 300,000. The Spanish period lasted from 1769-1822, the Mexican period lasted from 1822 to 1848, and the American period lasted from 1848 to the present.

The Spanish, who set up a colonial system of government and introduced Catholicism, claimed California. The Catholic Church established a series of 21 missions. Many of the Indigenous people were basically captives of the missions (hence the name "Mission Indians" for many of the California tribes) and were forced to do manual labor for the Spanish colonial government and the Catholic Church. The missions were forced labor camps, and with the brutal force of Spanish soldiers the friars were able to enslave many of the tribes. This lasted until 1836, when the Indians were allowed their freedom.

After 1848, with the Treaty of Guadalupe Hidalgo, California came under the jurisdiction of the United States. The Indigenous people had been exposed to disease forced labor, and, beginning in the mid-nineteenth century, the California Gold Rush. Many of the tribes suffered, and some consolidated with one another.

Southern California tribes use the gourd rattle as their primary instrument. The drum did not come into use among southern California tribes until after 1848, the beginning of the American period. For the tribes in Southern California, one of the important genres of music is the Bird songs. The songs number in the thousands and are presented as part of a series or cycle and sometimes part of a larger ceremonial. Some of the song texts are in ancient languages, while others are not—a testament to the antiquity of the genre. The songs are chants, but the mythology implied by the chant has great cultural significance (Siva 1989). The Bird songs in essence tell the complete creation and migration story for the Cahuilla, Serrano, and other Southern California tribes.

The musical structure of individual Bird songs reflects paired phrases and symmetrical organization. There is usually one song leader and a chorus of singers who all have rattles. There is a regular pulse or meter with syncopation. These songs accompany dance. The song leader knows hundreds of these songs, and they are learned through long apprenticeships and practice. The songs are diatonic, meaning they employ notes or scale degrees that are also found in Western European musical traditions. The Bird songs are performed from dusk until dawn, and the song leader and his singers must have great stamina and powers of memorization. The songs last about three to four minutes, so that in the course of an all-night performance many songs are sung. (Suggested listening: Louis Ballard, 2004, *Two Mojave Bird Dance Songs*, Canyon Records C6050.)

Although the repertoire of the Bird songs was beginning to wane, the genre has experienced a virtual renaissance, and now it is common to see Bird singers at many gatherings and to see young Bird singers learning their cultural patrimony.

## Great Basin

Major tribes in the Great Basin include the Northern Paiute, Southern Paiute, Owens Valley Paiute, Washoe, Northern Shoshone and Bannock, Eastern Shoshone, Western Shoshone, Ute, and Kawaiisu. The tribes in this region lived in relative isolation until the discovery of gold in California in the mid-nineteenth century. During the subsequent period they experienced epidemic diseases and loss of land.

The tribes in the Great Basin and Plateau are often overlooked but have remarkable cultural and musical practices. The Great Basin is the place of origin of major religious movements, namely the Ghost Dance and the Bear Dance. Perhaps due to the relative isolation of these regions into the nineteenth century and the ethnocentric judgment of outsiders who did not recognize the depth of spiritual conviction of the tribes in these areas, there exists a false impression that these are "barren" regions. Nothing could be further from the truth.

In 1869 a new messianic movement arose called the Ghost Dance, which spread to northern California tribes by the 1870s. A Northern Paiute prophet named Wodziwob had a dream about the Ghost Dance. This vision included music and a circle dance of men and women who would hold hands moving clockwise. Wodziwob understood his vision to be a message about world renewal and salvation. He shared his vision and the songs and dances he learned, and the Ghost Dance movement was started.

The Ghost Dance had to be performed five nights in a row, and the dancers would often go into a trance-like state and have visions. The Ghost Dance, if performed correctly, would bring back the recently deceased tribal members and restore balance to their world.

The Ghost Dance movement would spread to the Great Basin tribes, and

> ...by May 1870 the severely deprived Northern Shoshone and Bannock from the Fort Hall Reservation and the Eastern Shoshone from Wind River Reservation had become active proselytizers for the religion... The Ghost Dances of the early 1870's represent the first joint ceremonial undertakings of Ute and Northern Shoshone. (Jorgenson, 661)

In 1889, a new prophet named Wovoka emerged and renewed the Ghost Dance religion, after which it spread to the Plains tribes like wildfire. Wovoka was a Northern Paiute prophet who received visions. The Ghost Dance religion is one of the few proselytizing Native American religious movements. It was born out of the desperation of the early reservation movements in the late nineteenth century. Wovoka's interpretation was slightly varied from Wodziwob's initial ideology of the previous decade. It emphasized living in peace with the Euro-Americans and among themselves. Wovoka's ideal was that if the Native Americans practiced the Ghost Dance, they would be united with their deceased loved ones and bring peace to the world. (Jorgenson, ibid., 662).

Musically, Ghost Dance songs are sung monophonically with no instruments. The songs contain vocables, and special regalia are made for the dancers. Once the movement spread to the Plains tribes it took on newer meaning. It was believed that Ghost Dance regalia would be bulletproof. Tragically, this was not the case. In 1890 as Plains people gathered to participate in a Ghost Dance, they were attacked and killed by the United States Cavalry in what is now known as the Wounded Knee massacre. (Suggested listening examples: *Music of the American Indian*, Olympic Records, 1976)

## The Native American Church

The Native American Church, also called Peyote Religion, is another example of pan-tribal religious practices. The origins of the Native American Church are probably centered in the region of present-day Northern Mexico and Southern Texas/New Mexico, where an Indigenous cactus called peyote grows. The cactus is used in religious ceremonies in tribes throughout the United States, but especially in the Great Basin, Southwest, and Southern Plains areas. Native American Church combines Indigenous and Christian belief systems. It is the only syncretic religion in North America.

There are some variations in the Native American Church, but these are slight. The gatherings take place usually in teepees, and there is a Roadman or leader and his assistants. The gathering uses tobacco, peyote, and music, which are viewed as prayer. The instruments used for the ceremony are the water drum and rattle, which are accompanied by religious accoutrements such as an eagle feather fan and special staff. During the all-night gatherings, as the prayers/songs begin, they are sung in groups of four.

During the early part of the ceremony the participants consume their first serving of peyote, and the leader or Roadman picks up his staff, fan, and gourd rattle, and begins to sing, while accompanied by the drum. Everyone present joins in the song or prayer. He sings four songs. The Roadman then passes his staff, rattle, and fan clockwise, followed by the drum, and the next person sings four songs. This continues around the circle. The event lasts all night.

Musically the chants or prayers of the Native American Church are extremely fast with tempos at about 170-200 beats per minute. The rapid drumbeat and rattle are played at these very fast tempos with a steady beat. The sung phrases are usually in a narrow range of not more than a fourth. The water drum is a "tuned" instrument; depending on the depth of the water the pitch varies. The drum, the rattle, and the other religious accoutrements are viewed as sacred and not used for any other events. They are especially decorated with specific iconography that is used in the Native American Church. (Suggested listening: Primeaux and Mike, *Walk in Beauty: Healing Songs of the Native American Church*, 1995; *Navajo Peyote Ceremonial Songs*, 1979, Indian House Records.)

The Native American Church came under fire from the United States government because of the use of peyote. It was outlawed by most of the western states, including Utah, Nevada, California, and Colorado. There was also controversy in the tribes where the Native American Church had followers because of its pan-tribal origins. In most cases the Native American Church went underground. In the 1970s and 1980s legal battles took place to defend the use of peyote in the Native American Church. Anthropologists such as Warren d'Azevedo and Omer Stewart testified in major court cases that the use of Peyote was a legitimate religious practice. In 1978 the U.S. Congress passed the American Indian Religious Freedom Act or Public Law 95-341, in part due to the suppression of Indigenous religions such as the Native American Church (Jorgenson, 680-681).

## CONTEMPORARY NATIVE AMERICAN MUSIC

Contemporary Native American music can be viewed in two major waves, the first beginning in the 1960s and the second beginning in the 1990s. This is a very exciting time for contemporary Native American music because of the level of creativity and accessibility for non-Natives to the new genres and sounds being created. There is now a Native American category for the Grammy Awards; in Canada there is a category in the Juno Awards for Indigenous contemporary music.

## The First Wave

In the 1960s a revival of folk music in the United States and Canada and new awareness of the Indigenous and aboriginal peoples led to the commercial and critical success of such performers as Buffy St. Marie, and musical groups such as XIT, Red Bone, Floyd Westerman, Jesse Ed Davis III, and others. What is interesting about contemporary Native American music is that individuals, rather than the genre, are at the forefront, and the biographies of these individuals are fascinating.

Buffy St. Marie is certainly the original pioneer in the area of popular music. She was born on the Creek reservation in Saskatchewan, Canada, but was adopted and raised in the United States. She initially recorded her first album in 1964, which featured her as a folk singer and song writer. Her career skyrocketed in the later part of the 1960s, and she became well-known as a writer of protest songs and love songs. Performers such as Janis Joplin, Barbra Streisand, Elvis Presley, Neil Diamond, Tracy Chapman, and others recorded some of St. Marie's songs. St. Marie continues to write songs and had her most recent hit in 1996 with "Star Walker." She won an Academy Award in 1982 for her song "Up Where We Belong," as recorded by Joe Cocker and Jennifer Warnes for the film *An Officer and a Gentleman*. St. Marie also had a five-year stint on Sesame Street in the late 1970s. She helped establish a new category in the prestigious Juno Awards in Canada, the category for best music of First Nations people. She holds a position of Adjunct Professor at York University in Toronto, Canada.

Jessie Edwin Davis III (Comanche/Kiowa) is an unsung hero of early Native American popular music. Davis was a guitarist and singer who was born in Oklahoma in 1944 and died in Venice, California, in 1988. His first album was a self-titled record released in 1970 (Atco Records SD33-346) and including eight songs, with guest performers such as Eric Clapton, Leon Russell, and Gram Parsons. Davis played guitar and keyboards, sang, and had been playing in the London music scene in the late 1960s. He recorded and performed with Taj Mahal (he is featured in Taj Mahal's three-CD anthology *In Progress and in Motion: 1965-1998*). Davis also recorded with Dr. John, George Harrison (*Concert for Bangladesh*), Jackson Brown (*Saturate Before Using*), John Lennon (*Walls and Bridges*), Lightnin' Hopkins and John Lee Hooker, and with John Trudell (*AKA Graffiti Man* and *Heart Jump Bouquet*). Davis performed and collaborated with the best rockers and blues men of his generation. John Lennon said that Davis was his favorite guitarist (Trudell 1989).

Rock and roll groups also emerged from the 1960s and 1970s. Red Bone formed in the late 1960s, and their 1971 release *Message from a Drum* received

## SELECTED LIST OF NATIVE AMERICAN MUSIC EVENTS

The following list includes major regional gatherings that feature primarily powwow music. There are many other types of Native American music/dance events and it is difficult to include them all.

Denver March Powwow
   Third weekend each March
   Denver Coliseum, Denver, CO
   http://www.denvermarchpowwow.org
http://www.gatheringofnations.com/
   Gathering of Nations Powwow
   Albuquerque, New Mexico (last weekend every April)
http://www.readearth.org
   Red Earth Festival
   Oklahoma City, Oklahoma
   First weekend every June
The Crow Fair is middle weekend of August and is one of the oldest powwow gatherings.
   Sponsored by the Crow Agency in Montana.
   For information call: 406-638-3719, Fax: 406-638-3880, Visit Montana site.
   Crow Tribal Office, PO Box 159 Crow Agency, MT 59022
   http://visitmt.com/categories/moreinfo.asp?IDRRecordID=8832&SiteID=1
Schemitzun Intertribal Pow-wow. The Mashantucket Pequot Tribal Nation sponsors this annual
   events the last weekend in August in North Stonington, CT. For more information, call the
   Schemitzun Hotline 1-800-224-CORN.
   http://www.foxwoods.com/TheMashantucketPequots/Links/
Oklahoma has a large number of dance festivals and gatherings that include Powwow events, but
   also Stomp dance activities. The following link lists events.
   http://www.oklahomamusicguide.com/americanindianmusicevents.htm

## LIST OF ALASKA DANCE FESTIVALS

Alaska Federation of Natives
   Quyana Celebrations. Event occurs in third week of October in Anchorage, Alaska
   http://www.nativefederation.org/convention/quyana.php
Festival of Native Arts, University of Alaska, Fairbanks. Mid-March each year the event features
   Alaska Native dance groups from all over the State. Fairbanks, Alaska on the University campus.
   http://www.alaska.edu/uaf/festival/
Camai Festival, occurs in the last week of March in Bethel, Alaska
   http://www.bethelarts.com/
Athabascan Fiddling Festival occurs each November in Fairbanks, Alaska
   http://www.fiddlechicks.com/athabascan/index.htm
Celebration occurs on even years in Juneau, Alaska during the first week in June and features
   Tlingit, Haida and Tsimshian performers.
   http://www.sealaskaheritage.org
Kivgiq occurs every other year in Barrow, Alaska in January.
   http://www.co.north-slope.ak.us/nsb/70.htm

critical and commercial success, especially with the hit song "Witch Queen of New Orleans." The band members consisted of Lolly Vegas, Pat Vegas, Tony Bellamy, and Pete DePoe, hailing from California.

XIT was formed in the early 1970s as a "concept band," meaning the founders, namely Tom Bee, had a message to present in the medium of rock and roll. The title of their first album, *Plight of the Redman*, says it all. Released in 1972, the album was a commentary on the state of Native Americans, which had come to the forefront with the political actions of groups such as the American Indian Movement. It was during this period that the average American became aware that Native Americans were still around and because of their colonial history were actively fighting for their survival. XIT featured Tom Bee (Navajo), who wrote the lyrics, with music by Mike Valvano and featuring musicians such as A. Michael Martin, Leeja Herrera, Jonec Suazo, and R.C. Carliss, Jr. Tom Bee later started SOAR, a recording studio based in Albuquerque, New Mexico.

Floyd Crow Westerman (Lakota), a singer/guitarist, released an album in the 1970s called *Custer Died for Your Sins*, inspired by Vine Deloria, Jr.'s book of the same name. Like XIT, Westerman's music was a political and social commentary. The sentiments of the album were reflecting the cultural revolution that was occurring in the United States in the late 1960s, where issues such as civil rights were tearing the nation apart. The American Indian Movement or AIM was a political organization that came to international prominence during this period. Vine Deloria, Jr. (Lakota) was an academic who began publishing books such as *Custer Died for Your Sins*, *God is Red*, and other publications that were dispelling the myth that Native Americans simply existed in a romanticized version of the nineteenth century. The ugliness of colonialism, bitter reservation history, and other issues were presented in all their starkness in not only Deloria's books, but in the recordings by Westerman and others. The titles of Westerman's songs illustrate this: "Missionaries," "Red, White, and Black," "Here come the Anthros," and "B.I.A." Westerman continues to actively perform and also acted in well-known Hollywood movies such as *Dances With Wolves* and the television series *The X Files*.

The 1980s continued to reflect the growing number of Native American contemporary performers. In the 1980s there were performers whose primary audience was other Native Americans. These included Paul Ortega (Mescalero Apache), Joanne Shenandoah (Oneida), and Keith Secola (Anishinabe). These performers also received critical acclaim for their original sound from non-Native audiences and reached some commercial success. Paul Ortega recorded *Loving Ways* with Joanne Shenandoah, and it is still very popular today 20 years after it was recorded. Shenandoah has recorded over a dozen commercial recordings, and tours the United States, Canada, and Europe to sellout audiences.

Canada was perhaps even more active than the United States in producing nationally successful First Nations groups, including the C-Weed Band, Shingoose, Laura Vinson, and others.

## The Second Wave

The 1990s witnessed a renaissance in the area of contemporary Native American music. Just as the First Wave had brought Native talent to the larger public, the Second Wave clearly established Native American contemporary music in the national and international arenas. Native artists were recognized for their contributions in the areas of rap and reggae, as well as in performance art.

Keith Secola (Anishinabe) and his group Alter-Native incorporated rock and roll, Native American flute, and Native percussion instruments. His song "NDN Kars" has become standard airplay on Native radio stations across Canada and the United States. His first group, called the Wild Band of Indians, was formed in 1988, and in 1992 he founded a new group called Akina; their CD entitled *Circle* included "NDN Kars." In 1995 he released a CD entitled *Wild Band of Indians*, and later *Fingermonkey*.

Sharon Burch (Navajo) is a composer who uses the Navajo language in many of her original songs. Her music reflects many of the traditional values of her tribe. Her solo endeavor entitled *Yazzie Girl* was a solo project that was influenced by the Navajo sacred prayers that are part of the Nightway ceremonies. Burch's music sounds original, and her CD *Touch the Sweet Earth* was awarded a 1995 INDIE Award by the National Association of Independent Records Distributors and Manufacturers. Burch is well-known in the folk music circuit and has also performed at the Kennedy Center and in the international arenas as well. Most of her recordings are produced by Canyon Records.

Red Thunder emerged in the early 1990s with a sound that was straight ahead rock and roll combined with Indigenous percussion and vocal elements. They reached acclaim in 1994 when they appeared on MTV and VH1 in public service announcements as well as special programs such as "Free Your Mind" and "Makoce Wakan—Sacred Earth," which focused on Native American sacred site issues and the relationship between spirituality and environment. The band consisted of Robby Romero (Apache/Chicano), Benito Concho (Taos Pueblo), and others.

Another well-known musician from Taos Pueblo is Robert Mirabal. He was first recognized as a traditional flute performer and composer, and developed elaborate theatrical presentations for his music, such as *Music from a Painted Cave*. Mirabal's music is more performance art, as he combines elements of theatre, narrative, dance, and music to convey his conceptual works. His productions have appeared on public television stations, and he has toured extensively in the United States and abroad. (Suggested video: *Music from a Painted Cave*, 2001.)

The new female group Walela has experienced great success under lead singer Rita Coolidge. Ulali is another female group that has wowed many audiences with their complex vocal performances. Their music is arranged for the three female singers, along with various types of percussion instruments.

Indigenous is a straight-ahead rock group with blues influences that released an album entitled *Things We Do* in 1998 (Pachyderm Records) and achieved popular and critical acclaim. They released a self-titled album in 2003 (Jive Records) and are a very popular North American touring band.

Casper Lomadawa is a Hopi musician who combines reggae with Hopi-influenced music. His CD entitled *Sounds of Reality* was released in 2000 (Third Mesa Music), and he is a major headliner in Native American music festivals around North America.

In 1998 the Native American Music Awards or Nammy's was established and had their first awards ceremony in May 1998 at the Foxwoods Resort and Casino in Connecticut. The winners that year included: Walela, "Warrior" Song of the Year; Joanne Shenendoah, Best Female Artist; R. Carlos Nakai, Best Male Artist; Litefoot, Best Rap Artist; Buffy Sainte-Marie, Best Pop Artist; Black Lodge Singers, Artist/Group of the year; Primeaux and Mike, Best Traditional Album (*Peyote Songs*); Black Lodge Singers, Best Powwow Album (*Enter the Circle*); Joanne Shenendoah, Best Children's Album; Record of the Year, *American Warriors, Songs of Indian Veterans* (various artists). The Nammy's have grown, and they have had subsequent annual awards ceremonies. In 2002 the prestigious Grammy Awards established a Native American category, and they have given awards to Primeaux and Mike and the Black Eagle Singers.

Native American groups continue to push the envelope by playing various types of genres including reggae, blues, jazz, metal, and traditional. With the establishment of two major music awards—the Nammy and the Grammy—Native American contemporary performers are performing for many types of audiences.

## NOTES

1. The terms most common in the United States are American Indian or Native American, and in Canada, First Nations and Aboriginal.

2. Each world is associated with a color, such as black, blue, or yellow, and accounts for how certain geographic places are sacred, when certain animals, plants, and insects appeared, and the relationship of deities, holy people, and the first man, first woman, and their offspring.

3. Tlingit means "people" and indicates the tribe and the language spoken, the same with Dine (Navajo), Miccosukee (Seminole), and others. Yup'ik, a cultural group in Alaska, translates their term (Yup'ik) to "real people."

4. Some tribes have been forcibly relocated to live in different areas then they originally occupied; other tribes are now using their own self-designative term for their tribe, rather than the pejorative word. For example, the Cherokee of the Southeast were removed to Oklahoma, which is in the Southern Plains.

5. The Spanish expeditions were military expeditions, and their main goal was to claim land for the Spanish crown, set up military settlements to either enslave or control the Indigenous peoples, and obtain silver, gold, and other commodities. The United States grew in 1803 with the Louisiana Purchase, in 1848 with the Treaty of Guadalupe Hidalgo, and again in 1867 with the purchase of Alaska.

6. One of the deciding factors in Spain's victory over the Aztecs was the introduction of smallpox, which wiped out 50 percent of the Indigenous population, making it much easier for the Spanish to maintain their control of the region.

7. The Northeast can be divided into three geographic regions that include the a) Coastal Region (eastern seaboard from Nova Scotia to North Carolina), b) Saint Lawrence Lowlands Region (Massachusetts to Delaware), and c) the Great Lakes-Riverine Region (Ohio Valley/upper Great Lakes). The main language families included Iroquoian, Algonquian, and Siouan. There are hundreds of tribes that inhabited this area and flourished, combining agriculture with hunting practices.

8. The Indigenous tribes in the Northeast had a religion and political organization entered on gatherings in very large longhouses—hence the term "People of the Longhouse." The Cherokee, Choctaw, Chickasaw, Seminole, and Creek constituted a large population and lived in what later became Georgia, Florida, North and South Carolina, Mississippi, Tennessee, and Louisiana. They developed their own written language, published their own newspaper, which impressed the Americans—who then called them the "Five Civilized tribes."Others included the Abenake and Wapenaki Confederacy, the Powhatan Confederacy, Panacook Federation of New England, the Three Fires of the Chippeawa, Ottawa, and Potawatomi, and the Illinois Confederacy/Tripartite Miamis.

9. "The early relations of the English colonies of Plymouth in New England and Jamestown in Virginia with the neighboring Indians were similar. The English relied on Indian hospitality, Indian food, and Indian advice, yet became increasingly overbearing, demanding, and insensitive to native rights (Smith 1910; Bradford 1952). Capt. Miles Standish for the Plymouth colony and Capt. John Smith for the Virginia colony moved into the hinterland browbeating native leaders, robbing Indian food caches, and obtaining food for their bickering comrades by trade or extortion. The peaceful relations early established between the races were strained by this behavior and awaited only an excess of zeal before war erupted." (Washburn, "Seventeenth-century Indian Wars," in *Handbook of North American Indians*, Vol. 15)

10. The French and British promised their Iroquois allies various rewards should they win. The war lasted from 1756-1763; the British won, but soon they were at war with the American colonists. Deciding which group to ally with further challenged the Iroquois Confederacy, and their Council Fires were again extinguished in 1777.

11. In 1838-39 the United States government forcibly removed most of the members of these tribes to present-day Oklahoma.

12. The women wear multiple turtle shell rattles on their lower legs.

13. The term "Sioux" is another pejorative term that was coined by French-Canadians who heard the term from the Ojibway (Nadowesioux), which meant "enemy/snake." The Sioux were in reality seven different tribes that had a population of over 20,000.

14. Some tribes refer to it as a "Prayer Dress."

15. There are 11 different Athabascan languages spoken in Alaska and each dialect also represents a unique culture area.

16. One can compare this to the differences between classical composers—such as Beethoven and Schubert, or Mozart and Clementi.

17. *Cross cousins* is a term used by anthropologists to describe the first cousin who is the child of the mother's brother or of the father's sister.

18. San Juan Pueblo has recently changed its name to *Oke Owinge*, its traditional name.

19. Kivas are the ceremonial houses used by religious societies of the Pueblos.

20. The Apache and Navajo speak Athabascan languages, but they are not mutually intelligible. Similarly, English and Dutch are closely related within the same language family but are not mutually intelligible.

## BIBLIOGRAPHY

Black Bear, Ben, Sr. and R.D. Theisz. *Songs and Dances of the Lakota: Cokatakiya Waci Uwo! Come Out to the Center and Dance!* Rosebud, South Dakota: Sinte Gleska College, 1976.

Cajete, Gregory A. *Native Science: Natural Laws of Interdependence.* Santa Fe: Clearlight Publishers, 2000.

Garcia, Peter, Joe M. Abeyta, Cirpirano Garcia, Jerry Garcia, Carpio Trujillo, and Rohn R. Trujillo. *Turtle Dance Songs of San Juan Pueblo.* LP liner notes. Taos: Indian House Records, 1972.

Grinde, Donald A., Jr. and Bruce E. Johansen. *Exemplar of Liberty: Native America and the Evolution of Democracy.* UCLA American Indian Studies Center, 1991.

Help, Marilyn and Ellen McCullough-Brabson. *We'll Be in Your Mountains, We'll Be in Your Songs: A Navajo Woman Sings.* Albuquerque: University of New Mexico Press, 2001.

Heth, Charlotte, ed. *Selected Reports in Ethnomusicology.* Volume III, No. 2. Los Angeles: University of California, 1980.

Heth, Charlotte, ed. *Native American Dance: Ceremonies and Social Traditions.* Smithsonian National Museum of the American Indian and Starwood, 1992.

Jorgenson, Joseph G. "Ghost Dance, Bear Dance, and Sun Dance." In *Handbook of North American Indians, Volume 11, the Great Basin.* Edited by Warren L. d'Azevedo. Washington, D.C.: Smithsonian Institution, 1986.

La Vigna, Maria. "Music for a Winter Ceremony: The Turtle Dance Songs of Oke Owinge," *Selected Reports in Ethnomusicology,* Volume III, No 2. Los Angeles: University of California, 1980.

McAllester, David and Douglas F. Mitchell. "Navajo Music." In *Handbook of North American Indians,* Volume 10, edited by Alfonso Ortiz. Washington, D.C.: Smithsonian, 1983.

McAllester, David. "North America/Native America/Navajo." In *Worlds of Music: An Introduction to the Music of the World's People,* 3rd edition, edited by Jeff Todd Titon. New York: Schirmer Books, 1996.

Ortiz, Alfonso. "Introduction." In *Handbook of North American Indians, Volume 9 and 10.* Edited by William Sturtevant. Washington, D.C.: Smithsonian Institution, 1979.

Siva, Ernest. Personal Interview, Los Angeles, California, 1989.

Swetzell, Rina and Dave Warren. "Shadeh." In *Native American Dance: Ceremonies and Social Traditions,* edited by Charlotte Heth. Washington, D.C.: Smithsonian National Museum of the American Indian, 1992: 93.

Tooker, Elizabeth. "The League of the Iroquois: Its History, Politics, and Ritual." In *Handbook of the North American Indian,* Volume 15, Northeast, Volume Editor Bruce G. Trigger. Washington, D.C.: Smithsonian Institution, 1978

Trudell, John. Personal Interview, Los Angeles, California, 1989.

Wallace, Anthony F.C. *The Death and Rebirth of the Seneca,* New York: Vintage Books, 1969.

## RECORDINGS

Ballard, Louis. *Two Mojave Bird Dance Songs.* Canyon Records C6050. 2004.
*Caddo Tribal Dances.* Indian House SC300. 1955.

Heth, Charlotte. *Songs and Dances of the Eastern Indians from Medicine Spring & Allegany*. New World Records 337. 1985.

Heth, Charlotte. *Songs of Love, Luck, Animals and Magic: Music of the Yurok and Tolowa Indians* (Sound Recording). Recorded Anthology of American Music, New York. 1977.

Heth, Charlotte. *Songs of the Muskogee Creek*, Parts 1 and 2. 1985.

Heth, Charlotte. *Ceremonial Music of Oke Owinge* (videorecording). Office of Instructional Development, American Indian Studies Publications, University of California, Los Angeles. 1978/1989.

Heth, Charlotte. *Music in the World of the Yurok and Tolowa Indians* (videorecording). Office of Instructional Development, American Indian Studies Publications, University of California, Los Angeles. 1978.

Primeaux and Mike *Walk In Beauty: Healing Songs of the Native American Church*. Phoenix Arizona, Canyon Records, 1995.

*Song of the Indian*. 197-. Canyon Records

Stevenson, Robert. *Music in Aztec and Inca Territory*. Berkeley: University of California Press, 1968.

*Stomp Dance—Volume 1: Muskogee, Seminole, Yuchi*. Jimmie Skeeeter, Oscar Pigeon, Vernon D. Atkiins, William M. Beaver, John Mcnac, Harry Bell. Recorded at Okemah, Oklahoma May 5, 1978, Indian House IH 3003, Taos, 1978.

*Traditional Apache Songs*. Canyon Records, 1970

*Turtle Dance Songs of San Juan Pueblo*. Indian House records IH 1101. 1972.

Westerman, Floyd. *Custer Died for your Sins*, LP. New York: Perception Records, 197-.

## FILMS

*American Indian Dance Theatre, Volume 1: Finding the Circle*. Canyon Records, Phoenix, Arizona, 1996.

*American Indian Dance Theatre, Volume 2: Dances for the New Generation*. Canyon Records Phoenix, AZ, 1996.

*Into the Circle: An Introduction to Native American Powwows and Celebrations*. Full Circle Comunications, Tulsa, Oklahoma, 1992.

Heth, Charlotte. *Ceremonial Music of Oke Owinge* (videorecording). Office of Instructional Development, American Indian Studies Publications, University of California, Los Angeles 1978/1989.

Heth, Charlotte. *Music in the World of the Yurok and Tolowa Indians* (videorecording). Office of Instructional Development, American Indian Studies Publications, University of California, Los Angeles, 1978.

Heth,, Charlotte. *Music of Sacred Fire: the Dance of the Oklahoma Cherokee* (videorecording). Ofice of Instructional Development, American Indian Studies Center Publications, University of California, Los Angeles, 1978.

Heth, Charlotte. *Navajo Traditional Music: Squaw Dance and Ribbon Dance* (videorecording). Office of Instructional Development, American Indian Studies Center Publications, University of California, Los Angeles, 1978.

Mirabal, Robert. *Music from a Painted Cave*. Connecticut Public Television, Native American Public Telecommunications, Producer, JoAnne Young, Director, Dennis Glore, 2001.

## WEBSITES

www.Cherokee.org.
www.powwows.com.
www.navajo.org.
www.malimuseum.org (Southern California tribes).

# 5

# Polka and Tamburitza: Ethnic Music and Dance Traditions in the Upper Midwest

Like gigantic, striped mushrooms, the polka festival's tents rose up on the grassy knolls surrounding Proch's Ballroom. The hot summer air of northwestern Wisconsin was heavy both with July's humidity and the aromas from bratwurst and burgers grilling in the nearby village of campers and RVs. We left the car on the recently-mowed hayfield now serving as a parking lot and trudged toward the big tents. From a distance, the music streaming from the three separate dance tents blended into a single mélange. Even in this homogenized form, I could still make out the madcap rollicking sense of the music—tubas bouncing like trained elephants, trumpets, saxes and clarinets blending in chorus to form a single rich-textured voice, and concertinas, the old plate reed squeezeboxes ringing in the high registers like musical toys, the mellower tapered reed boxes gently crooning out old-time melodies.

As we approached one of the dance floors, the sound of Karl and the Country Dutchmen began to drown out the music from the other tents. Concertina player Karl Hartwich, a lanky farm boy born in western Illinois, was churning out a steamy version of his signature tune, "Dance Hall Polka," an old Czech number. His casual dress, cutoff shorts, a T-shirt, and clod-hopper boots, belied his true seriousness about music and did not diminish the intensity of his stage presence. The fingers on both his hands flitted effortlessly over the concertina keys encasing the straightforward melody in syncopated, improvised runs. With his entire band playing without any sheet music, Karl projected complete control over the six-piece ensemble—tuba, drums, and a chording piano for rhythm, plus two brass and reed multi-instrumentalists who, switching from trumpets to clarinets, traded melody and counter melody parts with Karl's concertina. Even as he executed difficult passages on his instrument, Karl directed the band with his body language, grunting dramatically on one-beat breaks, calling out key changes, all the while smiling and nodding greetings to dancers as they passed by the stage.

We joined the swirling circling dancers who filled the creaking floor with rustling crinolines and the swishing slide of dance shoes. We were in a sea of brightly colored outfits—many dancers were wearing polka club vests edged in rick-rack, emblazoned with the names and logos of groups like the Polka Lovers Klub of America (PoLK of A), the Wisconsin Polka Boosters, or the Happy Hoppers. Dancers circled the floor, the skillful dancers bobbing in the "hop style" polka, in double time to the music. At the corners of the floor, the very best dancers, skilled couples usually in coordinated outfits, moved out of the circling flow for a moment to execute fancy high kicks and jitterbug-style polka moves they obviously had practiced at home. We smiled at our partners, young and old together, and kept moving around the dance floor as if on a carousel slowly spinning and spinning for as long as Karl provided the infectious polka beat.

A few hours later, in the early evening, Brian Brueggen and his Mississippi Valley Dutchmen were on stage playing up a storm, when a real storm blew up, a real gully washer. The skies darkened way too soon for July as big thunderheads raced over; streaks of lightning and deafening peals of thunder loosed the big drops that the heavy air had promised all day. Brian and the band played more wildly than ever; someone hollered an ironic request for "Rain Rain Polka," a well known standard. We stopped dancing only long enough to roll down the sides of the tent. While sheets of rain slapped the canvas, we danced on in the faint glow of a few bare incandescent light bulbs. Now we danced circle two-steps (mixers that reminded us that we were all in this mess together) with gleeful abandon as if the world outside could be floating away but in the tent, our circling musical universe could go on forever.

It's a fond memory from the Ellsworth Polka Fest, one of many such recollections from my lifelong infatuation with Midwestern music traditions. My musical voyage began as a little kid at Croatian picnics in Chicago. I remember feeling surprised to see my Aunt Tonka suddenly open her mouth wide and to hear her let out an impassioned shriek, "Yu-yu-yu-yu-yu," as she danced an intricate *kolo* line dance, a tongue-twister for the feet, to the likewise intricate tinkling of the Skertich Brothers tamburitza combo's strings. As an adult I frequented my neighborhood's small corner taverns on Milwaukee's predominantly Polish Southside where the little concertina and drums duos like Concertina Millie Kaminski or Al Roberts Gostomski were all that was needed to keep the patrons' toes tapping as they sipped tap beer on barstools, or to keep three or four couples twirling on a tiny vinyl-tiled dance floor. As the state folklorist for Wisconsin for more than 20 years, my path has led on to country crossroads and small town centers all over Wisconsin and in its neighboring states, where venerable and spacious ballrooms, with gleaming hardwood floors, resounded to the pulsating rhythms of old-time dance bands. As a radio program producer and on-air host, Midwestern old time musicians sought me out, thanking me for playing their stuff and pressing promo copies of their latest recordings in my hand. As a musician, usually a sideman but also sometimes as a bandleader, I've played my button accordion atop a hayrick stage for a country pig roast, clunked banjo rhythm behind skilled concertina players in taverns and halls, and tickled the strings of my tamburitza in church basements as well as in fancy hotel ballrooms. There may be a paucity of written sources about these traditions, especially synthetic works, so mainly I am writing from my personal experience of these musical worlds.

## ETHNICITY IN MIDWESTERN TRADITIONAL MUSIC

The traditional musics of the Midwest (and it is imperative to use the plural "musics") ultimately spring from the vibrant cultures of the region's ethnic communities.

When one opens *The Atlas of Ethnic Diversity in Wisconsin* (University of Wisconsin Press, Madison, 1998) to page 70, a striking statistic stands out. In the 1990 U.S. Census, out of a population of nearly five million, only 76,558 people indicated their ethnicity as unhyphenated "American"—just 1.57 percent. On a small U.S. map in the upper left hand corner of the page, maroon colored circles on each state's map indicate the size of their unhyphenated "American" populations. The states of the South and the East Coast are nearly obliterated in maroon while in the Midwest, there is very little of that color on Wisconsin, Minnesota, Iowa, Nebraska, and the Dakotas. There's a bit more on Michigan, Illinois, and Ohio, while Indiana is virtually all maroon. The Wisconsin statistic is significant, and the map is literally a graphic indication of an important feature of Midwestern culture. Many Midwesterners tend to be conscious of their Old World origins. Of course, this heritage-consciousness has a direct bearing on their various traditional cultural practices, handicrafts, foodways, holiday celebrations, and of course, the traditional music that characterize the region.

The part of the region with the very little maroon circles is known as the Upper Midwest, and here the sense of ethnic identity is very much present in most of the population. Upper Midwesterners think of themselves, for example, as German-Americans, Polish-Americans, Luxemburger-Americans, or through inter-marriage, as a combination of these and/or a host of other hyphenated American nationalities. In the Upper Midwest, people often will ask the ethnic provenance of your last name if it is not already obvious. A typical reply might be something like this: "'Lervik' is Norwegian. Actually I'm Norwegian and Swiss on my father's side, but my mother is German and

Cornish." The responder might practice a few traditions from one, two, or even all of these backgrounds—attend a Norwegian lutefisk dinner, dance a Swiss laendler at the New Glarus Hotel to a yodeling accordionist's music, enjoy playing the German card game Sheepshead (*Schapkopf*) with friends and for a hearty meal, bake Cornish pasties, meat pies containing beef, pork, potatoes, and rutabaga.

Ethnicity pervades the various activities of Upper Midwestern life, including traditional music, of course. In this article there will be several of the ethnically named musical traditions of the Upper Midwest focusing on the European-American traditions of communities that immigrated to the Midwest during the nineteenth and early twentieth centuries. Of course there are many other ethnic musical traditions present in the Midwest, but these are the main ones to focus on here. I'll emphasize the four distinct polka music traditions—German, Czech, Polish, and Slovenian—but also discuss Scandinavian and Eastern European musics that rely less on polka's characteristic 2/4 tempo.

## WHERE IS THE UPPER MIDWEST?

Cultural regions seldom follow exactly along state lines. The term "Upper Midwest" has come into use to name a distinction Midwesterners understand. There is a noticeable difference between the culture of the "Lower Midwest," southern portions of states like Ohio, Illinois, most of Indiana and Missouri, and that of "the Uppers," Minnesota, Wisconsin, Michigan, and the northern portions of Illinois, Ohio, Iowa. The Jackson & Perkins rose growers Web site aptly calls the Lower Midwest "where the South meets the North." While they are referring to climate, the statement is also true of culture. Lower Midwestern traditional culture has a lot in common with the Upland South—the vernacular accent, the old time fiddle music, and lots of residents who characterize themselves as unhyphenated Americans. The Upper Midwest, the true North, is culturally a very heterogeneous region, with communities that have retained consciousness of their heterogeneity through several generations in America.

There can be no precise map dividing the Upper and Lower Midwest. For 14 years (1986–2000), in the standard intro to my weekly public radio show "Down Home Dairyland," to give a general idea of the Upper Midwestern geographic area where the music came from, listeners heard "from Detroit to the Dakotas, from Chicago to Chequamegon Bay" (on Lake Superior). Sometimes the boundary expanded east of Detroit into northern Ohio, but the Dakotas-Detroit alliteration sounded good on the radio. The geographic focus of this article is the same as for the Down Home Dairyland program.

## REGIONAL TRADITIONS WITH ETHNIC NAMES

One would be hard-pressed to name only a single musical example that would be emblematic of the Upper Midwest. Much as the population continues to recognize its aforementioned heterogeneity of origin, the traditional music forms heard in the Upper Midwest are very heterogeneous as well. Quite often the musical traditions bear an obviously ethnic name: Slovenian-style polka, Hungarian *csardas* music, Swedish fiddling. Sometimes the ethnic provenance is made more obscure in the generally used term: Bohemian brass bands, Dutchman music, tamburitza music. In these cases, the Czech-Americans from Bohemia (Cechy, the western province of today's Czech Republic, which was a part of the Austro-Hungarian Empire at the time the pioneers of these farming communities immigrated to the United States) have been more apt to call their music by the name of their European ancestors' home region than the term "Czech." The name of Dutchman music, a genre of German-American music that originated in Minnesota, has nothing to do with Hollanders; "Dutch" is from the American corruption of "Deutsch," meaning German. Tamburitza music, played mostly by Croatian- and Serbian-Americans, is named for the family of fretted stringed instruments used in this idiom, avoiding nationality entirely in the musical genre's designation.

Despite ethnic or ethnic-referent names, many of the musical traditions involve participants from a variety of ethnic backgrounds. Slovenian-style polka is played, of course, by members of that small Slavic ethnic group. However, because of the nationwide popularity of its best-known exponent, Frankie Yankovic, Slovenian polka became the favored regional polka style in many places, especially in industrial cities like Cleveland, Milwaukee, and Duluth, and in rural areas of Wisconsin, Minnesota, and Michigan. In these places there are numerous "Yankovic-style" bands with no Slovenes whatsoever.

In many areas, one ethnically-named traditional music has become the conventional form of music at weddings, anniversaries, and old-time dance parties. For example, in northeastern Wisconsin, Czech immigrants established a strong musical tradition of Bohemian brass bands. Their music became accepted by the rest of the area's population, primarily Germans, Belgians, Danes, and Poles. In fact, trumpeter Romy Gosz, an icon of that music style, the leader of the most famous Bohemian polka band from the 1930s to the 1960s, was not Czech but of German background. Today, an outstanding northeastern Wisconsin Bohemian polka band is directed by Clete Bellin, a proud Walloon Belgian. Clete is fluent in the Walloon dialect of French, has a beautiful singing voice, and knows many old Walloon songs. Nonetheless, when he sings with his Bohemian band he sings in very accurate, well pronounced Czech, having been carefully coached in the language by Czech friends.

Stevens Point in central Wisconsin is predominantly Polish-American, but in that area two polka styles co-exist—"Dutchman" German-style and Chicago Polish-style polka. Despite the fact that most of their members are Polish-American, bands like the Jolly Chaps and the Polka Stars play in the Dutchman style, a legacy of the popularity of Whoopee John and of the Six Fat Dutchmen, touring bands from Minnesota who in Stevens Point played dances and were heard on radio broadcasts from Minnesota stations. Stevens

Point's Polka Stars have recorded the well known Polish folk song *"Pitala sie pani,"* singing in Polish to German-American Dutchman-style accompaniment. The Dutchman polka style dominated in central Wisconsin from the 1930s until the 1960s when a local band, the Happy Notes led by Norm Dombrowski, sought to emulate the Polish-style polkas of Chicago's Little Wally. Gradually the Polish style gained ground in the area until now it is more frequently heard there than the Dutchman bands.

Tamburitza music, played on a family of acoustic fretted stringed instruments ranging from smaller than a mandolin to as large as a string bass, has not become the predominant music in any geographic zone. It thrives in festive events of the Croatian and Serbian communities. Nevertheless, a significant number of musicians from other ethnic backgrounds made important contributions to the tradition: Steve Makarewitch of Gary, Indiana, was a Ruthenian. His forebears hailed from eastern Slovakia. Nonetheless he became noted as an outstanding *primaš*, a player of the highest pitched lead instrument of the tamburitza family. Chicago's Kontraband ensemble features Robi Sestili, an Italian-American who grew up with the tamburitza tradition. His father Bob Sestili was a longtime bass player in Western Pennsylvania tamburitza groups. Milwaukee youth tamburitza instructor Julie Kutz Ewend is of German and Polish background, and her mother Joan Kutz, though not Croatian, has long served as the president of the Croatian Fraternal Union's Junior Cultural Federation, the most important organization promoting instruction of youth in tamburitza music.

The Midwestern ethnic musical subcultures usually feature two distinct types of ensembles: amateur music and/or dance groups that perform on stage, presenting arranged and choreographed versions of the singing, instrumental music, and/or dance of their ethnic group; and professional and semi-professional music groups that play for pay at the festive events of the ethnic communities. Amateur music and dance societies have existed in the Midwest since the nineteenth century. Typically they are a large group featuring a score or more participants, clad in folk costumes from Old World villages or replicas sewn in America. Such groups assert that they are preserving the "authentic" musical and dance heritage from the mother country. The professional bands, in contrast, tend to be much smaller—from a solo accordionist to a trio to a six or seven piece band. The degree to which they foreground ethnic heritage in their performances varies from band to band and even from performance to performance by the same band, depending upon the particular audience. Sometimes they may emphasize the ethnic heritage aspect of what they perform. At other times they stress their eclecticism and modernity. Often they are just playing for informal dancing or to entertain a tavern crowd.

A case in point would be the Goose Island Ramblers, a "Norwegian Polkabilly" trio from Madison, Wisconsin, led by K. Wendell Whitford from the late 1930s until 1999. Whitford was of English background but grew up on a farm in predominantly Norwegian southeastern Dane County, learning fiddle tunes from his Norwegian neighbors. He also learned to sing and play guitar, reproducing the sentimental ballads of Bradley Kincaid and other Southern crooners, which he heard on the radio. Whitford also composed several original ballads in that idiom. The Ramblers' lineup with the greatest longevity included two Norwegians, fiddler George Gilbertsen and accordionist Bruce Bollerud, along with Whitford. Bollerud was a farm boy from Hollandale who learned a lot of music from the Norwegian immigrant farm hands who worked in his parents' dairy operation. Gilbertsen was a fiddle prodigy who already in his early teens began playing (contrary to the liquor laws) in taverns in his native neighborhood, the industrial east side of Madison.

During the 1960s and 1970s, the Ramblers had steady Friday night gigs at two Madison taverns, Glen and Ann's and later Johnny's Packer Inn. They attracted a very devoted crowd of followers who came nearly every Friday night. The musical favorites and ethnic proclivities of their audience were varied. Thus their eclectic repertoire included old time country music songs and hoedown tunes, German, Polish, and Slovenian polkas, Norwegian schottisches and waltzes, and several localized parodies of well known popular or country songs. The performances included many comedic elements. They rang cowbells at the close of numbers, or they tooted on bird calls and howled like dogs if the song lyrics mentioned those animals. Bruce feigned extreme drunkenness when performing the county music chestnut "Mountain Dew" or the German-American dialect song "Milwaukee Waltz." He brought several hats and caps to the gigs—a cowboy hat, a Norwegian farm hand's work hat, a railroad engineer's cap—donning the hat appropriate to the tune being played. George tied on a bonnet fitted with long yellow yarn braids and an apron to become the amorous Norwegian widow "Mrs. Johnson" (pronounced Yahn-sohn), or while playing dobro on "Norwegian War Chant" (a parody of "Hawaiian War Chant"). George donned a "Viking" helmet fashioned from a milk pail and a couple cow horns.

Their performances clearly denote the Norwegian ethnic identity of the band—including Whitford's "Norwegian by association" status. Bruce Bollerud, who is a fluent Norwegian speaker, sings several songs in that language. Even the name of the band derives from a local toponym that is a corruption of the Norwegian "gode land." Nonetheless, the German and Polish numbers in the Ramblers' repertoire represent a nod to the multi-ethnic composition of the working-class Madison populace that comprised the bulk of their audience, and the country music repertoire represented a shared American popular culture that fit the musical aesthetics of their ethnic performances.

Neither strictly "authentic" ethnic display nor de-ethnicized mainstream culture, the Goose Island Ramblers performances embody the ethnic versus mainstream dialectic that so many Upper Midwestern bands navigate. Another would be the most influential Polish-American band of the later twentieth century, Eddie Blazonczyk's Versatones. They move from Polish ethnic pride when Eddie sings folk songs with his beautiful voice in perfect Polish, to asserting American identity with their cover of a Merle Haggard country hit, played in their Polish-American polka style. Rather than wearing Polish folk costumes, the band, whose very name was chosen to suggest their versatility, sports matching Hawaiian shirts, dress that now has become standard for Polish polka bands, perhaps symbolizing an American "party animal" identity.

The ethnic versus mainstream dialectic implies a temporal dialectic as well. Foregrounding ethnicity usually embodies a venerable old heritage, representative of an imagined golden era from the community's past. Mainstream popular culture equals modernity. There are several ways in which Midwestern ethnic bands can invoke varying degrees of an old-timey nature or show their up-to-date acumen. Singing song lyrics in a European language other than English or feigning an immigrant's thick accent in non-native English or a Celtic brogue typically denotes the past, an old time heritage. Singing a recent pop song or Nashville-sound hit denotes modernity. But an "American" old-timeyness can also be invoked by singing decades-old pop or country chestnuts like "You Are My Sunshine" or "In the Good Old Summertime."

The instruments used also can denote traditionality or modernity. The degree to which changing instrumental technology has been accepted into a music tradition varies quite a bit within and between the Upper Midwestern ethnic music genres. Slovenian-American polka was profoundly modernized by Frankie Yankovic, who as a boy in the 1930s, with the connivance of his understanding mother, overcame the strident opposition of his father to allow him to acquire and play a modern piano keyboard accordion instead of the traditional diatonic Alpine button box. Yankovic later introduced electronic accordions and the Solovox, an early electronic organ, into his Slovenian polka style. Other bandleaders in this style introduced raunchy-toned saxophone playing, reminiscent of 1950s rock and roll, supplanting the more traditional clarinet.

For more than two decades beginning in the late 1940s, these modernized polka bands were all the rage in the Slovenian ethnic community, and their music also "crossed over" to enjoy a broad mainstream following in the commercial music industry. Nonetheless, during the heritage-conscious 1970s there was a resurgence of interest in the button accordion. Button box clubs were formed (at first) primarily in Slovenian ethnic communities, in many cases with instigation from the ethnic fraternal SNPJ (Slovenian National Benefit Society). Today in the Slovenian polka scene, contemporary "Yankovic-style" bands using everything from MIDI-units to occasional drum machine units coexist with button box clubs who play acoustic instruments whose basic technology is a century and a half old. And to invoke an element of older traditionality, the accordionists in some Yankovic-style polka bands have learned to play a few numbers on the Alpine button accordion and will strap on that instrument for a tune or two during their performances.

Polemics about the appropriateness of instrumental innovations are particularly fierce among players in genres where the instrument itself is defined as the item of revered heritage and defines the genre—such as the Hardanger fiddle and the tamburitza. You couldn't substitute an electric fiddle or even a normal violin for a Hardanger fiddle. Playing that specific instrument is the point. It is an ornate type of violin with a flatter bridge and fingerboard featuring five sympathetic vibration strings which pass under the fingerboard. The oldest still-extant Hardanger fiddles date from the mid-seventeenth century. Hardanger fiddle is considered by many to be the national instrument of Norway and therefore a part of Norwegian-American heritage.

The various-sized tamburitza instruments likewise define the music genre. The archetypical ensemble features the five different-sized tamburitza fretted string instruments. But other instruments have crept into use in tamburitza combos, sometimes sparking controversy. Players disagree about the appropriateness of substituting a normal string bass for the fretted, steel-stringed *berde*. The violin and the accordion have been accepted in some bands as long as the tamburitza sound is still prominent. Since the 1970s, there have been a few groups that use the rhythm section of a pop or rock band—electric bass, rhythm guitar, and a drum set with a plugged-in tamburitza playing the lead part. Some tamburitza enthusiasts refer to these groups pejoratively as "boom-boom bands," while others are more positive, feeling this type of music provides a way to attract to tamburitza events more young people who are used to a rock-style "bottom" on the music.

## POLKA FROM EUROPE TO AMERICA

Many of the European-American dance music traditions in the Midwest, though quite distinct, are often lumped together, referred to as "polka bands." Before taking a closer look at the distinct and separate polka traditions, it may be helpful to say a few words about polka in general. The polka suddenly emerged in the 1840s and quickly swept all over Europe. Initially it was popular with the elite class, but during the second half of the nineteenth century the polka spread to the common people, urbanites first and eventually to peasants. The exact origin of this lively dance is hard to pinpoint. Several versions of an origin legend for the polka have appeared in print. The legends usually ascribe invention of the dance to a nameless Czech servant girl whose Austrian employer, also nameless, and usually a schoolteacher, noted it down. Next, the polka was being played and danced all over Europe and beyond. Of course, the legend's historical veracity is suspect. How did a single girl demonstrate a couples' dance? What kind of written dance notation could this schoolteacher have known? And how could enough other people read that notation to start a sudden international dance fad? Nonetheless, the legend was good hype to promote a popular craze reflective of the Romantic-era infatuation that the European intellectuals then had for an idealized view of the peasantry. It is notable, however, that in order to become significant, the Slavic peasant girl's polka dance still needed to be validated (in writing) by the learned Austrian man.

In the mid-nineteenth century, the ongoing Industrial Revolution was producing a new urban and small town middle class that was receptive to new cultural expressions reflecting their lives. Whoever may have been polka's original creator cannot be known, but clearly this provocative new music and dance spoke to the spirit of the times. Thus, the polka is an early example of a popular culture dance fad—a couples' dance, a break from earlier traditional line dances. The United States also was rapidly industrializing at this time, and streams of immigrants from Europe crossed the Atlantic. Since the polka happened to be widely popular at the time they journeyed to the United States, the nineteenth century immigrants from central Europe brought with them an affinity for that dance and its associated music. Once in America, several central European ethnic groups continued to emphasize polka music and dancing in the festive events of their communities. In some cases, their continuing devotion to polka in the United States outstripped that of their co-nationals in the homeland, where subsequent dance fads overshadowed the polka. Several immigrant groups in America defined the polka as an element of their ethnic identity, preserving its importance in the New World community.

## ACCORDIONS AND CONCERTINAS

The musical instruments most commonly associated with the polka are the free reed squeezeboxes, accordions, and concertinas. As early as the 1820s, tinkerers in England, France, and Germany began to experiment with making a new type of musical instrument based on the recently acquired European acquaintance with the Chinese free reed instrument the *sheng*. Applying the industrial notion of mechanization, they joined bellows, springs, and levers with the metal reeds to create mechanical instruments on which one musician could replace a small ensemble of earlier instruments. With the right hand, a squeezebox player had melody and harmony; on the left, rhythm chords and bass notes. Small manufacturers of these automatic one-man-band instruments sprang up, making them available and relatively inexpensive. Moreover, compared to an organ or piano, a squeezebox was highly portable and, mounted in sturdy wooden boxes, not too fragile. Squeezeboxes were a prized possession carried in many an immigrant's baggage or ordered from an Old World maker as soon as finances allowed.

Thus, the American polka traditions so prevalent in the Upper Midwest are a result of a confluence of three streams emanating from the cultural and social changes in an industrializing world—the mid-nineteenth century polka dance fad in Europe, mass immigration from Europe to the United States, and ready availability of the newly invented accordions and concertinas.

## AMERICAN POLKA TRADITIONS

Germans, Czechs, Swiss, Poles, and Slovenians have been the most active in perpetuating polka traditions in the Midwest. Also, many Swedes, Norwegians, Danes, Finns, Belgians, Dutch, Ukrainians, Italians, Croatians, and other European-Americans identify with and participate in polka activities, and musicians from those groups have made significant contributions to Midwestern polka.

The nineteenth century polka craze also entered Mexico from Europe, and Mexican musicians in Texas have interacted with musical German, Polish, and Czech immigrants there to shape the polka style of the Texas-Mexican *conjuntos* (bands). During the twentieth century, Mexican-Americans have migrated to many areas of the Midwest, bringing with them the Southwestern *conjunto* style of polka music and dancing.

Folklorists generally like to stress the cultural community-based creative process, often de-emphasizing the role of individual artists. Nonetheless, in music traditions, ever since the phonograph and radio made it possible for outstanding musicians to be heard nearly everywhere, individual trendsetting musicians have frequently defined the paradigm of musical idioms. This text will focus upon those individuals, the paradigm-definers of the contemporary forms of polka and related ethnic musical genres. Unlike Bill Monroe and B. B. King, who have had enormous influence on bluegrass and blues, respectively, the contributions of polka and ethnic musical pioneers are still too little known outside of their in-groups.

Early recordings of polka music can be found on 78-rpm discs produced at the beginning of the twentieth century. Some were recorded in Europe and marketed to the American ethnic communities, while others were recordings of immigrant musicians made mostly in New York and Chicago. The earliest recordings reveal a very diverse array of instrumentation and performance styles. Polkas were played, for example, by large brass bands, by solo accordionists, or by fiddle and concertina duos. The labels on the discs frequently were in languages other than English, and often the immigrants' musics differed little from their European antecedents. After several decades of gestation in the Midwestern environment, distinctive American polka traditions began to emerge by the late 1920s. The 1930s, 1940s, and 1950s proved to be the decades in which the music played by key influential bands became the models that defined the four main American polka styles—German, Polish, Bohemian, and Slovenian. Each style evolved a standard instrumental lineup, a core repertoire, and a distinct set of musical aesthetics.

In the same era that the distinct styles were emerging, the polka also achieved its greatest prominence in American commercial music. By the mid-1930s, the records of Manitowoc, Wisconsin's premier trumpet player Romy Gosz gained widespread attention for his Bohemian Czech style of polka. The "Beer Barrel Polka" was a popular sensation in 1938–39 in versions by the Will Glahe band and especially the later vocal version by the Andrews Sisters. During the World War II era, ironically, the German-American music of Minnesota's "Whoopee John" Wilfahrt began to attain national popularity. His Decca recordings of "Clarinet Polka" and "Mariechen Waltz" were million sellers. The musical career of Cleveland's Frankie Yankovic, perhaps the most widely known popular polka musician, had to wait until after he completed his service in the U.S. Army. He nearly lost his hands to severe frostbite in the

Battle of the Bulge. Refusing amputation, he was fortunate that his accordion-playing hands recovered, enabling him to play his huge post-war hits: "Just Because," a re-worked hillbilly number, and "Blue Skirt Waltz," an old Czech tune with new Tin Pan Alley lyrics. A few years younger than Yankovic, Little Wally Jagiello emerged in the late 1940s as the teenaged musical sensation of Chicago's Polish community. For nearly 20 years Lil' Wally set the standard for the folksy, improvisational, so-called "Chicago" or "honky" Polish polka style—played in small combos of two to six pieces. But in the 1960s, a younger fellow Chicagoan, Eddie Blazonczyk, updated the honky style that has defined the paradigm for Polish-American polka bands ever since.

The interest in polka on the part of the commercial music world waned by the later 1950s. Elvis Presley became a sensation, and rock and roll became the next music craze, relegating polka to the popular music margins. Although exiled from the mainstream media, polka has continued to thrive and evolve as the bands continued to play and record, but not so much in the popular music industry as in the ethnic communities and on ethnic record labels. It was back where the music originated.

## POLKA TODAY

Nowadays polka continues to be played and danced to in corner taverns in blue-collar urban neighborhoods and at crossroads road houses in rural areas. However, fewer and fewer of these venues offer live music and dancing, so in order to hear and dance to their favorite music, polka dancers have established clubs to promote their avocation. The polka dance clubs or ballroom operators organize dozens of polka festivals throughout the Upper Midwest concentrated in the summer months. Some are national in scope—like the International Polka Association's festival each August in the Chicago area. Others, like the Mid-Winter Polka Fest at the Chandelier Ballroom in Hartford, Wisconsin, draw from a more limited geographic area. There are retiree dancing enthusiasts who travel all summer by RV from one polka fest to another.

Most festivals emphasize a single style of polka—German, Polish, Slovenian, or Czech. But some larger polka festivals may broaden the offering. The Gibbon Polka Festival in Minnesota emphasizes Dutchman music but also hires some Slovenian bands and occasionally a Polish band. The Central Wisconsin Polka Fest in Merrill usually has an equal number of Polish and German bands on two separate stages. To draw an audience, the festivals compete to hire the most popular dance bands in their featured styles. They also stress the quality of the dance floor to lure the avid dancers. It is expected that polka festival participants will spend most of their time dancing, four or more hours straight, with only brief respites to sip drinks, munch sausages, and rest the feet.

At festivals, on the edge of the stage or on a folding table beside the dance floor, there will be schedules of the bands' future gigs and lots of fliers proclaiming the stellar lineup at upcoming polka festivals. Monthly and bi-weekly newsletters and newspapers like the *Polka News*, *Music and Dance News*, and the *Wisconsin Polka Boosters Newsletter* list dozens of opportunities to polka.

Mainstream record companies like Mercury and Capitol dropped polka artists during the 1960s, leaving the polka labels that existed then, like Polka-land in Sheboygan and Jay Jay in Chicago, to be the sole disseminators. New successful polka labels also arose during the 1960s: Bel-Aire in Chicago, and Dana in Massachusetts. Today, polka fans complain that they can find little or none of their favorite music in record stores. They have to seek out an ethnic specialty store that handles, for example, Polish or German souvenirs to find a rack of recordings. Today most polka bands produce their own recordings, which they sell at their gigs or provide copies to be marketed through mail-order and online polka outlets.

## GERMAN POLKA

The origin of Dutchman music may well have been in 1904 when Barbara Portner Wilfahrt, a farm woman from Sigel Township on the plains of southern Minnesota, made what must have been a difficult decision. She spent $3 of the scant cash assets that a farm family would have had on...a concertina. Some might have viewed it as an extravagance for a family that included more than 10 children, but Barbara was from musical stock, German

Whoopee John and his band photographed at the WTCN studios in 1937. Front row, L to R: Harold "Andy" Anderson, Theodore "Teddy" Hofmeister, Hugo "Hooks" Hofmeister, Whoopee John W. Wilfahrt. Back row, L to R: Donald "PeeWee" Rice, Otto "Ottie" Hofmeister, Patrick "Pat" Wilfahrt. Edna Istel on piano. Photo courtesy of Dennis Brown.

immigrants from Bohemia, a very musical place. And she sensed that her 11-year-old son John Anthony had some of her family's innate musical talent in him. Her maternal instinct was on target. One day as she was doing her housework, she was unconsciously humming a folk tune from Bohemia, "Mariechen Waltz." To her astonished delight, John picked up the squeezebox and played the tune, matching her humming note for note. This story became a family anecdote, and that waltz eventually became the theme song for his world-famous ensemble, the Whoopee John Band.

In the 1860s, Germans from Bohemia began immigrating to Sigel Township, southwest of the town of New Ulm in Brown County, Minnesota. By the 1880s some had migrated into New Ulm, particularly to the *Gansviertel* or Goosetown neighborhood. The earlier German immigrants who had settled the town a decade or two before the "Bohemians" began to arrive and who congregated around the *Turnverein* gymnastic society's Turner's Hall viewed the newcomers as bumpkins. Nonetheless, by the middle of the twentieth century it was the music originated by these rubes from Bohemia that became a national phenomenon and put New Ulm on the map as the "Polka Capital of the Nation."

After a few years of practicing in the family grain bin, at the age of 15 John Wilfahrt performed for parties as a soloist on concertina, and by 1909 he had formed a trio with his brother Edwin on clarinet and a cousin Edwin Kretsch on trumpet. By 1915 the band grew to six players. By the later 1920s, the group became consistently known as the Whoopee John Band. Concerning that nickname, there is an anecdote that John's band arrived late to an engagement, prompting an enthusiastic fan to shout, "Whoopee, John is here!" The nickname may have stuck more because of the whooping "yoo hoo hoo" yodels with which John accented his performances.

By the 1930s the Whoopee John Band had an 11-member lineup that was to characterize it henceforth and set the ideal standard for "Dutchman" bands for years to come—three brass, three reeds, tuba, drums, banjo, piano, and concertina. The band emulated the trappings of professionalism used by the popular Big Band dance ensembles of that era. The sidemen tended to dress in matching suits and sat behind painted bandstands emblazoned with the band's name or logo, sometimes including the call letters of radio stations that broadcast their performances. Their regional/ethnic character usually was confined to the character of bandleader Whoopee John himself. By the 1930s he tended to front the band dressed in knickers and flower-ornamented suspenders—mimicking lederhosen—and a plumed Jaeger's hat. Though he still played the concertina, the instrument became less prominent musically in his band's brass and reed dominated arrangements, and more of a showbiz prop. He extended the concertina's long bellows with a flourish and sometimes whirled the entire instrument over his head. Like the popular big bands of that era, the brass and reed instruments produced a blended melodic sound, but the rhythm section was different. The oompah rhythm produced by tuba, piano, banjo, and drums defined Whoopee John as a polka band.

L to R: Al Kopotski, Eddie Wilfahrt, John Wilfahrt, Jr. (Whoopee John), Otto Stueber, and John "Boom Boom" Bauer. Ernst Wilfahut and Louis Soukup's wedding, 1924. Photo courtesy of Dennis Brown.

Professional touring bands like Whoopee John's had become possible owing to technological advances: radio, recordings, automobiles, and better roads. The advent of radio and improvements in phonograph records in the 1920s fundamentally altered the environment in which Midwestern traditional musicians performed. Before radio and widespread use of records, local dance bands formed with whatever instruments and players were available, and played the tunes that were known in local tradition or that someone had acquired sheet music for. In old photographs of wedding parties, the musicians came in myriad combinations, and early recordings from the first two decades of the twentieth century reveal many idiosyncratic styles of play. Radio and records made it possible for certain influential ensembles like Whoopee John's to set a standard for a musical genre. Musicians heard the popular radio entertainers, bought their records, and these influenced them when forming their own combos. Whoopee John recorded prolifically, initially for Okeh, Vocalion, Brunswick, and Columbia; then after 1938 he recorded over 200 records for Decca. In all, the band recorded more than 1,000 sides. The instrumentation, the core repertoire, and even the typical type of arrangement for Dutchman music was originally set by the Whoopee John Band. The name of the genre, however, came from a later upstart band from New Ulm, formed in 1932 by tuba player Harold Loeffelmacher—the Six Fat Dutchmen, incidentally, a band that usually featured not six but at least eight or nine musicians. Loeffelmacher was a tuba player, so in addition to contributing the Dutchman name to the genre, the Six Fats sound also gave additional emphasis to rollicking, bouncy tuba lines from the bandleader's instrument.

It was possible to pick up Whoopee John's radio broadcasts from Minneapolis stations WTCN and WCCO in several surrounding states. Automobiles,

L to R: Ray Ries, Hugo Hofmeister, Whoopee John (also known as John Wilfahrt, Jr.), Emil "Rumpfy" Domeier, Bennie Kitzberger, and Otto Stueber. Wedding reception on a farm, 1928. Photo courtesy of Dennis Brown.

trailers, buses, and paved highways made it possible for the band to travel to gigs in the entire area in which the radio broadcasts were heard—especially Minnesota, the Dakotas, Nebraska, Iowa, Wisconsin, and northern Illinois. Throughout this area, additional Dutchman-style bands proliferated: Fezz Fritsche and the Goosetown Band, the Emil Domeier Band, Elmer Scheid and his Hoolerie Band, the Jolly Lumberjacks, Ray Dorschner and the Rainbow Valley Dutchmen, and Paulsen's Dutchmen, to name just a few. These bands often featured a smaller lineup, but stylistically they tended to emulate the style's pioneer bands, Whoopee John and the Six Fat Dutchmen.

John Wilfahrt passed away in 1961, but the band had incredible longevity. John's sons Patrick and Dennis continued to run the band until the end of the 1960s. In 1970, another Minnesota musician, Vern Steffel, purchased the band's arrangements and operated the reborn Whoopee John Band on-and-off until the early 1990s.

Even as the originally influential bands Whoopee John and the Six Fat Dutchmen continued to tour, the Dutchman style was evolving in other stylistic directions. Whoopee John's instrument, the Chemnitzer concertina, which had assumed no more than a minor role in the arrangements played by his band, re-emerged to become the most important Dutchman instrument. With improved sound systems, it became possible to effectively amplify the concertina—no longer overpowered by the trumpets and saxophones. Elmer Scheid, also from New Ulm, was one of the first outstanding concertina players to reclaim a major role for his instrument in the band's sound. Syl Liebl, who as a teenager moved from southern Minnesota to West Salem, Wisconsin, proved to be the seminal figure inspiring a younger generation of Dutchman musicians to take the music in a new direction. Whoopee John and the Six Fats were polished bands. They played from written arrangements. It was smaller, less prominent local bands, especially in rural areas, that continued to play by ear. Jim Kirchstein, the owner-operator of Cuca Records in Sauk City, Wisconsin, recalled that Syl's Jolly Swiss Boys, a five or six piece group, had an uncanny ability to play spontaneously. Syl would call out the name of a number and they all just started to play, the concertina trading solos with the wind instruments until the number reached its culmination and they'd effortlessly end together. Kirchstein remembered that they recorded most of the tunes in one take on the several albums they did on Cuca in the 1960s and 1970s. Syl's concertina playing was visceral, like singing, listeners said. His improvised grace notes and riffs between melodic lines were unprecedented. His band's infectious improvised music was more appealing to some younger musicians, especially Karl Hartwich, from Trempealeau, Wisconsin, and a pair of first cousins, Brian and Gary Brueggen from Cashton, Wisconsin. Karl, born in 1961, after an apprenticeship involving sitting in with Syl's band, started his own group at age 13 with his mother Norma on tuba. He quickly became a sensation. Building upon Syl Liebl's style, Karl emphasized the riffs and accentuated syncopation and generally made the music burst with life and enthusiasm. He has had 30 years of touring with his band the Country Dutchmen, although only in his mid-40s, and is widely acknowledged as the finest player ever of the Chemnitzer concertina in the Dutchman style.

Another outstanding Chemnitzer concertina player, Brian Brueggen comes from a family that has contributed five generations of musicians to their western Wisconsin rural community, going back to the mid-nineteenth century. Brian served his musical apprenticeship in his father's and uncles' band, the Ridgeland Dutchmen. After graduating from high school, Brian left Wisconsin to play with an Ohio polka band, but in the mid-1980s he was persuaded by his father to return, with the promise that they'd start a new group—Brian and the Mississippi Valley Dutchmen, a band that has been popular for more than 20 years. Brian's younger cousin Gary Brueggen assumed leadership of the Ridgeland Dutchmen family band and has likewise become an exceptional concertinist. Going by the showbiz nickname of "Wisconsin's Concertina Kid," Gary's band dispenses with the brass and reed instruments, concentrating on the concertina to be the sole lead instrument in the ensemble.

The Chemnitzer concertina has become more and more the defining instrument of the Dutchman style of German-American polka, and small combos of a concertina plus bass horn and drums have become the minimal Dutchman band. Despite the Chemnitzer's obscurity to the general public (the uninitiated often call it an accordion!) and no formal infrastructure for learning to play it, new young Chemnitzer prodigies have continued to emerge. The latest is John Dietz, a former Minnesotan in his twenties, now living in West Bend,

Wisconsin. His skillful and innovative play confirms the sentiment tattooed on his forearm—"Music is my life."

## POLISH POLKA

Eddie Blazonczyk didn't have to seek out the finest Polish-American polka music; it came to him. When he was still a small child in the 1950s in his father Fred Blazonczyk's Chicago tavern, the Mountaineer Bar, he could hear the top-notch polka bands—Lil' Wally Marion Lush, Steve Adamczyk, Eddie Lash, and others—as they entertained the Southside's working class Poles. A high proportion of his patrons, like Blazonczyk himself, had roots in southern Poland's Tatras Mountains region, an area where the people are noted for their devotion to music, dance, and the traditional way of life. They are known in Polish as *"Gorale"* (mountaineers), they have a distinctive dialect, costumes, and customs, and they share many cultural traits with the Slovaks who live just over the mountain on the southern slopes of the Tatras.

The great Polish music didn't stop coming to Eddie even when, during his boyhood, the senior Blazonczyk moved the family up to the north woods hamlet of Hiles, Wisconsin. Chicago Polish bands made the trek up to the Blazonczyk's tavern there as well, bringing a taste of Polonia to the numerous Gorale Poles who inhabit that area.

Eddie always had musical talent. As a small boy in Chicago, he donned the Gorale embroidered felt pants, vest, and the wide-brimmed hat to sing and dance in the community folk dance ensemble lead by his mother Antoinette. He learned concertina, drums, guitar, and eventually settled on the electric bass guitar as his main instrument. All the while he developed his considerable vocalizing skills, singing beautifully both in English and Polish.

As a teen in the late 1950s and early 1960s Eddie flirted with a career in Rockabilly music. At first his group was nicknamed Eddie B. & the Hillcroppers after the day jobs of the young fellows in the band—working in a pulp lumber operation. Eddie B. & the Bel-Aires the band got so far as an appearance on Dick Clark's "American Bandstand" television program, broadcast live from Philadelphia, before Antoinette persuaded her gifted son to devote his notable talents to Polish music.

In 1962 Eddie moved back to Chicago from northern Wisconsin, taking a job at Mercury Records. His purpose was to learn as much as possible about the records business to prepare himself for starting his own Polish-American recording company. He did so, establishing Bel-Aire Records in 1964—to record his own recently formed polka band, the Versatones, as well as the many other Polish polka groups in Chicago and the Midwest.

When he created the Versatones in 1963, Eddie had a specific musical sound in mind; he wanted a style in between that of a couple of his idols, between the passionate "honky style" of Lil' Wally and the more disciplined approach of Steve Adamczyk. Chicago Polish bands of that era had recently emerged as the performers of the dominant popular polka style among Polish-Americans across the United States. Previously in the 1940s and 1950s, large, more orchestral groups were all the rage. They were led by such bandleaders as Frank Wojnarowski, Gene Wisniewski, Bernie Witkowski, and Ray Henry, and mainly they were based on the East Coast (New York, Connecticut, Massachussetts). Like the popular Big Band jazz groups of their era, the Polish bands featured 10 or more musicians, plenty of brass and reed players, and were distinguished in their instrumental lineup from the "American" dance bands only by the obligatory use of an accordion. Seated behind painted bandstands, using written arrangements, the Polish big bands performed fast tempo hot polkas and mellow waltzes, featuring vocalists who sang everything from old Polish folk songs to American pop standards.

But in the 1950s the musical world was changing. Better sound amplification made it possible for a small combo—perhaps no more than a squeezebox, bass and drums—to make a big enough sound to rock a ballroom. Thus, in the early 1950s, a Chicago teenager, Lil' Wally Jagiello of Gorale heritage shook up the Polish-American music scene, alternating between his impassioned singing, insistent drumming, and funky concertina playing. In a role comparable to that of his contemporary Elvis Presley in popular music, Lil' Wally had a raw, rootsy musical power to win over the Polish music audience to his small five piece combo sound.

The term "honky" adhered to his style, perhaps due to the honking tone of the saxophone in his combos. (And probably totally unrelated to the term "honky tonk" as applied around the same time to a piano style and a subgenre of country music.) In honky-style combos, the brass and reed players typically play polyphonically, interweaving their parts like musicians in a Dixieland jazz band. They regularly lay out for concertina solos and occasionally even drum solos. In his honky style, Lil' Wally and his followers stuck to a polka tempo that was slower than the Eastern Polish big bands, facilitating a later development of a new double-time polka dancing technique, "hop style," also called the "Chicago hop." Hopping vertically instead of gliding horizontally, skilled dancers execute jitterbug-like hand dancing moves.

Soon the honky style spread to bands in Polish communities across the United States, even to the eastern homeland of the orchestral Polish bands. The style's march across the continent can be traced by noting the appearance of the Chicago style's Chemnitzer concertina in the Polish polka bands. That type of concertina (previously discussed in connection with German polka) was manufactured in Chicago by the Star Concertina Company. It was adopted early on by Midwestern Poles as well as Germans. As early as 1926 the exuberant concertina playing of Milwaukee's Sosnowski Trio and that of Chicago's Bruno Rudzinski can be heard on 78 rpm discs. During the 1950s and 1960s, the concertina became a dominant voice in Polish-American music, relegating the remaining accordions to a secondary role of playing chordal rhythmic bellows shaking.

By the mid-1960s, when Eddie Blazonczyk was establishing Bel-Aire Records and the Versatones, he felt that the Polish polka landscape was ripe for another tectonic shift. Although he and his band continued to play and record some honky-style material (and even some old Gorale folksongs), Eddie wanted to create a recognizably new and unique sound. Thus he "cleaned up" the polyphonic interplay of brass and reeds, emphasizing unison passages by a pair of trumpets. To pump up the excitement, he increased the use of accordion bellows shaking and turned up his bass guitar so loud that he seldom needed even to pluck the strings with his right hand. The right hand was free to gesture, enhancing the expressiveness of his singing performances. The bass notes still rang out as he "hammered on" the frets with the fingers of his left hand. The hot bass, punched-up rhythm, and loud overall volume level appealed to an audience now accustomed to rock and roll, a trend that has continued to this day and is in small part responsible for the Polish polka scene retaining a sizeable and enthusiastic younger audience. It is ironic that the polka style Eddie pioneered with the Versatones is usually nicknamed "Dyno" or "Push" after the band names of a couple of his early followers, the Chicago Push and the Dynatones from Buffalo.

In his illustrious career, Blazonczyk and his Versatones were the primary ambassadors of Polish-American polka, touring constantly and playing well over 200 road gigs per year. Many of the top Polish polka musicians like Jerry Darlak and Ed Siwiec completed musical apprenticeships as sidemen in Eddie's band. The Versatones have recorded more than 50 LPs and CDs, helping define the core repertoire of Polish-American polka music and bringing adapted country material from artists like Merle Haggard and Buck Owens into the accepted polka repertoire.

With able direction from Eddie's wife, Tish Blazonczyk, Bel-Aire's business expanded beyond recording and publishing records into polka-oriented tourism. Bel-Aire puts a great emphasis on organizing polka cruises, European trips, and other outings with the band. They also organize Polka Fireworks, one of the largest annual polka festivals in the Seven Springs Resort in Pennsylvania.

Eddie has been the recipient of virtually every honor that the Polish polka organizations have to offer. He is a member of the Polka Hall of Fame. The Versatones' recordings have been perennial Grammy award nominees, and Eddie won that prestigious award in 1985. In 1998 Eddie Blazonczyk was awarded the National Heritage Fellowship by the National Endowment for the Arts. In 2002 the band was prominently featured in a PBS documentary titled *Polka Passion*.

The stress of life on the road has taken a toll on Eddie's health, forcing him to curtail and eventually cease his performing with the band in 2002. Nonetheless, the Versatones continue to perform and tour under the direction of Eddie Blazonczyk, Jr. "Junior" worked his way into the ensemble as a sideman, usually playing concertina, but also adding fiddle on a few numbers, a new instrument in the Versatones ensemble. Like Hank Williams, Jr., Blazonczyk, Jr. has a very tough act to follow, but he is rising to the occasion. The band continues to be one of the top Polish bands in the country.

Today there is a burgeoning Polish-American polka scene, especially strong in the Northeast and the Great Lakes states. Today there are dozens of Polish-style polka bands in the United States, most of them playing in the "dyno" style Eddie Blazonczyk originated.

## SLOVENIAN POLKA

On an amazing musical Friday in Milwaukee during the summer of 1985, Lojze Slak, Slovenia's most renowned button accordion player, was in town, playing in the afternoon at a picnic grove on the western outskirts of town. He was on tour from Europe with a small instrumental group and a quartet of male singers. They wore Slovenian folk costumes—dark vests over white shirts with billowing sleeves, the corners of colorful fringed kerchiefs protruding at both shoulders from under their vests. Under a huge striped tent and on a stage of unfinished lumber, Slak played for picnickers from the local Slovenian community. Slak's straightforward accompaniment of the singers and his clear renditions of Alpine melodies were models of tasteful reserve by a master musician who didn't need to show off his prodigious skill. Following the performance by Slak's group, the chairs were cleared away and couples waltzed and polkaed to a dozen ornate Alpine button boxes played by Slak's acolytes, members of the Chicago Slovene Button Box Club.

That same evening, to the east in the industrial suburb of West Allis, in Perko's Lounge, close to the Allis-Chalmers tractor plant, accordionist Gary Frank was playing for the bar's working-class patrons. He played a set of his country songs adapted to accordion, jazz standards as well as the polkas and waltzes that Frankie Yankovic had made famous. Moving on later in the evening to the Blue Canary, a smorgasbord restaurant and dancehall near Milwaukee's airport, concertina player Don Gralak, a young Polish-American, swung through an eclectic medley of Slovenian-style polka including such disparate tunes as "Under the Double Eagle" and the theme from the "Benny Hill" TV show.

In 1985 and to this day, the Slovenian style of polka is comprised of two main musical directions—a multi-ethnic contemporary music in a style made famous since the 1940s by Frankie Yankovic and an assertively ethnic traditional music played in participatory button box clubs grounded in the Slovenian-American community.

Slovenia is a small nation located in the eastern Alps, bordering Austria, Italy, Croatia, and Hungary. Immigrating to the United States around the turn of the twentieth century, Slovenians found work in the coal, iron, and copper mines of Pennsylvania and the Upper Midwest, and also in the steel mills of the "Rust Belt" from Pittsburgh through Ohio to Illinois and all the way to Fontana, California. Music played a big part in their ethnic culture. They have a strong tradition of informal harmony singing, and at the time of their immigration, small diatonic button accordions were all the rage in their Alpine homeland. A squeezebox was a treasured possession in many an immigrant's baggage.

The small Slovenian ethnic group has had a huge musical influence in America, exemplified by the career of Frankie Yankovic. Frank Yankovic was born in Davis, West Virginia, the son of Andy Yankovic and Rose (Mele) Yankovic. Andy and Rose were not acquainted in Slovenia. They both happened to immigrate to the United States in 1903, and they met and married in West Virginia in 1910.

Andy worked in a lumber camp but supplemented his income making untaxed liquor. When Frank was just an infant, his father had to flee from the authorities from West Virginia to Cleveland. The family settled in the large Slovenian immigrant community of Collinwood on that industrial city's east side. Andy worked as a crane operator, and later was a partner in a hardware store while Rose ran a boarding house in their home, feeding, lodging, and laundering for a half dozen young Slovenian men.

From early childhood, Frank's life was filled with Slovenian folk music. After meals his father and the boarders would lift their voices in Alpine-style harmonies, often accompanied by a small diatonic button accordion played by boarder Max Zelodec. Impressed by the esteem Max received, young Frank persuaded the accordionist to give him a few lessons. Frank learned quickly, and by the age of nine he was performing in the neighborhood with his own "button box."

By his teens, Frank felt frustrated by the limitations of the little squeeze box. Frank was growing up in America in the 1920s, a time when recently invented media, radio and phonograph records, were broadening the nation's musical horizons. In addition to Slovenian folk songs, Frank also was exposed to the popular music and jazz that were sweeping the country. He yearned for a piano keyboard accordion, a modern instrument capable of playing tunes with jazzy chord progressions—impossible on the limited button box. But Frank's father Andy was a stern traditionalist and forbade him from obtaining a piano accordion. In 1931, when Frank was 16, his mother Rose had to engage in a little family subterfuge. She acquired the instrument, secreting it at Frank's older sister Mary's house, where he worked hard to learn to play it. Finally on Christmas Eve, Frank strolled into the family holiday gathering, playing on the modern instrument "Maricka pegla," one of his father's favorite Slovenian polkas, whereupon Andy relented in his opposition.

The incident is symbolic of the thrust of Frank Yankovic's musical creativity. He was firmly grounded in Slovenian ethnic musical traditions but also was a first-generation American who wanted to create a music that reflected his own times and milieu but nonetheless mediated between the musical aesthetics of his own generation and those of his parents' generation. That he was very successful in doing so is evident in his career.

In his teens and twenties during the 1930s, Frank strove with dogged determination to establish his small polka band and honed his unique sound, blending American and European elements. He tended to play the lead accordion parts on Old World melodies. In his earliest bands he traded lead parts with a sax player but later employed a second accordionist to play improvised runs and riffs between and around the melodic lines. His rhythm section took a page from Dixieland jazz, including a snappy tenor banjo and a string bass player who played in the jazzy "walking bass" style.

He managed to secure a regular spot on local radio and cut four very successful self-produced 78 rpm discs when the major labels rebuffed him. Frank married June Erwith in 1940, a marriage that lasted 28 years. They had eight children. In the early years Frank had to keep day jobs as a milkman, a pattern maker, and accordion teacher. In 1941 Frank purchased a tavern, arranging a grand opening party on December 6—one day before the attack on Pearl Harbor. During the War years, the Yankovic Bar provided his family with steady income and was a venue for his band. It quickly became the hangout of Cleveland's finest polka musicians, such as Johnny Pecon, Kenny Bass, and Eddie Habat.

In 1943 Frank joined the Army. On one afternoon during a two-week furlough before shipping out to Europe in 1944, Frank rounded up banjoist Joe Miklavic, bassist Johnny Hokavar, and pianist Al Naglitch for a recording session. They cut 32 sides with no rehearsal and one take per tune. In these sessions the saxophone part was omitted and Frank never used the instrument in his band henceforth, emphasizing an accordion-based sound.

Frank suffered severe frostbite during the Battle of the Bulge. A doctor recommended that his hands and feet be amputated, as gangrene had set in. Frank refused the amputation, and fortunately his extremities began to recover. An old accordion was rounded up; playing it was therapeutic, and before long Frank was entertaining the hospital. Upon his release from the hospital he was assigned to special services to entertain the troops with a five-piece band. His Army experience, entertaining men of varied backgrounds from all parts of the country, provided him with insights that helped advance his musical career as soon as he came home from the Army in December 1945. Although Frank never ceased singing some vocals in Slovenian, he realized he needed to develop English lyrics for his tunes in order to reach a broader audience and to enable fans to easily identify and request a favorite number.

Frank's definitive sound emerged when he added a second accordionist, Johnny Pecon, who added exciting improvised riffs, and Frank began to employ the Solovox, an early portable electronic organ. Pecon taught Frank a country tune he had learned while serving in the Seabees, "Just Because." They reworked the number in polka style and it became the band's signature tune. When Columbia Records officials were reluctant to let Frank record "Just Because" at a December 1947 recording session because as a country tune it hadn't been a hit, he argued, kicked chairs, and threw sheet music around the room. Finally they relented when Frank offered to buy 10,000 copies of the record himself. The record was hugely popular, quickly sold a million copies, and launched the popular polka craze of the late 1940s and early 1950s. Also in 1948, Frank was declared "America's Polka King" at a "battle of the bands" event in the Milwaukee Auditorium.

Columbia wanted him to tour extensively, so Frank sold the tavern and devoted the rest of his career exclusively to the music business. His fame increased. In 1949 his recording of "Blue Skirt Waltz" was the year's second biggest seller. His sidemen from Cleveland's Slovenian community balked at the 300 days per year of one-nighters that became Frank's way of life for decades to come, so he engaged professional musicians who had no previous polka experience. His definitive band during his peak period from 1949–1954 included Tops Cardone, accordion; Carl Paradiso, banjo; Buddy Griebel, piano; and Al Leslie, bass. In the early 1950s in Hollywood they played prestigious venues, made five short films for Universal Studios, and recorded with Doris Day as vocalist.

Over the years there was a lot of turnover in sidemen due to the band's grueling touring schedule. Typically they drove over 100,000 miles per year. Thus the Yankovic band became an incubator for outstanding musicians. Joe Sekardi, Frankie Kramer, Richie Vadnal, Roger Bright, Jim Maupin, and Joey Miskulin are a few of the Yankovic accordionists who have had a big impact on the polka world.

The touring took a toll on family life. Frank and June divorced in the late 1960s, and Frank's second marriage in the 1970s produced two children but also ended in divorce. He met his third wife, Ida, at his 70th birthday celebration in 1985. They married in 1987. Ida took an active role in Frank's band business, traveling with the band and taking responsibility for sales of his recordings.

In 1986 NARAS initiated a polka category for the Grammy awards, and it was no surprise that Frank Yankovic was the first recipient of the award for his album *70 years of Hits*. In December 1994, an hour-long documentary on Frank's life was shown nationally on PBS. Frank remained an active musician virtually until the time of his passing in 1998. Hundreds of bands perpetuate the polka style he codified. His hometown of Cleveland remains the most active center of this musical style, followed closely by Milwaukee, Pittsburgh, Chicago, and northern Minnesota.

In the heritage-conscious 1970s, there began a resurgence of interest in the instrument that Yankovic had abandoned—the button box. Beginning in the late 1960s, another Cleveland Slovenian named Frank, Frank Novak, recorded several influential LP albums of button box tunes. Around this time an ethnic fraternal organization, the Slovene National Benefit Society, usually known by its Slovenian initials SNPJ (*Slovenska Narodna Potporna Jednota*), sought to emulate the musical success of a similar organization, the Croatian Fraternal Union (CFU). For decades the CFU had supported the formation of youth tamburitza orchestras featuring the fretted stringed instruments that are a prominent symbol of Croatian ethnic identity. More than 30 youth tamburitza orchestras were in the CFU Junior Cultural Federation, bringing a lot of vitality to the fraternal organization. Since the Alpine diatonic button accordion is a potent symbol of Slovenian ethnic identity, the leaders of SNPJ sought to stimulate the formation of button box ensembles in their youth circles. Thus, the older style is being preserved in the Slovenian ethnic community while the Yankovic style remains popular both within and beyond the ethnic group.

## CZECH POLKA

In Slovan, Wisconsin, on most any Sunday afternoon of the year, travelers will be greeted by the sight of dancing couples twirling in the Country Inn to a unique sound: raucous trumpets, quavering clarinets, or billowing saxophones playing old folk tunes originally from Bohemia, the western province of the Czech Republic, and the region from which most of the Czech immigrants in Wisconsin came. The rhythm provided by the oom-pah of a tuba, a piano clunking chords, and the tapping of drums will most likely be a polka or a waltz, or maybe a "modern" foxtrot from the 1930s.

There are still about a dozen bands in northeastern Wisconsin playing Czech-American traditional dance music, and most of them take their turn playing in Slovan. Locally they are termed "Bohemian bands." The community's elders can remember a time when there were at least three times as many Bohemian bands active in the area and somewhere to go dancing nearly every night of the week.

Although diminished by changing times, nonetheless this Czech dance music tradition lives on in the Midwest. It is especially in demand at weddings, anniversaries, and church festivals, and in the last 20 years there has been an increase in polka festivals and ethnic heritage fests. Although this treatment will focus on northeastern Wisconsin, other regional styles of Czech polka can also be found wherever Czech-American rural communities were founded: in northern Iowa, southern Minnesota, a few places in Michigan and Ohio. There are very active and important Czech polka music scenes in eastern Nebraska and in central and southeastern sections of Texas.

## THE MARCHING BANDS

When they first arrived in the nineteenth century, the Czech pioneers faced rugged circumstances in the rural Midwest. But as soon as conditions improved, the Czech communities established brass marching bands, a type of music that was wildly popular in the old homeland at the time they left. A town band was considered a prerequisite for civilized life. From the 1890s through the 1920s, nearly every little Czech farming community in eastern Wisconsin had its band: the Pilsen Brass Band, The Hoppe Band, the Schauer Band, the Blahnik Band, the Luxemburg Brass Band, and dozens more. The musicians were not only of Czech heritage. This music was warmly accepted also by members of the other nationalities in northeastern Wisconsin, especially the Belgians, Germans, and Poles, who had similar musical traditions in their own ancestral homelands. Mostly self-taught, these farmer and small town dweller musicians played from the heart. Like New Orleans brass bands, the Bohemian bands had a raw, gutsy energy and a brassy and reedy texture.

A lot of resources were invested in establishing a band—instruments had to be purchased, of course, but also, when they could be afforded, dressy military-style uniforms gave the band a professional look. The musical arrangements were very important. Some were purchased from Vitak and Elsnic, a Czech music publisher in Chicago. Others obtained hand-notated sheet music from Joseph Buchta, a gifted Czech-born band arranger who had settled in Idaho.

## THE DANCE BANDS

As ballroom dancing became a popular phenomenon in the 1920s and 1930s, the emphasis shifted from marching to dance bands and dance halls. In 1921, Paul Gosz from the Manitowoc County hamlet of Rockwood started a family band that ultimately was to become, under the leadership of his son Romy, the model for the so-called Wisconsin Bohemian style of polka band. Paul Gosz's band featuring his sons Frank, Mike, George, and Romy doubled as a barn-storming basketball team! After playing a local team, the boys would take out the instruments and play for dancing on the basketball court. It was a six or seven piece combo. There were two trumpeters, two clarinet/sax players, and for rhythm, a tuba, piano, and drum. Initially Romy was the piano player. He had a lot of natural musical talent. After only one piano lesson, he notified his teacher, Mrs. Charles Kirchen, that he couldn't make it to his second lesson that Saturday because he had to play for a dance.

In 1924 Paul left the band to son George's leadership. In 1928, when he opened a tavern, George turned over the bandleader job to his little brother Romy. Romy switched to trumpet in 1931 and it was soon obvious that he had a phenomenal lip, terrific volume, and a unique tone. His personal style was unmistakable. Like a jazz trumpeter, Romy played with emotional abandon, unconcerned about conventional notions of technique. A Mishicot, Wisconsin musician, Larry Hlinak, once described a conversation among polka musicians about Romy. One player asserted that a lip like Romy's only comes around once in 50 years. Another musician corrected him, "No it's more like once in 500 years."

Soon many musicians, mostly in Wisconsin but some as far away as Iowa and Minnesota, emulated the Romy Gosz sound. In addition to his prodigious talent on the trumpet, Romy Gosz was also known for his penchant for wild living. He passed away in 1966 at the age of 56, but many Gosz-sounding bands continue to perform.

Several of his former sidemen and other musical admirers formed their own bands, and the Manitowoc and Kewaunee County area became extremely rich in dance bands. Rudy Plochar, Dick Rodgers, Elroy Berkholtz, Gordy Reckelberg, Jerry Goetsch, Louis Zdrazil, Jerry Voelker, and Gene Heier are several of the bandleaders whose music followed the style established by Romy Gosz. Even in the pre-Interstate highway era, the more popular of these bands fanned out to play venues all over Wisconsin and in neighboring states.

The brass and reed instruments could be used either to play the traditional polka repertoire, usually termed "old time music" by the locals, or they could play the current popular dance tunes of the Big Band era, called "moderns." A particular band might place an emphasis on either "old time" or "modern," but most played some of each type of repertoire.

The old time dances have retained a recognizable format, which in many cases was codified by local musicians' union rules. A prerequisite for a professional look has been a set of bandstands, usually painted with the band's name and/or logo. At most dances, the old time bands played a set of three tunes of a particular tempo in a row—three polkas, three waltzes or laendlers, and maybe a set of fox trots or schottisches. Most in attendance remained out on the dance floor during the set, returning to their tables only briefly between sets to take a sip of their drinks. Many couples were proud to assert that they danced to every number during a four hour event.

At venues where many of the patrons were acquainted, mixer dances were popular. One of the most common was the circle two-step, which required a caller, but there were also the waltz quadrille and the circle schottische. At weddings, especially, the Flying Dutchman (also called the butterfly dance) was a must. Danced in threesomes, it alternated between a waltz and a fast polka tempo. During the fast tempo, partners swung each other wildly with elbows hooked. If they lost their hold, partners flew across the floor!

During the 1950s and 1960s a second very popular style of Czech polka also emerged from the same area of Wisconsin. Bandleader Lawrence Duchow from Potter, Wisconsin, established the Red Raven Orchestra, a larger ensemble with a smoother sound, influenced by the Big Band dance bands. He toured widely and even established a regular polka night gig at Chicago's Trianon Ballroom, a prestigious mainstream venue. Duchow's band business had problems with the IRS, and Duchow fled abroad, but bandleaders like Lee Rollins and Jay Wells continued to play in his style. In a controversial move, Wells even appropriated the Red Raven Orchestra's name.

The most recent development in Czech polka from Wisconsin has resulted from the 1980s tours of ensembles like Budvarka, Veselka, and Morovanka from the old homeland. Cletus Bellin, a sideman in a number of northeastern Wisconsin bands, was impressed by their sound and established the Clete Bellin Band in the late 1980s to emulate their European style of play. With Clete's fine Czech language vocals and the band's crisp and intricate arrangements, the band currently is one of the most popular Czech polka bands in the United States.

## TAMBURITZA

Romy Gosz set the paradigm for the Bohemian style in the 1930s, Yankovic did it for Slovenian style in the 1940s, and Eddie Blazonczyk did it for Polish style in the 1960s, but for tamburitza, despite a century of being played in America, the current standard was set more recently, in the 1980s by Pittsburgh's Jerry Grcevich.

Western Pennsylvania, where Jerry Grcevich has lived all his life, has more tamburitza players per square mile than any place outside of Croatia, and many argue that Jerry is the best player of them all. The greater Pittsburgh area and the surrounding mill and mining towns are home to the largest Croatian-American ethnic community. The prospect of work in Pennsylvania's steel mills and coal mines was a magnet to South Slavic immigrants leaving impoverished villages in the Austro-Hungarian Empire, and the most numerous among these were the Croatians.

Croatian-Americans have made the tamburitza tradition their most visible and emphasized symbol of ethnic identity. In Europe and in America, members of Croatia's neighboring Slavic nationalities also play this family of fretted stringed instruments: there have been many important Serbian and Bosnian tamburitza players, and tamburitzas are also played in one region of Slovenia. Nonetheless, since the mid-nineteenth century, it was Croatians who invested the most effort in advancing the tamburitza and the song and dance traditions with which the instrument is associated.

Owing to a strong, ethnic, community-based infrastructure, the tamburitza tradition remains very strong, even among the third and fourth generations born in America. Since the beginning of the twentieth century, in the United States and Canada, Croatian ethnic communities have nurtured active youth orchestras most frequently supported by lodges of the Croatian Fraternal Union. Over the decades, the singing of traditional folk songs and dancing choreographed versions of folk dances became integral to their performances. In Pittsburgh, the Duquesne University Tamburitzans, a touring collegiate ensemble that performs eastern European music and dance, was established in 1937. Hundreds of graduates of Duquesne's "Tammies" remained active life-long ethnic musicians and/or teachers of youth orchestras. The network of youth groups, called "junior tammies," became *de facto* minor leagues for Duquesne. In the 1960s, the Croatian Fraternal Union organized its Junior Cultural Federation to support the work of the youth tamburitza ensembles, providing resources and organizing an annual festival.

Jerry Grcevich was born in East Pittsburgh in 1951. His family was deeply involved in tamburitza music. Jerry's maternal grandfather Marko Sumrak was a noted tamburitza player. Jerry's uncle Marko Grcevich was a musician who played in the tamburitza combo "Sloboda" (Freedom) led by his brother, Jerry's father, Joe Grcevich. Joe also served for many years as the music director of the St. George Junior Tamburitzans in Cokeburg, Pennsylvania. In the Grcevich household, playing music was just something that was done, and Jerry got an early start.

In the 1960s he started playing with the St. George Junior Tamburitzans. As a teenager he also played in his father's group Sloboda, where he gained poise, technique, and professional experience. Beginning in 1969, the St. George group made several tours to Croatia and Serbia. On the first trip, in the city of Novi Sad, Jerry met Janika Balaz, the renowned Romany (Gypsy) musician and bandleader, who was considered the finest *primas* of his era. The *primas* plays the *prim*, the soprano melodic instrument, the smallest and most challenging of the tamburitza family. Janika recognized Jerry's potential, and Jerry became determined to be a fine *primas*. Janika's orchestra performed for many years in the restaurant in the old Austrian fortress on the Danube at Petrovaradin. There Jerry also met Zvonko Bogdan, the noted vocalist and composer of traditional-style songs, who frequently performed to Janika's accompaniment in Petrovaradin. Zvonko also became a major influence upon Jerry in the areas of singing and composition. Years later, Jerry accompanied Zvonko on several concert tours of the United States and Canada. During one sojourn in the United States, Zvonko recorded an album of traditional and original songs with Jerry.

That album was made in Jerry's own studio, where he has produced several other recordings, both of traditional music and of his own compositions. One of his best known songs, "Ja cu se vratiti" (I will return), was composed at the end of the 1980s in collaboration with the Croatian singer Miroslav Skoro, who at that time was living in the United States. The lyrics were prescient. The wars that followed the breakup of Yugoslavia began shortly after this recording was made. The words to the song express a yearning for home and the desire to return. It became a hit in Croatia and an unofficial anthem for the war's refugees and displaced persons, making Jerry the first American-born tamburitza musician to gain widespread recognition in Croatia.

For several years Jerry performed with Joe Kirin's "Slanina" (Bacon) orchestra from Chicago, including two performances in the "Folk Masters" series at Wolf Trap and at National Folk Festivals in Chattanooga and Dayton. Since 1993 he has led his own combo, comprising Vjeko Dimter, Bob Sestili, Steve Wagner, and Marko Dreher.

Jerry has become a bridge between the American and Croatian tamburitza musical scenes. He makes frequent extended visits to Croatia, where he is involved with a widening circle of the finest tamburitza musicians there. In 1994 he was honored at the biggest Croatian festival of tamburitza music in Slavonska Pozega for his efforts to preserve Croatian music and culture in North America.

A new generation of tamburitza musicians is emerging. Perhaps the most talented is Peter Kosovec. Along with players like Ryan Werner of Milwaukee and Robi Sestili of Pittsburgh, Peter is one of an amazing crop of young American primaši that have emerged in the past few years. The Kosovec family of Detroit has had a long-time influence upon the American tamburitza scene. Peter's grandfather Ludwig was a leader of the Detroit Tamburitza Symphony. His father Kenneth has been a member of noted combos "Lira," and "Momci" with his brother Dennis. Ken was also the instructor for the youth group Detroit Star Tamburitzans. His mother Bonnie is an excellent vocalist. Peter was born in 1980, and he got an early start in music. He recalls the moment at age five when his father put an instrument in his hand: "I remember the exact time he gave me the tambura in my living room. It's the same one I use today" (Mikolajek, 2001).

After a few years in the Detroit junior group, his talent was obvious. He recorded his first CD in his basement studio at the age of 13, sharing vocal tasks with his mother and his sister Sonja. He and Sonja, as well as his cousin David, became members of the Duquesne University ensemble.

Because of his precocious virtuosity and his self-produced sound-on-sound recordings, Peter is like the next generation's Jerry Grcevich; however, there also are significant differences. Jerry developed his amazing talents in a greater degree of isolation. Before the 1990s, he seemed to be something of a reclusive genius. Through the 1980s, tamburitza enthusiasts waited for Jerry's inspiring self-produced recordings to emerge from his home studio. As a Duquesne Tamburitzan, Peter's musical skills were showcased in live shows far and wide. After graduation he remained in Pittsburgh, forming a combo with the potent name Otrov. (It means "poison" in Croatian.) Today the American tamburitza tradition is healthy and shows no signs of decline. Young people continue to learn to play the tambura in more than 30 youth groups, mostly associated with the CFU Junior Cultural Federation. And youthful professional combos are making their mark. At the 2003 Tamburitza Extravaganza in Chicago, the teenaged members of the youngest participating professional combo, "Mladi Fakini" from Milwaukee, were greeted with much enthusiasm.

## BIBLIOGRAPHY

Bohlman, Philip. "Music in the Culture of German-Americans in North-Central Wisconsin." Master's thesis, University of Illinois, Champaign-Urbana, 1980.

Brown, Dennis. "Whoopee John: His Musical Story." Lakefield, Minnesota: undated self-published booklet (circa 1990).

Keil, Charles , Angeliki V. Keil, and Dick Blau. *Polka Happiness*. Temple University Press: Philadelphia, 1992.

Keil, Charles. "Slovenian Style in Milwaukee." In *Folk Music and Modern Sound*, edited byWilliam Ferris and Mary L. Hunt, 32–59. Jackson: University of Mississippi Press, 1982.

Greene, Victor. *A Passion for Polka*. Berkely: University of California Press, 1992.

Leary, James P. "Polka Music in a Polka State." In *Wisconsin Folklore*, edited by James P. Leary, 268–283. Madison: University of Wisconsin Press, 1998.

Leary, James P. "The German Concertina in the Upper Midwest." In *Land Without Nightingales: Music in the Making of German-America*, edited by Philip V. Bohlman and Otto Holzapfel, 191–232. Madison: Max Kade Institute for German- American Studies, 2002.

Leary, James P. "Czech Polka Styles in the U.S.: From America's Dairyland to the Lone Star State." In *Czech Music in Texas: A Sesquicentennial Symposium*, edited by Clinton Machann, 79–95. College Station, TX: Komensky Press, 1988.

Leary, James P., and Richard March. *Down Home Dairyland: A Listener's Guide*. Madison: University of Wisconsin-Extension, 1996.

Leary, James P., and Richard March. "Dutchman Bands: Genre, Ethnicity and Pluralism." In *Creative Ethnicity* eited by Stephen Stern and John Allan Cicala, 21–43. Logan, UT: Utah State University Press, 1991.

Lornell, Kip. "The Early Career of Whoopee John Wilfahrt." *JEMF Quarterly* Vol. XXI No. 75/76, 1989, pp. 51–53.

March, Richard. "Slovenian Polka Music." *JEMF Quarterly* Vol. XXI No. 75/76, 1989, pp. 47–50.

March, Richard. "Polkas in Wisconsin Music." In *The Illustrated History of Wisconsin Music*, edited by Michael G. Corenthal, 385–397. Milwaukee: MGC Publications, 1991.

March, Richard. "Tamburitza." In *American Folklore*, edited by Jan Harold Brunvand (Garland Publishing, New York, 1996) pp. 702–703.

March, Richard. "My Little Global Village (*Selo moje malo*): Contemporary Tambura Music-Making in the United States" (English version of the article is online at http://www.tamburaland.com/events/richardmarch1.html. Croatian version is in Narodna Umjetnost 40/2 [Zagreb, 2003]).

March, Richard. "Deep Polka: Dance Music from the Midwest." Smithsonian Folkways SF CD 40088, CD booklet, 1998.

March, Richard. "Deeper Polka: More Dance Music from the Midwest." Smithsonian Folkways SF CD 40140, CD booklet, 2003.

March, Richard. "Wisconsin Remains Polka Country." In *Wisconsin Folklife: A Celebration of Wisconsin Traditions*. Madison: Wisconsin Academy of Sciences, Arts and Letters, 1998. 18–21.

Yankovic, Frank, and Robert Dolgan. *The Polka King: The Life of Frankie Yankovic.* Cleveland, OH:Dillon and Liederbach, 1977.

## RECORDINGS

Very few recordings are available in the idioms discussed in this article through standard music industry sources. There is an esoteric distribution network for polka and tamburitza music. Many of the recordings are self-produced by the musicians. Lately it has become much easier to buy the recordings through Internet sites.For a musical overview, the two Smithsonian Folkways compilations are convenient and available on the Smithsonian Folkways Web site: http://www.folkways.si.edu/index.html

*Deep Polka: Dance Music from the Midwest.* Smithsonian Folkways SF CD 40088 (1998)

*Deeper Polka: More Dance Music from the Midwest.* Smithsonian Folkways SFW CD 40140 (2002)

Recordings of the individual polka bands or reissues of older music can be found either at Polkamart or Nancy's Place for Polkas, two very reliable online sources:

Polkamart: http://www.polkamart.com

Nancy's Place: http://www.polkas.com

Contemporary tamburitza recordings are available through Tamburaland, and reissues of older material through Balkan Records.

Tamburaland: http://www.tamburaland.com

Balkan Records: http://www.esotericsound.com/FolkMusic.htm

## Polish-style Polka

Eddie Blazonczyk's Versatones. *Live and Kickin'*. Bel-Aire Records BACD 4431 (2001).

Li'l Wally (Jagiello). *Fantasztyczne.* Jay Jay 5165.

## Slovenian-style Polka

Yankovic, Frank. *Greatest Hits, Volume 2.*
Steve Meisner Band, "Jammin' Polkas" HG 5045 CD (1996)

## Tamburitza

Grcevich, Jerry. *Daleko je Selo Moje.* (2001).
Kosovec, Peter. Kuda Idu Godine. Tamburaland Productions (2002).
*The Balkan Singles, Volume One.* Balkan Records.

## Dutchman-style Polka

Whoopee John. *CD No. 2.*
Karl and the Country Dutchmen. *Boys Day Out.*

## Czech/Bohemian-style Polka

Gosz, Romy. *1935–36.* Polkaland CD-602.
Mark Vyhlidal Band. *Just Doin' Our Thing.*

# Selected Bibliography

Ancelet, Barry Jean. *Musiciens Cadiens et Créoles: The Makers of Cajun Music*. Austin: University of Texas Press, 1984.

Ancelet, Barry Jean. *Cajun Music: Its Origins and Development*. Lafayette: Center for Louisiana Studies, University of Southwestern Louisiana, 1989.

Bernard, Shane K. *Swamp Pop: Cajun and Creole Rhythm and Blues*. Jackson: University Press of Mississippi, 1996,

Butcher, Vada E. & Wanda Brown. *Final Report to NEH: Ethnic Music in General Education*. Washington D.C.: 1977.

Chalmers, Wilma Grand. *$2 at the Door: Folk, Ethnic, and Bluegrass Music in the Northwest*. McMinnville, Or: Broadsheet Pubs., 1981.

*Ethnic Recordings in America: A Neglected Heritage*. Washington D.C.: Library of Congress, 1982.

Gombert, Greg. *A Guide to Native American Music Recordings*. Ft. Collins, CO.: Mult-Cultural Publishing, 1994.

Grame, Theodore C. *America's Ethnic Music*. Tarpon Springs, FL: Cultural Maintenance Assoc., 1976.

Greene, Victor. *A Passion for Polka: Old-Time Ethnic Music in America*. Berkeley & Los Angeles: University of California Press, 1992.

Greene, Victor. *A Singing Ambivalence: American Immigrants Between Old World and New, 1830-1930*. Kent & London: Kent State University Press, 2004.

Herndon, Marcia. *Native American Music*. Norwood, PA: Norwood Editions, 1980.

Herrera-Sobek, Maria. *Northward Bound: The Ethnic Immigrant Experience in Ballad and Song*. Bloomington and Indianapolis: Indiana University Press, 1993.

Koskoff, Ellen, ed. *Music Cultures in the United States: An Introduction*. New York & London: Routledge, 2005.

Lausevic, Mirjana. *Balkan Fascination: Creating an Alternative Music Culture in America*. Oxford University Press, 2007

Loeffler, Jack. *La Musica de los Viejitos: Hispano Folk Music of the Rio Grande del Norte*. Albuquerque: University of New Mexico Press, 1999.

Meek, Bill. *Songs of the Irish in America*. Dublin: Gilbert Dalton, 1978.

Moloney, Mick. *Far From the Shamrock Shore: The Story of Irish-American Immigration Through Song*. New York: Crown Publs., 2002; incl. CD.

O'Neill, Capt. Francis. *Irish Minstrels and Musicians: with Numerous Dissertations on Related Subjects*. Cork & Dublin: Mercier Press, 1987; reprint of 1913 edn.

Paredes, Américo. *"With His Pistol in His Hand": A Border Ballad and Its Hero*. Austin: University of Texas Press, 1958.

Paredes, Américo. *A Texas-Mexican Cancionero*. Urbana: University of Illinois Press, 1976.

Peña, Manuel. *The Texas-Mexican Conjunto: History of a Working-Class Music*. Austin: U. of Texas Press, 1985.

Robb, John Donald. *Hispanic Folk Music of New Mexico and the Southwest: A Self-Portrait of a People*. Norman: University of Oklahoma Press, 1980.

Robb, John Donald. *Hispanic Folk Songs of New Mexico*. Albuquerque: University of New Mexico Press, 1954, 1962.

Sapoznik, Henry. *Klezmer! Jewish Music from Old World to Our World*. New York: Schirmer, 1999.

Savoy, Ann Allen. *Cajun Music: A Reflection of a People*. Vol. 1. Eunice, LA: Bluebird Press, 1984, 1986.

Silverman, Jerry. *Mel Bay's Immigrant Songbook*. Pacific, Mo.: Mel Bay, 1992.

Slobin, Mark. *Tenement Songs: The Popular Music of the Jewish Immigrants*. Urbana: University of Illinois Press, 1982.

Smyth, Willie, and Esmé Ryan. *Spirit of the First People: Native American Musical Traditions of Washington State*. Seattle: University of Washington Press, 1999.

Spottswood, Richard K. *Ethnic Music on Records*, 7 vols. Urbana: University of Illinois Press, 1990.

Tawa, Nicholas. *A Sound of Strangers: Musical Cuture, Acculturation, and the Post-Civil War Ethnic American*. Metuchen, NJ, & London: Scarecrow Press, 1982.

Vernon, Paul. *Ethnic and Vernacular Music, 1898-1960: A Resource and Guide to Recordings*. Westport, CT: Greenwood Press, Discographies, No. 62; 1995.

Williams, William H.A. *'Twas Only an Irishman's Dream: The Image of Ireland and the Irish in American Popular Song Lyrics, 1800-1920*. Urbana: University of Illinois Press, 1996.

Wright, Rochelle, and Robert L. Wright. *Danish Emigrant Ballads and Songs*. Carbondale & Edwardsville: So. Ill. Univ. Press, 1983.

Wright, Robert L. *Irish Emigrant Ballads and Songs*. Bowling Green: Bowling Green University Popular Press, 1975.

Wright-McLeod, Brian. *Encyclopedia of Native Music: More than a Century of Recordings from Wax Cylinder to the Internet*. Tucson: University of Arizona Press, 2005.

# Index

# About the Editor and Contributors

## THE EDITOR

NORM COHEN is the author of *Long Steel Rail: The Railroad in American Folk-song* (1981) and *Traditional Anglo-American Folk Music: An Annotated Discography of Published Recordings* (1994). He has edited and/or annotated two dozen albums, and written extensively on various aspects of folk, country, and popular music. He is a retired chemist and currently teaches physical science in Portland, Oregon. His previous book for Greenwood is *Folk Music: A Regional Exploration* (2005).

## THE CONTRIBUTORS

KEVIN S. FONTENOT is an instructor at Tulane University's School of Continuing Education, where he teaches Louisiana and United States history. Fontenot is completing his doctorate in history at Tulane. His dissertation is a biographical study of the life of Louisiana governor and country music star Jimmie H. Davis. Fontenot has published articles in *Country Music Annual*, the *Journal of Country Music*, *The Jazz Archivist*, *Louisiana History*, *Journal of*

*Southern History*, and the *South Carolina Historical Quarterly*. He is the 2007 recipient of the John Dwayer Award for Excellence in Teaching, awarded by Tulane University's School of Continuing Studies.

Fontenot was born in Eunice, Louisiana, and grew up outside of Oberlin, Louisiana, in an area where Cajun and Anglo-American cultures merge.

STEVEN LOZA is Professor of Ethnomusicology at the University of California, Los Angeles, where he has been on the faculty since 1984. He has served as Director of the Arts of the Americas Institute at the University of New Mexico and has also taught at the University of Chile, Kanda University of International Studies in Japan, and at the Centro Nacional de las Artes in Mexico City. His books include *Barrio Rhythm: Mexican American Music in Los Angeles* and *Tito Puente and the Making of Latin Music*, both published by the University of Illinois Press. He has edited a number of anthologies, including two volumes of *Selected Reports in Ethnomusicology* (UCLA Ethnomusicology Publications), *Hacia una musicologia global: Clasicos y nuevos pensamientos sobre la etnomusicologia* (CENIDIM/INBA, Mexico, D.F., in press) and *Religion as Art: Gudalupe, Orishas, Sufi* (University of New Mexico Press). He has been the recipient of various fellowships and grants, including those of the Fullbright, Ford, and UC MEXUS foundations. He directed the UCLA Mexican Arts Series for ten years and is an accomplished musician and composer with two CDS on the Merrimack label.

RICHARD MARCH has a Ph.D. in Folklore from Indiana University. He has been the Traditional & Ethnic Arts Coordinator for Wisconsin Arts Board since 1983. He initiated folk arts programming, including apprenticeships, project grants, media efforts, international cultural exchanges and teachers' workshops. He did graduate study at the University of Zagreb in Croatia and worked as a researcher at the Institute of Folklore and Ethnography in Zagreb, conducting research in Croatia, Bosnia and Serbia. From 1986 to 2001 he produced and was the on-air host of a traditional music program "Down Home Dairyland" on Wisconsin Public Radio. Curriculum materials based on the radio show are distributed by the University of Wisconsin. He developed two CDs for Smithsonian Folkways, "Deep Polka" and "Deeper Polka," for Polkaland Records "Golden Horns on Green Fields," and for Arhoolie Records "Tamburitza!" "Wisconsin Folks," the folk arts education website of Wisconsin Arts Board, has been acclaimed.

PAUL F. WELLS is Director of the Center for Popular Music and Associate Professor of Music at Middle Tennessee State University. His research includes work on fiddling and fiddle tunes, bluegrass music, music of the Civil War, Irish traditional music, early country music, and the history of music publishing. He currently is editing a volume of American fiddle tunes for the series *Music of the United States of America*. Wells is a past-president of the Society for American Music and active in a number of other professional organizations. He plays

American, Canadian, and Irish traditional music on fiddle, flute, guitar, mandolin, and banjo.

MARIA WILLIAMS is Tlingit and of the Deishitaan clan and a child of the Killer Whale clan. She was born and raised in Anchorage, Alaska. She received her M.A. and PhD in Music, specializing in Ethnomusicology from the University of California, Los Angeles. She currently teaches at the University of New Mexico and continues to work with tribal communities in Alaska as well as in New Mexico in addition to her teaching and research obligations.